RADICAL *Review*
HISTORY
Issue | 148

Feminists Confront State Violence

Issue Editors: Anne Gray Fischer, Sara Matthiesen, and Marisol LeBrón

Making Our Way Out

*Anne Gray Fischer, Sara Matthiesen,
and Marisol LeBrón*

Pat Parker searched for an escape from the state in her 1978 poem "Where Do You Go to Become a Noncitizen?" In one stanza, she wrote:

The A.P.A. finally said all gays aren't ill
Yet ain't no refunds on their psychiatry bills.
A federal judge says MCC is valid—a reality
Yet it won't keep the pigs from hurting you or me.
I wanna resign; I want out.[1]

Parker registers her suspicion of inclusive liberal reforms in the specific context of the postwar United States. She marks the formal end of the pathologization of homosexuality with a reminder that such recognition does not disrupt a for-profit system of health care. And the state's willingness to legitimate queer worship in the Metropolitan Community Church does not offer any protection to live free from police violence. But Parker's desire for noncitizenship transcends US borders: throughout her poem, she indicts Queen Elizabeth, Ford Motors, and the CIA, naming the persecution, abandonment, and exploitation of the people and the land caught in the grooves of global capital. In this way, Parker refuses the superficial incorporation of her Black lesbian identity in service to what Erica R. Edwards calls "the long war on terror" that powers US imperialism.[2] Trapped between the violence of statecraft and the vulnerability of statelessness, Parker writes:

Radical History Review
Issue 148 (January 2024)   DOI 10.1215/01636545-10846766
© 2024 by MARHO: The Radical Historians' Organization, Inc.

Please lead me to the place
Give my letter to a smiling face
I want to resign; I want out.

What political horizons have guided feminists in their search for a way out of state-sponsored violence? In this issue of *Radical History Review*, readers will find feminists confronting proliferating forms of state harm: dictatorship in Iran, settler colonialism and misogyny in Palestine, economic austerity and the criminalization of reproductive rights in Latin America, sexual policing in South Africa, and incarceration in the United States during the AIDS epidemic, to name a few. These diverse histories of activism illustrate how gender and sexuality—in their historically and culturally specific forms—are consistently mobilized to enact violence and justify abandonment. Taken collectively, these contributions respond to Parker's question—"Where do we go?"—by articulating a key insight of abolition feminism: interpersonal gender-based violence cannot be theorized separately from structural violence.[3] Feminists must oppose both in their struggle toward a horizon of well-being and safety for all.

It is in the *how* of finding a way out, of building the place Parker longs for inside the world we have now, that these histories raise pressing questions about strategies forged from the political horizon of abolition feminism. If abolition feminism is, as Ruth Wilson Gilmore notes, "about affirming life-building institutions," then this issue asks about the capacity of the state to affirm life, given its structural investments in violence and the strategies available for winning redress from the institutions that exist.[4] In one sense, the massive and multiscaled scope of state violence—religious and racist genocide, medical apartheid, colonial dispossession, global austerity, and capitalist resource extraction that accelerates our climate catastrophe—indexes the immense potential of state infrastructures. Global systems that can accumulate and wield such sprawling powers might instead be used to redistribute resources on that same scale. In another sense, this analysis exposes a fundamental contradiction: how, and why, make demands for the equitable distribution of care, safety, and life on a state that unequally distributes violence, immiseration, and death? Or, as Edwards and Randi Gill-Sadler ask in their essay, "If state violence is articulated as policy that *cares* and protection that *kills*, how do we imagine the care that . . . *radically remakes worlds?*"

This issue, animated by an abolitionist faith that there is an "affirming life-building" place, offers an archive of feminist strategies, practices, and visions that struggle to radically remake worlds from inside this one. When read together, they stake two claims: there are significant limits to the state's capacity to care; and it is necessary to maneuver within those limits in an effort to practice what Heather Berg calls "politics for the meantime."[5] Emily K. Hobson and Mónica A. Jiménez, for example, demonstrate in their contributions that radical care is possible from within confinement, and that feminists, in the words of Jiménez, "resist US colonial structures even while being held deeply within them." Hobson's contribution, drawn from a larger project on incarcerated people's organizing against HIV/AIDS inside prisons and jails across the United States, focuses on how organizers used the AIDS Memorial Quilt "both to mourn and to organize." Hobson intervenes in the false dichotomy between caregiving and activism that has pervaded the historiography of AIDS organizing to definitively argue for caregiving as a form of political action. This claim is illustrated by Hobson's astute reading of quilt squares created largely in women's prisons. As HIV/AIDS organizers' work increased in tandem with government officials' neglect, the complexity and quality of their art increased, evidencing how their access to self-expression was hard-won. Incarcerated women in the maximum security wing of the Federal Correctional Institution, Marianna, summarized their organizing efforts with the phrase "While we are in prison, we are still free to love."

The failure of the carceral state to extinguish solidarity is also illustrated by Jiménez's biographical history of her great-aunt Monserrate del Valle, "Titi Monse," a Puerto Rican nationalist arrested in 1950 for attempting to overthrow the US government. "Searching for Monse" explores the difficulty of tracing the life of a possibly illiterate revolutionary who deliberately did not record her political activities to evade government surveillance, and who did not speak of revolution after starting a new life in New York City. But Jiménez "finds" Monse in the Arecibo Women's Jail, where she spent two years before a jury found insufficient evidence to convict her under an antisedition law. During this period, incarcerated nationalists relied on one another and other incarcerated women to survive their conditions of confinement; through their care they also refused "to allow the colonial state to demean them or their dignity."

Beyond prison walls, feminist activists in essays by Kaysha Corinealdi, Romina A. Green Rioja, and Spencer Beswick developed multipronged strategies to build what Beswick describes as "feminist dual power" modeled on Zapatista women's revolutionary work in Chiapas: building grassroots feminist infrastructure to "meet needs outside of the state and capitalism" alongside "genuine democratic institutions . . . that directly challenge the hegemony" of the state. As Corinealdi writes, early twentieth-century Afro-Panamanian communities "survived and sometimes even thrived . . . *in spite of* the state, not because of state interest or investment." In her essay, Corinealdi documents how Felicia Santizo and Sara Sotillo, two Black feminist educators in Panama, mobilized working women to set their own agendas for collective care. They redistributed access to basic social goods, including food and literacy, and they organized for dignified working conditions for teachers. Across more than two decades of organizing, Santizo and Sotillo created flourishing community-based mutual aid programs to "[work] around the state." When they confronted "'prevailing circumstances'"—economic crisis, antifeminist backlash, and anticommunist repression—"'which we cannot fight, much less escape,'" they led feminist organizations and teachers unions that issued unrelenting demands for "what the state owed" their communities.

In Green Rioja's essay, the economic austerity of late twentieth-century Argentina catalyzed working-class women to build dual power within nested sites of capital abandonment, criminalization of reproductive health care, and a patriarchal labor movement—organizing that, in turn, transformed the scope and power of the country's feminist movement. During the neoliberal economic crisis of the 1990s, as rising numbers of working-class women joined the paid labor force, they were forced to "choose between having an illegal abortion that could lead to their death or giving birth to a future starving child." Poor Argentine women connected their struggles for control over their reproductive autonomy with their economic conditions, which were ignored or ridiculed by sexist, male-dominated worker organizations: "Do you speak in assembly meetings? Did you decide on your maternity?," one flier for the first assembly of *piqueteras*, or unemployed women, asked. Through this analysis, women consolidated their understanding of themselves as political subjects by creating *espacios de mujeres* (women's spaces), taking over a factory, and fortifying the feminist movement with class-centered politics.

Reproductive autonomy was also central to anarcha-feminist analysis of structural patriarchal and capitalist violence in the 1990s United States. In his essay, Beswick highlights the important contribution that feminists in the Love and Rage Revolutionary Anarchist Federation made to the struggle for abortion access during this period, rejecting law as the terrain of battle and the state as an avenue for the protection of rights. "Our freedom will not come through the passage of yet more laws but through the building of communities strong enough to defend themselves against anti-choice and anti-queer terror, rape, battery, child abuse and police harassment," Love and Ragers wrote. Rather than direct their organization's demands at a state that "would never protect them," Love and Ragers built dual power by physically defending embattled abortion clinics against antiabortion activists' violence—in this way defending the limited right to reproductive health care ostensibly protected in *Roe v. Wade*. Second, the organization empowered women to provide their own "basic gynecological care" through self-help groups and "public cervix announcements" detailing "how to end early term pregnancies safely with a group of friends." Between fighting in the streets and running menstrual extraction tutorials, anarcha-feminists argued that building "women's capacity to care for their own bodies and reproduction materially lessens state power."

If these histories demonstrate the necessity of "working around the state" to make care, bodily autonomy, and worker power possible, essays by Gill-Sadler and Edwards and by Berg argue that radical care is also engendered through community defense. Gill-Sadler and Edwards read Toni Cade Bambara's cultural production, with particular attention to her filmmaking, to explore how Bambara, in concert with other Black feminist cultural workers, refused the 1960s turn to "warfare that governance wraps in care." Thinking with Bambara's speculative practice of "living in," Gill-Sadler and Edwards elucidate "a radical Black feminist geometry of power" that exposes state-sponsored care as surveillance and minoritarian upward mobility as capitalist exploitation while imagining "horizontal power that privileges radical collective care." Bambara's work does not make reparative appeals to a shape-shifting state that evades accountability for its continued violence. Rather, she first exposes this violence as a matter of course, as in her 1987 film *The Bombing of Osage Avenue*, which invites viewers to see the 1985 bombing of Philadelphia's MOVE organization as yet another horror manifested from deep legacies of a settler-colonial, white supremacist police state. She then replaces violence and violence-as-care with a narrative of "living in" in her speculative treatment for a never-produced film, *Come as You Are*, in which several characters facing homelessness take over a luxury apartment complex and experiment with "contra-state forms of care and repair."

From Black feminist cultural workers who imagine and represent alternative radical forms of care, the issue turns to sex worker abolitionists working collectively in community defense groups so that they can, in the words of the Clandestine Whores Network, "refuse our deaths." For Berg's interlocutors, appeals to "[humanize . . .] the sex worker" by resisting racism, transphobia, and whorephobia to win the dubious protections of the state are a dead end—quite literally, since it is the state that "makes sex workers available for death." This structural reality compounds sex workers' vulnerability to individual attacks because "citizens take cues [from the state] about who is available for disposal." It is at this point that the sex workers in Berg's archive linger over the limits of the abolitionist project of transformative justice, which insists on targeting structures, not individuals. As one of Berg's interviewees asks, "What about individual abusers who form a structure?" Contemplating what it means to practice collective defense against rapists and murderers—both police and johns—sex worker abolitionists read "historical resources for navigating tactical ambivalence in the present" to produce "a sex worker theory of transformative justice." Berg's essay explores the question of whether "stop[ping] the war on whores" will require stopping not only violent structures but also the individuals who do the state's work for it.

India Thusi's essay grounds the politics of sexual policing in South Africa and documents how sex workers "manage the risks" of their criminalized labor. Reporting on contemporary campaigns to repeal prostitution laws, Thusi asks what the possibilities for sex worker safety and defense might look like after decriminalization. While Thusi argues that decriminalization would not eliminate the structural harms of economic exploitation and gender-based violence, abolishing criminal sanctions "might be the necessary first step for sex workers to live in a material world where they feel safer and in better control of their lives."

Anticolonial feminist movements against femicide and authoritarianism further expose how varied systems of inequality threaten interpersonal safety. Essays by Jennifer Mogannam and Manijeh Moradian demonstrate how recent feminist uprisings in Palestine and Iran were ignited by the murders of Israa Gharib and Jina (Mahsa) Amini, respectively. Mogannam demonstrates that in Palestine the nationwide protest organized under the slogan "No free homeland without free women" represents "a twofold challenge to the patriarchal order": a blow against Zionist colonialism carried out through gender-based violence and economic deprivation, and a rejection of social and legal tolerance of femicide in Palestinian society and political culture. The rallying cry of young women in Iran—"Women, Life, Freedom"—mobilized wide swaths of the population who embraced the feminist insight that gender and sexual oppression are, as Moradian points out, "central to the operations and structures of authoritarian power as a whole." Moradian states that the movement in Iran is "the culmination of many decades of organizing," though she also insists that the "feminist understanding of the goals of revolution" is "unprecedented in the history of Iran." Like the Plurinational Meeting of Women, Lesbians, Trans, Bisexual, Intersexual, and Nonbinary in Argentina, in Green Rioja's essay, this feminist understanding includes "the decriminalization of any gender or sexual orientation" and explicitly names the LGTBQIA+ community. Gender and sexual liberation, rather than mere equality, is the demand. Mogannam's essay, in contrast, understands the 2021 emergence of the Palestinian Feminist Collective as a moment in the long history of "Palestinian women's and feminist organizing," and her essay illustrates that "a Palestinian anticolonial feminist politics" has existed since "Western forms of colonialism were imposed on the lands and peoples of Palestine." Indeed, the history offered by Mogannam lays claim to a decidedly decolonial feminism that rejects associations with Western imperialism and accounts "for very real material conditions being felt by women and queer Palestinians," arguing that liberation means freedom from colonialism and patriarchy.

The essays in this issue draw on diverse and innovative archives of feminist strategies for confronting state violence. They move between scales of biography, radical cells, worker collectives, and social movements. In a visual essay, Jessie B. Ramey and Catherine A. Evans illustrate the importance of archives that work at the scale of a single life. The Kipp Dawson Papers at the University of Pittsburgh and over thirty interviews with Dawson amplify lessons drawn from a lifetime of resisting multiple forms of state violence—including the repression and criminalization of organizing efforts. Ramey and Evans approach their history of Dawson, a leader in overlapping movements for justice in the United States since 1960, through the framework of "radical collaboration" that, like Bambara's cultural production, rejects vertical power. Dawson's lifetime of activism in civil rights, antiwar, feminist, gay liberation, labor, and education justice movements exposes a state that distributes violence alongside limited rights. Dawson's antiwar organizing was partly sabotaged by the COINTELPRO strategy of sowing divisions within movements, leading to her expulsion from the West Coast Spring Mobilization Committee to End the War in Vietnam. She was repeatedly laid off from the mines during her thirteen years as a coal worker and labor organizer, and her career as a public school teacher was marked by numerous efforts to resist massive state divestment from public education. At the same time, her successful fight in the courts to have her queer family recognized by the state legalized gay families in Pennsylvania. Dawson offers lessons for facing down nimble and relentless structural oppressions that echo the radical care articulated in other essays. "When people can experience and feel the beauty of struggling together for one another and leave behind the 'me-myself-and-I' paradigm at the heart of exploitation and isolated misery, all good things are possible."

Gill-Sadler and Edwards characterize those who "live into" horizontal power as "creative combatants," quoting Bambara's foreword to *This Bridge Called My Back*: "women determined to be a danger to our enemies."[6] Drawing on the abolitionist feminist vision of building a life-affirming presence, the feminists featured here have practiced care that endangers the state. Collectively, these histories offer one snapshot of the enduring work of feminists who recognized, as Sotillo reminds us in Corinealdi's essay, "that individual actions are lost to oblivion, while those based in cooperation live on." There are also armies of creative combatants outside the frame, studying, adapting, and creating strategies to be dangerous to the state. Feminism has been a central force in combating state power even when, as Mogannam points out about the Palestinian context, there exist "multidirectional challenges to the concept and language of feminism." The essays in this issue offer a rejoinder to any version of feminism that colludes with imperialism, neoliberalism, global capital, and carcerality in pursuit of equality rather than remaking worlds, or that claims feminism for a singular subject of "woman" rather than gender liberation for all. The anticolonial, abolitionist, anticapitalist feminist maneuvering collected here aims to fuel "the momentum for more feminism" that Green Rioja sees as characteristic of the feminist movement in Argentina. Such momentum holds the promise of not only undermining state power but also making radical, collective care the revolutionary strategy that can build a world from inside this one. As the Clandestine Whores Network puts it in Berg's essay: "Tonight is a great night to refuse our deaths."

Anne Gray Fischer is an assistant professor of gender history at the University of Texas at Dallas. She is the author of *The Streets Belong to Us: Sex, Race, and Police Power from Segregation to Gentrification* (2022).

Sara Matthiesen is an associate professor of history and women's, gender, and sexuality studies at George Washington University. She is the author of *Reproduction Reconceived: Family Making and the Limits of Choice after* Roe v. Wade (2021), which won the 2022 Sara A. Whaley Prize from the National Women's Studies Association.

Marisol LeBrón is an associate professor of feminist studies and critical race and ethnic studies at the University of California, Santa Cruz. She is the author of *Against Muerto Rico: Lessons from the Verano Boricua/Contra Muerto Rico: Lecciones del Verano Boricua* (2021) and *Policing Life and Death: Race, Violence, and Resistance in Puerto Rico* (2019). With Yarimar Bonilla, she is the editor of *Aftershocks of Disaster: Puerto Rico before and after the Storm* (2019).

Notes

1. Enszer, *Complete Works of Pat Parker*, 69–70.
2. Edwards, *Other Side of Terror*, 2.
3. Davis et al., *Abolition. Feminism. Now.*
4. Quoted in Davis et al., *Abolition. Feminism. Now.*, 51.
5. Berg, *Porn Work*, 9.
6. Bambara, foreword, viii. Bambara credits June Jordan for this formulation.

References

Bambara, Toni Cade. Foreword to *This Bridge Called My Back: Writings by Radical Women of Color*, edited by Cherríe Moraga and Gloria Anzaldúa, xiii–xvii. Watertown, MA: Persephone, 1981.

Berg, Heather. *Porn Work: Sex, Labor, and Late Capitalism*. Chapel Hill: University of North Carolina Press, 2021.

Davis, Angela Y., Gina Dent, Erica R. Meiners, and Beth E. Richie. *Abolition. Feminism. Now.* Chicago: Haymarket Books, 2022.

Edwards, Erica. *The Other Side of Terror: Black Women and the Culture of US Empire*. New York: New York University Press, 2021.

Enszer, Julie R., ed. *The Complete Works of Pat Parker*. Dover, FL: A Midsummer Night's Press and Sinister Wisdom, 2016.

The AIDS Quilt in Prison

Care Work in and against the Carceral State

Emily K. Hobson

A fireworks pattern of brightly colored paint bursts out from behind gray bars sewn onto a rectangle of black fabric measuring three by six feet. Small black hearts in the field of paint hold forty-four handwritten names. A weeping heart, whose red color pops against the black fabric, breaks through the bars, while above them, a white dove carries in its beak a flowing banner that reads, "Although our bodies are confined in prison, our hearts are free to be with our loved ones who have died with AIDS." The quilt makers record themselves at bottom right: "By Women Prisoners, Shawnee Unit, Marianna, Florida" (fig. 1).

This sewn and painted memorial, now joined into block 3240 of the AIDS Memorial Quilt, was crafted in 1993 by thirteen people in the Shawnee control unit (high-security surveillance wing) of the Federal Correctional Institution (FCI) Marianna, located seventy miles west of Tallahassee, Florida.[1] Beginning in 1991, incarcerated women in the Shawnee Unit organized an AIDS Awareness Group to advance knowledge about HIV transmission, testing, and treatment and to support their peers in the prison who were living with HIV and AIDS. The group's quilt makers drew together a range of tools and skills to make their panel, using toothbrushes and combs to splatter the paint that made the fireworks design, masking off the black hearts as negative space amid the paint, and embroidering the intersections of the prison bars to appear three-dimensional. On October 12, 1993, they displayed their quilt inside the prison in a memorial

Radical History Review
Issue 148 (January 2024)   DOI 10.1215/01636545-10846780
© 2024 by MARHO: The Radical Historians' Organization, Inc.

Figure 1. "Women Prisoners of Marianna Florida," received February 1994 from FCI Marianna, panel 7 of block 3240, AIDS Quilt. Image courtesy of AIDS Memorial Quilt.

that honored friends, family, and fellow incarcerated people who had died of AIDS or who were living with HIV.[2]

The incarcerated quilt makers at Marianna sought to communicate to audiences both in prison and beyond. Through words and design, they asserted mourning as a form of resistance to imprisonment and an expression of solidarity across prison walls. They echoed this with the tagline in their memorial program: "While we are in prison, we are still free to love." The quilt makers' letter to the national offices of the AIDS Quilt gave further evidence of their goals: "The heart behind bars design is one familiar to prisoners around the country. We are strengthened by the knowledge that women and men in other prisons are organizing themselves to fight AIDS as we are. We hope other prisoners will see our panel and take strength from it, too."

Their hope was well founded: across the late 1980s and 1990s, incarcerated people organized against HIV/AIDS in dozens of prisons and jails across the United States. Black, Latinx, and white, these HIV/AIDS activists in women's and men's prisons led peer education, pushed for medical access and compassionate release, built inside-outside correspondence and publication networks, and supported each other and their loved ones through tactics ranging from infirmary visits to fundraising walkathons on prison yards. They also, and especially in women's prisons, crafted contributions to the AIDS Quilt. Incarcerated activists used quilt making both to mourn and to organize, and facing rigid constraints on expression, they worked through rather than against the perceived sentimentality of the Quilt.

Over the height of the AIDS crisis in the United States, people in prisons created and sent at least 134 contributions to the AIDS Quilt.[3] These quilts were overwhelmingly (101 of the total) made in women's prisons, and mostly in the early 1990s in New York State, where the epidemic's impacts among women and especially Black and Latinx women proved among the starkest in the country. Prison quilts honored subjects ranging from individuals to whole neighborhoods and collectively recorded over fifteen hundred names. These are conservative figures, as it remains difficult to enumerate all the prison quilts created or all of the people they honor. The databases of the AIDS Quilt record the names visible on a quilt and what person or organization sent it, if known, but many prison quilts list only first names, and many names are difficult to read because they were handwritten or inscribed with ink that has bled or faded over time.[4] Quilt makers did not always credit themselves as creators or make it explicit that they were quilting from a prison or jail. Further, a handful of prison quilts described in archival or published sources cannot be located in the AIDS Quilt databases, suggesting that at least a few were created but never sent to the Quilt's national office.

The scale and gendered patterns of prison quilts remain clear nonetheless. They represent a tiny fraction of the nearly fifty thousand total panels of the AIDS Quilt but were a persistent tool in incarcerated people's responses to the epidemic, one that both reflected and catalyzed organizing. The quilts' center of gravity in women's prisons likewise reflected their significance to the politics of HIV/AIDS. Prison quilts exemplified the interconnections that energized the AIDS movement, threading together protest and caregiving; mobilization and emotion; and queer, feminist, and antiracist politics.

The largest group of prison quilts (fifty-one) were created by members of AIDS Counseling and Education (ACE), an AIDS peer education project organized by people at Bedford Hills Correctional Facility, a women's prison in Westchester County, New York.[5] Located ninety minutes by train or car from midtown Manhattan, Bedford Hills had long been the site of incarcerated people's organizing and had drawn involvement from both reformers and radicals.[6] Two of ACE's leaders, Kathy Boudin and Judy Clark, were former members of the Weather Underground who were incarcerated on charges stemming from the 1981 Brink's robbery, which had been intended to support revolutionary activities led by the Black Liberation Army.[7] Another well-known ACE leader was Katrina Haslip, who after being released from Bedford Hills in 1990 became an active voice of the campaign to demand that the Centers for Disease Control expand the definition of AIDS to better address the epidemic among women, poor people, and people using injection drugs.[8] Boudin, Clark, Haslip, and others' networks across anti-imperialist, Black, feminist, queer, and other movements connected AIDS prison activism nationally through inside-outside ties.[9] These ties bolstered AIDS peer education—and quilt making—in other prisons, including federal women's prisons. While incarcerated people also crafted quilts in sites where they did not or could not launch sustained organizing, the quilts from Bedford Hills and federal women's prisons stand out in both number and content. Incarcerated activists used quilt making to make their losses visible, to build communities of advocacy and support, and to voice connections to home communities, the broader AIDS movement, and their freedom dreams.

AIDS, Incarceration, and Caregiving

The course and effects of the HIV/AIDS epidemic in the United States have been deeply intertwined with the feminization of poverty, the growth of mass incarceration, and other conditions of what Sara Matthiesen has characterized as state neglect and Ruth Wilson Gilmore has termed the "anti-state state." Matthiesen's concept names the pattern of policies that, since the 1970s, have withdrawn support for care labor and implemented obstacles to family making, through which the US state has "necessarily produced new forms of reproductive labor through its own negligence."[10] Gilmore's framework describes "people and parties who gain state power by denouncing state power," specifically by increasing reliance on prisons and jails while eradicating social welfare supports.[11] These racialized and gendered developments have held profound consequences for public health, including as related to HIV/AIDS. For example, the most significant federal source of funding against the epidemic, the 1990 Ryan White Comprehensive AIDS Resources Emergency (CARE) Act, furthered a shift from public spending to charities and required states to implement HIV criminalization laws.

By the mid-1980s the AIDS crisis was intensifying in prisons and among Black, Latinx, and poor people, both queer and straight, with particular effects among people using injection drugs and their sexual partners. Women, equated in this era with people assigned female, constituted a growing number of those affected. By 1990 New York and New Jersey registered AIDS as the third-leading cause of death for all women aged fifteen to forty-four and as the leading cause of death for Black women in that age group; New York found that 20 percent of people entering women's prisons and 11.5 percent of those entering men's prisons tested positive for HIV.[12] Transmission inside prison was one problem, but it also became clear that incarcerated people with HIV typically contracted the virus before prison, with their criminalization often related to and occurring in the same contexts as their HIV risk. Both inside and outside prisons, the AIDS crisis propelled people into what Celeste Watkins-Hayes terms the "transformative project" of addressing HIV as a personal and collective outcome of "injuries of inequality."[13]

AIDS activists in women's prisons challenged carceral conditions that facilitated HIV stigma and illness, including isolation, high stress, breaches of confidentiality, and medical neglect. Through peer workshops and counseling, they identified their HIV risk factors as including histories of injection drug use, their own or a lover's; unprotected sex with men, for some including sex work or transactional sex; and sex with women, which many saw as a concern given both the community prevalence of the virus and the lack of research into lesbian transmission and women's HIV. They discussed how opportunistic diseases, made more widespread by poor health care and living conditions, accelerated the progression from HIV to AIDS and how racism and sexism kept people from diagnosis, treatment, and services.

AIDS prison activists worked in dialogue with allies on the outside, particularly women's and prison caucuses of the AIDS Coalition to Unleash Power (ACT UP), AIDS organizations in communities of color and those serving women, and legal advocates ranging from the ACLU to the HIV Law Project. Many of these allies understood AIDS as creating a crisis of caregiving due to the disabling nature of the disease, the lack of adequate care and services, and the effects of these problems in families.[14] Activists in women's prisons built on this analysis by noting that incarceration, too, created a caregiving crisis that converged with AIDS. Most women in prisons were mothers, and most others provided caregiving labor in their families. Their incarceration denied their loved ones economic, emotional, and physical support. Those living with HIV especially feared losing parental rights due to their viral status if they did not die before they could return home.[15]

In this context, AIDS activists in women's prisons took up caregiving as both a (gendered) problem and a (gendered) solution, developing incisive critiques of state neglect while caring for each other. They did so within a carceral system that defined "rehabilitation" through gender normativity and domestic labor even as it moved, across these years of prison expansion, toward a warehousing model.[16] ACE member Roslyn Smith recalls with visceral detail changing her sick friends' diapers and cleaning up their diarrhea, noting that people had to sit in their feces when locked down overnight and adding, "the administration didn't really help us."[17] Later Bedford Hills' medical director relied on ACE to provide round-the-clock care for women who were ill or dying.[18] Amid these circumstances, ACE expressed frustration that "volunteerism is put forward by the government as the answer" to the epidemic, arguing that this imposed an ever more inequitable burden of unpaid labor on women in "the communities worst hit by HIV/AIDS [that] already have the least support and resources." They said that in fighting AIDS in prison, "we carry the weight of our oppression as women, as well as the oppression of racism, poverty, shrinking social services, hopelessness, and the drug epidemic." Or, as they put it most simply, "our story is the story of the AIDS epidemic among women."[19]

While caregiving was central to the AIDS movement, some imagined it in opposition to activism and as inherently less radical. Such juxtaposition could help spark protest by naming AIDS as a crisis whose needs outpaced services. But the gendered and racialized hierarchies that structured contrasts between activism and caregiving privileged masculinized, public, and rational action over feminized, domestic, and emotional labor.[20] As Larry Kramer put it in *The Normal Heart*, "I thought I was starting with a bunch of Ralph Naders and Green Berets, and the first instant they have to take a stand on a political issue and fight, almost in front of my eyes they turn into a bunch of nurses' aides."[21] The supposed binary between activism and caregiving was belied by many continuities, including direct action to fund

AIDS services and treatment; challenges to the racist, classist, and sexist practices of some AIDS organizations; and access policies to welcome sick and vulnerable people into direct action, among other examples.[22] AIDS prison organizing offered a further challenge to this binary, drawing attention to a context in which it was particularly apparent that providing AIDS care might be a way to challenge state power, as well as that care labor and organizing overlapped.

Incarcerated HIV/AIDS activists risked both prohibition and co-optation by prison authorities. Simply discussing HIV could breach prison rules against sex and drugs, but prison administrations treated incarcerated people's leadership, circulation across housing units and racial groups, and communication with outside supporters as the biggest threats. Administrators at times banned AIDS peer education outright or sought to repress projects by transferring leaders to another prison (this could backfire as activists shared information in new sites).[23] More commonly, administrators worked to control projects by requiring peer counselors to complete many layers of certification or by assigning supervision by psychologists or chaplains.[24] By 1990, 96 percent of federal and state prison systems claimed HIV education in at least one facility, but this figure included states with just one program in one prison and counted everything from an occasional video screening to extensive programs led by incarcerated people.[25]

While ACE won more autonomy than any other prison AIDS project, it also continually contended with carceral control. The founders of ACE approached Elaine Lord, the superintendent of Bedford Hills, with their idea for a project in the fall of 1987. She told them to submit a formal written proposal, which they did, and she approved it. Yet soon after this, she banned ACE from operating altogether, claiming suspicions over drugs.[26] She then renewed her approval with constraints that made it nearly impossible for ACE to meet, to correspond with outside groups, or to carry out peer education. Finally, in November 1988, Lord authorized ACE to operate under the supervision of the prison's new medical director, who had been hired to meet the terms of *Todaro v. Ward* (1977), a class action suit compelling Bedford Hills to improve its medical care.[27] ACE now began an extensive program of workshops and counseling. In the fall of 1989, through a grant from the New York AIDS Institute, Lord hired two nonincarcerated staff to serve as ACE's director and temporary coordinator. Under the terms of the grant, ACE became a project of the Women and AIDS Resource Network and the Columbia University School of Public Health and was charged with crafting a model AIDS program for New York prisons. It also won permission to convert a room into an office and to hire some incarcerated participants as "ACE staff," a role that was counted as a prison job.[28]

As ACE participants later reflected, institutional approval and space simultaneously strengthened their work and changed it, including by generating tensions over decision-making, resources, and power.[29] These stresses refracted the contradictions of care work within and against the carceral state. As traced through the AIDS prison movement, incarcerated people's caregiving for and with one another was at once an urgent intervention to ease suffering, a means of organizing community against the atomization of confinement, and a form of labor that authorities might seek to co-opt. Prison quilts were shaped by these same contradictions and bore marks of carceral control. Yet, as tools for collective expression under the cover of sentiment and feminine craftwork, prison quilts held potentially subversive power to challenge the widening meanings of HIV/AIDS.

The AIDS Quilt and Prison Art

Prison quilts challenged common assumptions about the AIDS Quilt writ large. As Nino Testa recounts, the AIDS Quilt has been viewed alternately as "a powerful ambassador and transformational work of communal mourning" and as "maudlin," infantilizing, depoliticizing, degaying, and nationalist.[30] Initiated in 1987, with its first 1,920 panels displayed in Washington, DC, during the second National March on Washington for Lesbian and Gay Rights, the AIDS Quilt gained considerable public visibility and support. By the spring of 1988 it had been taken on a twenty-city national tour that raised nearly half a million dollars for AIDS service organizations and drew new panels from around the country. By 1989 it had become the subject of an Academy Award–winning documentary, *Common Threads*, and over time it toured internationally and won repeated displays on the National Mall.[31]

ACT UP's mobilizations of anger and grief contrasted with the AIDS Quilt both affectively and in orientation to the nation's capital.[32] By the early 1990s, many in ACT UP were organizing political funerals to mourn and to call for accountability, drawing inspiration from sources that ranged from the antiapartheid movement to the artist David Wojnarowicz's provocation "If I die of AIDS—forget burial—just drop my body on the steps of the FDA." In the 1992 Ashes Action, which ACT UP members explicitly contrasted to an AIDS Quilt display then occurring at the National Mall, activists carried their loved ones' cremains to the fence surrounding the White House and deposited the ashes on the lawn. The next year, following the wishes of the activist Tim Bailey, ACT UP members drove his casket from New Jersey to Washington, DC, where police fought mourners and at one point nearly pulled the casket to the ground.[33] In contrast to these confrontations, the AIDS Quilt could appear conciliatory and naive. Yet, as Testa holds, "activists worked with and against the Quilt in complicated ways that are not easily reduced to radical/sentimental binaries."[34] Some quilts expressed anger or cynicism, and some were carried in political funerals. Prison quilts were similarly complex.

Incarcerated quilt makers continually navigated constraints on their self-expression. Nicole Fleetwood and Rox Samer offer helpful guides in understanding these problems, as each examines how incarcerated people have used art and performance to sustain connections with the outside, to act queer, and otherwise to push back. For Fleetwood, the concept of carceral aesthetics frames visual art made in prison within the limits incarcerated people face on the materials they may use and the time and space they have to create, along with the threat of their artwork being confiscated, destroyed, or used to justify punishment. Drawing on dozens of interviews with incarcerated and formerly incarcerated artists, their family members, and prison art teachers, Fleetwood identifies art and artmaking as a source of "relational possibilities that disrupt the mandate of prison," including connections with loved ones and supporters.[35]

Moving from visual art to performance, Samer considers how incarcerated people have used theater and performance to enact queer and Black feminist refusals of carceral norms.[36] She highlights a feminist documentary video made in 1974 at Bedford Hills that records incarcerated women staging role-plays that were marked by affection, humor, and flirtation and that critiqued prisons' gender conformist strategies as well as the concept of rehabilitation itself.[37] Some fifteen years later, AIDS prison activists used plays and improv performance to challenge HIV stigma, dramatize the impacts of the epidemic, and demonstrate ways to negotiate safer sex and harm reduction.[38] Judy Clark, a leader of ACE, recalls that to evade the prison's rules against homosexuality, ACE would satirically stage discussions of safer sex in the setting of a nun's convent.[39] AIDS peer educators also infused queer potential into role-plays depicting straight relationships, making these cross-gender performances into sites of play and camp.

Incarcerated quilt makers generally relied on volunteers or prison staff to bring them quilting supplies, and they needed permission for all steps of their work, including gathering together, using tools, storing work in progress, and sending finished panels to the AIDS Quilt. Their final quilts reflect a range of circumstances for creation. Some are elaborately constructed, while others are made with ink markers rather than with the sharp tools necessary for cutting, sewing, and needlework. Prison quilts varied and changed over time in ways that underscore the uneven time, space, and materials incarcerated people won for self-expression.

The earliest prison quilts are typified by abstraction, a characteristic that may be explained in part by these quilts being made outside peer education or other organizing contexts. The first was received from a women's prison in Rhode Island in June 1988, just months into the AIDS Quilt's first national tour. Titled "Fellow Prisoners," it illustrates ten birds in flight, nine of them brightly colored and one in black, each bearing a single initial and breaking out of prison bars that are set against a white field.[40] A handful of other panels followed with similar themes of anonymity and flight. One received in June 1991 from the men's prison in Elmira, New York, represents butterflies breaking through bars.[41] Each butterfly is cut from colorful, patterned cloth and labeled by a first name as well as birth and death years. At the left, a brown chrysalis includes a name and birth year only, with no year of death. Presumably this person was sick when the quilt was created but had yet to make their final metamorphosis; perhaps they were the quilt maker. Without a full name, it is impossible to know when or whether they died.

The AIDS Quilt staged its first formal display in a prison on February 20 and 21, 1992, at California Medical Facility, a men's prison in Vacaville that held the state's largest number of incarcerated people with HIV/AIDS.[42] Incarcerated people had organized to bring about this event and, more broadly, to challenge the prison's medical neglect and lack of action on HIV/AIDS. Responding in part to their action, the prison's chaplain had launched a pastoral care program through which incarcerated people won approval to visit peers in the hospital ward, including to stay in patient rooms during count so that people would not be left to die alone.[43] The program's participants communicated with reporters and lawyers about the prison's conditions and reached out to the AIDS Quilt's national office to request the quilt's display. They also crafted their own quilt, a block measuring twelve by twelve feet (equivalent to eight panels) that depicted four faceless men, white, Latinx, Black, and Indigenous, dressed in prison uniforms and holding one another's hands, standing behind bars in front of a waving rainbow flag.[44] While this quilt openly depicted gay identity, multiracial unity, and affection, it also reflected censorship. As the activist Brian Carmichael recalls, "We fought with the prison bitterly about how many names they would let us include, because our count was approaching two hundred and fifty that had died there," but the prison allowed quilt makers to list just ninety-three of those who had died with AIDS at Vacaville from 1985 to 1992.[45]

The Vacaville quilt both commemorated a first in AIDS Quilt history and marked a turning point. By 1992, eleven years since the first published reports of the epidemic, HIV infections and AIDS deaths were rising sharply, including among women and communities of color. Many longtime AIDS activists had died, while others, propelled by grief and exhausted from years of sustained organizing, were turning to political funerals as a new tactic of protest and mourning. It was at this time that incarcerated people, especially in women's prisons, increasingly sent panels to the AIDS Quilt and increasingly quilted overt resistance and self-expression. Prison quilts proliferated, grew more personalized and less abstract, and drew connections to the wider AIDS movement. As the epidemic worsened and widened, people in women's prisons used quilt making to make their losses visible, to sustain bonds with their home communities, and, at the outer edge of possibility, to express an abolitionist imaginary.

Making Losses Visible and Sustaining Ties with Home

Quilts play a central role in the story of ACE at Bedford Hills. In the fall of 1987, after submitting a project proposal to the prison superintendent and while waiting for approval, ACE's cofounders worked informally to develop their knowledge, gathering in the prison library to read and to write information requests to hospitals and AIDS organizations. Further, using paints donated by an area church and working with the support of volunteers whose presence enabled them to meet, they began to make panels for women who had died with AIDS in the prison.[46] In February 1988 they set up tables covered with cloth and made fifteen panels that they displayed in a school building and in living units. Members of ACE later stated that "the quilt project was the final and maybe necessary step before the actual formation of ACE."[47] While the panels created in these initial sessions cannot be found in the AIDS Quilt's databases and may not have been sent to the its national office, ACE's account affirms the centrality of quilt making to their organizing.

As their origin story suggests, ACE members saw their efforts as autonomous and self-directed. While they sought out administrative approval to operate, they viewed the most crucial step in their organizing to be a shared sense of purpose and found that the AIDS Quilt helped catalyze that motivation. Because quilts expressed love rather than stigma, and because they prompted expressions of grief that revealed the epidemic's wide reach among incarcerated people and their communities, creating and displaying quilts opened up conversations about HIV risk, AIDS illness, and issues of sex, drugs, and perceived guilt and innocence. These conversations brought people together across differences of race, religion, sexuality, and viral status and encouraged them to think through their circumstances together. Indeed, although it was best recorded by ACE, quilt making propelled organizing in multiple prisons. Carmichael describes the AIDS Quilt's display and creation at Vacaville as "life-altering" and has detailed how it sparked a monthslong medication strike in the prison that by late 1992 had won better medical treatment and a prison hospice.[48]

After ACE won its office space at the end of 1989, it became an even more important hub for quilt making, drawing new participants and fielding panel requests from people who were dying. With space to store and display quilts, the office began to regularly host memorials, hanging panels on yarn looped through the small holes in the ceiling board.[49] As the scale of death inside and outside the prison grew, ACE's organizing offered a means to cope and to find some sense of agency against the epidemic, and ACE participants expressed their bonds with one another through their quilts.

In contrast to earlier prison quilts, which were generally anonymous and abstract, ACE made highly individualized panels: "For Sandy, there was a baseball diamond and her favorite song, 'Do Me Baby.' Fat Baby had her Newports; Diane loved horses and her quilt was a big horse."[50] Again, these specific panels cannot be located, but others attributed to ACE reflect the same style (fig. 2). ACE panels were typified by a name in large script together with depictions of the person's favorite things or accomplishments, such as a Model T car, a bag of rice and can of corned beef, a diploma, or status as ACE staff. Some details suggest items from the prison

Figure 2. Blocks 2881 (*left*) and 2882 (*right*), AIDS Quilt. Panels 1–7 of block 2881 (*all but the bottom right*) and panels 1–3 and 5–7 of block 2822 (*all but the center right and bottom right*) were received in 1993 from the ACE at Bedford Hills. Images courtesy of AIDS Memorial Quilt.

commissary, while others point to achievements or things missed from the outside. Around the names and painted items, quilt makers inscribed messages to say good-bye, memorializing women as they were known through AIDS prison organizing.

Quilts made in New York State women's prisons where people did not develop sustained organizing offer important comparisons to those made by ACE. Visually, these quilts suggest more circumscribed time, space, and materials to create.[51] They typically were made with markers rather than paint or sewing, lacked unified designs, and memorialized many people at once, with several names clustered together with decorative crosses, flowers, or animals. While evoking limits on creation, these quilts affirm common themes in how incarcerated women were experiencing and thinking about HIV/AIDS. For example, quilts made in the women's prisons at Taconic (Westchester County) and Suffolk County (Long Island) speak to home geographies in New York City. A detail from a panel made at Suffolk, which honors Ada or "Smiley," reads "St. Mary's, Alabama, Brooklyn, New York. Remembering all of you."[52] Another from Taconic recalls "South Jamaica, Queens. Sutphin Blvd. 150th St. 119th Ave. In memory of you all."[53] Similarly but at a greater scale, ACE curriculum analyzed the community effects of HIV/AIDS, and some veterans of ACE established ACE-OUT, a program in which formerly incarcerated women with HIV returned home and continued peer education in New York City.

Although not crafted in contexts of peer education, the quilts from Taconic and Suffolk did reflect support from outside allies. Suzanne Kessler, who served for six months as ACE's temporary coordinator, went on to volunteer at Taconic and assisted with quilts there, including by shipping them to the AIDS Quilt's national office.[54] An AIDS program at Cornell University supported the creation of the

Suffolk quilt and reported that incarcerated women's next project was to craft crib quilts for babies with AIDS.[55] ACE and other peer educators developed even stronger connections to outside work against AIDS. Members of ACE not only made baby quilts but also organized fundraising walkathons on the prison yard through which incarcerated people contributed funds from their commissary accounts to beneficiaries including Incarnation Children's Center, a New York City AIDS foster care home.[56] In the federal prison at Dublin, California, peer educators crafted a block (a twelve-by-twelve-foot quilt) decorated with stuffed animals, baby blocks, and the bilingual message "Our hearts cry for all the orphaned children / Nuestros corazones lloran por los niños huérfanos." This quilt was part of a triptych by Pleasanton AIDS Counseling and Education (PLACE, whose name reflected the Dublin prison's former name). Like ACE at Bedford Hills, PLACE organized workshops, peer counseling, and a walkathon that raised thousands of dollars.[57] Its walkathon specifically benefited AIDS care at the Children's Hospital of Oakland and the Ambassador Hotel, a residency in San Francisco's Tenderloin neighborhood that provided hospice to homeless people with AIDS.[58]

The relationships expressed through quilts were central to their meaning, and censorship of such bonds registered carceral control. Carmichael's story of the names on the Vacaville quilt reflected one kind of censorship of mourning. Another example appeared through "Women of Albion Correctional Facility," created in 1996 at a prison near Rochester, New York.[59] On its left, the Albion panel depicts a dozen figures resembling paper dolls behind bars; on the right, a dove flies above an explosion of color. As an accompanying letter explained, the paper dolls "represent the women's incarceration," while the right side "represent[s] the outside world." In the center of the panel, an appliquéd heart fastened shut with yellow yarn holds "a 2×3 foot 'remembrance cloth'" that was "made available to those in Albion's general population" to write names and messages, allowing more people to participate despite the "security environment." Yet, with the strip of cloth permanently hidden inside the quilt, its memories were kept quiet.

Prison quilts held their greatest power when created through organizing, a process that requires both building and naming relationships of common interest and shared goals. Underscoring this, some prison quilts named bonds across the wider AIDS movement, with several honoring fellow AIDS activists and at least one memorializing protest itself. Such quilts spoke to intertwined goals of survival and freedom and reflected how widely incarcerated activists envisioned their communities as well as how ambitiously they imagined their goals.

Drawing Movement Ties and Sewing an Abolitionist Imaginary

Prison quilts that honored activists and activism built on long-standing radical traditions of memorialization. Indeed, one of the earliest prison-related quilts was made by a nonincarcerated activist for a comrade who died behind bars. Created by Marion Banzhaf, who was radicalized in the 1970s as an abortion access organizer and anti-Klan activist and later became the executive director of the New Jersey Women and AIDS Network, it honored Kuwasi Balagoon, a member of the New York Black Panther Party who had been targeted by police as a member of the Panther 21, became a member of the Black Liberation Army, and was later convicted on charges stemming from the 1981 Brink's robbery, which also led to the incarceration of Kathy Boudin and Judy Clark at Bedford Hills.[60] Balagoon died of AIDS in prison in December 1986, and his death caught many by surprise. He has increasingly been claimed as a queer member of the Black liberation movement.[61] Balagoon's loss, and the discussions it generated inside the prison, propelled his codefendant David Gilbert, together with two other incarcerated leaders, Mujahid Farid and Angel Nieves, to organize the Prisoner Education Project on AIDS (PEPA) in the men's prison at Auburn, New York. Though short-lived, PEPA held lasting influence in ACE and other AIDS peer education projects.[62]

As AIDS prison activism grew, its quilt makers memorialized each other. Katrina Haslip became a prominent example. A jailhouse lawyer and a cofounder of ACE, she was released from Bedford Hills in 1990 and became active in the years-long campaign to, as its name and slogan stated, "Change the Definition" of AIDS. Led by women's caucuses of ACT UP in concert with the HIV Law Project, the campaign demanded that cervical cancer and other gynecological conditions, bacterial pneumonia, and tuberculosis be added to the AIDS diagnostic criteria so as to better recognize the epidemic in women and people assigned female, injection drug users, and people who experienced AIDS as a disease of poverty. One reason these changes mattered was that an AIDS diagnosis enabled people to access disability benefits. Haslip lived to win the campaign but died just weeks before the expanded definition went into effect, in deep poverty and with her death uncounted in the national tally of AIDS.[63] Surviving ACE members memorialized her with a quilt that honored her Muslim faith and her role as a Black woman in their multiracial organizing.[64] Haslip was also named in a quilt made by PLACE that honored women leaders of the AIDS prison movement around the country.[65]

Similarly, the quilt featured at the opening of this article, made in the federal prison at Marianna, Florida, reflected bonds with men across the AIDS movement (fig. 1). Names on this quilt included Elliot España, who had worked to support HIV peer education at the Washington, DC, jail; Mike Riegle, a writer and editor for the newspaper *Gay Community News* who had written an ongoing column on prison AIDS issues; and Kuwasi Balagoon. The Dublin, Marianna, and other quilts demonstrated that activists from different prisons knew about and mourned each other across space, time, and walls.

By far the most explicit imagination of freedom in a prison quilt came through a twelve-by-twelve-foot block completed in the women's federal prison at Danbury, Connecticut, in April 1996 (fig. 3). Seventy-seven people, many of them active in a peer education program called the AIDS Awareness Group, organized for six months to sew this block, which recognized 195 people who had died of AIDS.[66]

Figure 3. "Women Prisoners of FCI-Danbury 1996," received June 1996 from FCI Danbury, block 4640, AIDS Quilt. Image courtesy of AIDS Memorial Quilt.

Saturated with detail and composed of many layers of fabric, cord, and thread, the Danbury contribution became one of the heaviest single blocks ever contributed to the AIDS Quilt. When unveiled at Danbury for display, it produced near panic among prison authorities, who feared that its imagery coded plans for escape. The quilt contained no literal plot, but it did present a map of the prison, occupied its grounds with signs of protest, and daringly imagined a way out.

The Danbury quilt portrayed a prison that was built of AIDS memorials and whose grounds were filled with organizing and protest. The largest objects in its design, two rectangles and an L shape made of white fabric, represent prison housing and are labeled Units 6, 13, and 2. These buildings serve as canvases for sixty miniature, individualized quilt panels, which are neatly arranged on the white fabric as if they are cells on the housing blocks. Each miniature quilt is about six by ten inches and is intricately made with bits of cloth, cord, felt, glue, thread, buttons, and other materials. At the unit doors, around the buildings, and throughout the prison yard, spirited figures move about, gather, and hold protest signs. Two hold a quilt as a banner, recalling displays in political funerals. One holds a sign bearing a pink triangle and the phrase "Silence=Death." Two people walk around a track in the upper right, recalling the fundraising walkathons organized at Danbury, Bedford Hills, Dublin, and beyond. Another figure, holding a cigarette, most likely represents Susan Rosenberg, a political prisoner who was involved in the quilt's creation and whose papers and photos document its display.[67] Pathways, grass, and trees surround the buildings, with the yard enclosed by a fence made of fabric netting.

At the bottom of the Danbury quilt, two items sit just outside the fence: a gravestone that credits the quilt makers, and a tree graffitied with a pink triangle and the words "act up NOW! Jon Greenberg." Greenberg had been part of the ACT UP affinity group the Marys, which removed Tim Bailey's body from a New Jersey funeral home to drive it to Washington, DC. Before his death Greenberg had expressed an unforgettable wish for his remains: "I don't want an angry political funeral. I just want you to burn me in the street and eat my flesh."[68] The quilt was made of mourning yet communicated lively, rebellious action.

One detail suggests the reason the Danbury quilt made prison authorities so nervous when it was unveiled. The prison fence ends a few feet below the top of the quilt, with the rest of the fabric illustrating the sky and hills of the free world beyond. At the upper right, a small plane flies a banner bearing the famous words of labor organizer Mother Jones: "Pray for the dead and fight like hell for the living." Below this banner a helicopter hovers, extending a ladder to just above the prison fence. It is easy enough to imagine the tiny figures on the quilt coming to life, making their way to the fence, and climbing up to the ladder to fly away. Of course, the figures are affixed firmly to fabric and cannot move. Yet high above in the sky there is the sun. There are a gull and an eagle, another plane, a hot air balloon—so many things in flight.

What better example of the potential of quilt making to rage in grief and labor in care? Building on a history of quilts that memorialized individuals, neighborhoods, and a wider movement, the Danbury quilt affirms the power of a craft gendered as women's work to organize community, challenge structures of harm, and imagine freedom beyond both prison and AIDS.

Emily K. Hobson is an associate professor of history and of gender, race, and identity at the University of Nevada, Reno. She is the author of *Lavender and Red: Liberation and Solidarity in the Gay and Lesbian Left* (2016) and, with Dan Berger, editor of *Remaking Radicalism: A Grassroots Documentary Reader of the United States, 1973–2001* (2020). Hobson is active with Prison Health News and Return Strong NV.

Notes

My thanks to the editors and anonymous reviewers of this issue for their comments on this essay and to Myrl Beam, Salonee Bhaman, Nic John Ramos, and audiences at the University of Chicago and University of Nevada, Reno, for their responses to earlier drafts.

1. On Shawnee and other control units, see Gambill, "Shawnee"; and Baraldini et al., "Women's Control Unit."
2. Letter accompanying panel 7 of block 3240, AIDS Quilt, https://www.aidsmemorial.org/interactive-aids-quilt (accessed November 15, 2022).
3. The standard contribution to the Quilt is a panel measuring three by six feet, the approximate size of a grave. Eight panels are combined into a block of twelve by twelve feet; contributions can also be created at the size of a block. I use *Quilt* (capitalized) to refer to the AIDS Quilt as a whole; *quilt* (uncapitalized) or *contribution* to refer to any section designed on its own, whatever its size; and *panel* or *block* as appropriate.
4. The Quilt's public database, which includes names on each panel and low-resolution images, can be searched at https://www.aidsmemorial.org/interactive-aids-quilt. The Quilt's internal database adds who sent the panel or block (if known), when it was received, and whether a letter or any other materials were included.
5. ACE documented itself in ACE, *Breaking the Walls of Silence*; *ACE against the Odds* (dir. Debra Levine, 1996); *I'm You, You're Me: Women Surviving Prisons, Living with AIDS* (dir. Catherine Saalfield and Debra Levine, 1993); Clark and Boudin, "Community of Women Organize Themselves"; Boudin, "Resilience of the Written Off"; and Women of ACE, "Voices." ACE has received attention in Matthiesen, *Reproduction Reconceived*; Day, "Fire Inside"; Schulman, *Let the Record Show*; and the exhibitions *Metanoia: Transformation through AIDS Archives and Activism* (curated by Kat Cheairs, Alexandra Juhasz, Theodore [ted] Kerr, and Jawanza Williams, LGBT Community Center, New York, and ONE Archives, Los Angeles, 2019) and *Inside/Out: HIV/AIDS Prison Activism and Peer Organizing* (curated by Kat Cheairs, LGBT Community Center, New York, 2023).
6. Baylor, "Centering Women."
7. Berger, *Outlaws of America*.
8. See especially *Nothing without Us: Women in the Global Fight against AIDS* (dir. Harriet Hirshorn, 2017); and Schulman, *Let the Record Show*.
9. Hobson, "Fighting HIV/AIDS in Prison."
10. Matthiesen, *Reproduction Reconceived*, 11.
11. Gilmore, "In the Shadow of the Shadow State," 228; Gilmore, "Restating the Obvious," 261.
12. Lambert, "AIDS in Black Women Seen as Leading Killer"; ACE, *Breaking the Walls of Silence*, 24, citing New York State Department of Health AIDS Institute, *Focus on AIDS in New York State* (April 1994), 1, 3.
13. Watkins-Hayes, *Remaking a Life*.
14. Bell, "Rethinking the 'Straight State'"; Matthiesen, *Reproduction Reconceived*.
15. As discussed by Katrina Haslip in *I'm You, You're Me*.
16. Samer, *Lesbian Potentiality*; Berger and Losier, *Rethinking the American Prison Movement*.
17. Smith, interviewed by Cheairs.
18. ACE, *Breaking the Walls of Silence*, 134.
19. ACE, *Breaking the Walls of Silence*, 23, 354, 335.
20. Vider, *Queerness of Home*; Gould, *Moving Politics*.

21. Kramer, *Normal Heart*, act 2, scene 8.

22. Royles, *To Make the Wounded Whole*; Bost, *Evidence of Being*; Beam, "Caring for Each Other."

23. Gilbert, interviewed by Berger, "Grief and Organizing."

24. El-Sun White and Ramirez, "The Distance from Our Hearts to Our Minds."

25. Kaplan, "Organizing Inside." Especially early on, authorities often screened the fearmongering *AIDS: A Bad Way to Die* (dir. Taconic Video Center), made in 1986 at the New York men's prisons at Sing Sing and Taconic.

26. ACE, *Breaking the Walls of Silence*, 63, 66. In response, ACE crafted a participation contract that included commitments to confidentiality (not snitching) and to being sober while doing ACE work; they declined to ban drugs outright.

27. *Todaro v. Ward* is discussed in ACE, *Breaking the Walls of Silence*; and Baylor, "Centering Women."

28. ACE, *Breaking the Walls of Silence*, 61–62, 87. The medical director was Nereida Ferran; the director was Marie St. Cyr, head of the Women and AIDS Resource Network; and the temporary coordinator was Suzanne Kessler, a social psychologist.

29. These issues are addressed in ACE, *Breaking the Walls of Silence*.

30. Testa, "'If You Are Reading It, I Am Dead.'" See also Capozzola, "Very American Epidemic"; and Sturken, *Tangled Memories*.

31. "The History of the Quilt," National AIDS Memorial, https://www.aidsmemorial.org/quilt-history (accessed October 31, 2022).

32. Gould, *Moving Politics*, 230–32.

33. For clips of the Ashes Action, see *United in Anger: A History of ACT UP* (dir. Jim Hubbard and Sarah Schulman, 2012). On political funerals including Bailey's, see Royles, "Love and Rage"; and Levine, "How to Do Things with Dead Bodies."

34. Testa, "'If You Are Reading It, I Am Dead,'" 38.

35. Fleetwood, *Marking Time*, 2, 8, 25.

36. Samer, *Lesbian Potentiality*, 92.

37. The film is *Songs, Skits, Poetry, and Prison Life* (dir. Women of Bedford Hills Correctional Facility, 1974).

38. *I'm You, You're Me*; *ACE against the Odds*; Dimitria Simmons and Marilyn Buck, "Who Says I Have AIDS?" (1992), unpublished manuscript, Marilyn Buck Papers, Freedom Archives, Berkeley, CA; and Blunk, "Cause and Effect."

39. Judy Clark, interview by author, September 22, 2022.

40. "Fellow Prisoners," received June 1988 from ACI Women's Division Rhode Island (Providence), panel 8 of block 0551, AIDS Quilt.

41. "Elmira Correctional Facility," received June 1991 from STAP at Elmira Correctional Facility, New York, panel 8 of block 1782, AIDS Quilt.

42. Miller, "Imprisoned by Grief"; Carmichael, interviewed by Cheairs.

43. Law, "'Out of Flames and Fear'"; Carmichael, interviewed by Cheairs.

44. "California Medical Facility Vacaville," block 1943, AIDS Quilt.

45. Carmichael, interviewed by Cheairs; letters accompanying block 1943, AIDS Quilt.

46. Their requests generated a relationship to Montefiore Medical Center, some of whose staff later trained ACE members in HIV/AIDS education. The organization they met with was AIDS Related Community Services (ARCS, formerly Mid-Hudson AIDS Task Force), credited with the "Prisoners—Remember Their Voices" panel.

47. ACE, *Breaking the Walls of Silence*, 30, 15–16.

48. Law, "'Out of Flames and Fear.'"

49. ACE, *Breaking the Walls of Silence*, 106, 30. For an example of memorials in the office, see *ACE against the Odds* and "Carmen" (for Carmen Royster), received April 1995 from Bedford Hills, panel 2 of block 3946, AIDS Quilt.

50. ACE, *Breaking the Walls of Silence*, 15–16.

51. Differences can be seen by comparing the panels in block 3706, AIDS Quilt, received April 1995 and viewable through the online database of the AIDS Quilt. In this block, panels 1, 2, 4, 6, and 7 are from Bedford Hills, while panels 3 and 5 are from Taconic.

52. "Women's Health Forum, Suffolk County Correctional Facility," received July 1992, panel 4 of block 2473, AIDS Quilt.

53. "Taconic State Correctional Facility and Women of Albion State Correctional Facility," received April 1996, panels 4, 5, and 6 of block 4332, AIDS Quilt.

54. Suzanne Kessler, interview by author, August 15, 2022.

55. Letter accompanying panel 4 of block 2473, AIDS Quilt. These quilts were to be sent to the charities Hale House and Little Flower.

56. ACE, *Breaking the Walls of Silence*, 23, 115–16.

57. "Our Hearts Cry for All the Orphaned Children," received August 1993 from Pleasanton AIDS Counseling and Education (PLACE), FCI Dublin, California, block 3034, AIDS Quilt. The other panels in the triptych are blocks 3033 and 3035, AIDS Quilt.

58. PLACE, "Sponsor a Prisoners Fight AIDS Walkathon," n.d.; and Linda Evans, "PLACE Is for Us," in Prison Issues Committee ACT UP San Francisco, *Voices from Inside: Prisoners Respond to the AIDS Crisis* (1993), Laura Whitehorn Materials, Prisons Box, Subject Files, Interference Archive, Brooklyn, NY.

59. "Women of Albion Correctional Facility," received March 1998, panel 8 of block 5097, AIDS Quilt; accompanying letter, panel 8 of block 5097, AIDS Quilt.

60. "Kuwasi Balagoon," received June 1988, panel 2 of block 873, AIDS Quilt. Useful sources on Balagoon include Umoja, "Maroon"; Berger and Losier, *Rethinking the American Prison Movement*; and Meyer and Kersplebedeb, *Kuwasi Balagoon*.

61. Meyer and Kersplebedeb, *Kuwasi Balagoon*; Umoja, "Maroon"; Balagoon, "Love, Power, and Peace by Piece"; Gibson, "Kuwasi Balagoon."

62. Farid, "The Social Dimensions of AIDS in the Prisons," unpublished MS, December 1989, Gay Men's Health Crisis Records, Series X.A., Box 327, Folder 5, New York Public Library; Gilbert, interviewed by Berger, "Grief and Organizing"; Gilbert, "Struggle for AIDS Education in Prison"; Hobson, "Fighting HIV/AIDS in Prison."

63. See *United in Anger*; Schulman, *Let the Record Show*; *Nothing without Us*; ACT UP/New York Women and AIDS Book Group, *Women, AIDS, and Activism*; and Day, "Fire Inside."

64. "Katrina Haslip," received January 1993 from Bedford Hills Correctional Facility (created by members of ACE), panel 1 of block 2982, AIDS Quilt.

65. "For Women Prisoners / Para las mujeres prisioneras," received August 1993 from FCI Dublin and PLACE, block 3035, AIDS Quilt. Haslip was also named in panel 8 of block 3377, AIDS Quilt. On PLACE's quilts, see Evans, "PLACE Is for Us."

66. Rosenberg, *American Radical*, 274–77.

67. My thanks to Mark Lambert for calling my attention to details of these photos, held in the Susan Rosenberg Papers, Sophia Smith Collection, Smith College.

68. As quoted by The Marys, 1993, and cited in Levine, "How to Do Things with Dead Bodies."

References

ACE (AIDS Counseling and Education). *Breaking the Walls of Silence: AIDS and Women in a New York State Maximum-Security Prison*. Woodstock, NY: Overlook, 1998.

ACT UP/New York Women and AIDS Book Group, eds. *Women, AIDS, and Activism*. Boston: South End, 1990.

AIDS Memorial Quilt. https://www.aidsmemorial.org/interactive-aids-quilt (accessed November 15, 2022).

Balagoon, Rhamier Shaka. "Love, Power, and Peace by Piece." *Monthly Review Online*, March 1, 2022. https://mronline.org/2022/03/01/love-power-and-peace-by-piece/.

Baraldini, Silvia, Marilyn Buck, Susan Rosenberg, and Laura Whitehorn. "Women's Control Unit: Marianna, FL." In *Criminal Injustice: Confronting the Prison Crisis*, edited by Elihu Rosenblatt, 187–93. Boston: South End, 1996.

Baylor, Amber. "Centering Women in Prisoners' Rights Litigation." *Michigan Journal of Gender and Law* 25, no. 2 (2018): 109–59.

Beam, Joseph. "Caring for Each Other." In *Remaking Radicalism: A Grassroots Documentary Reader of the United States, 1973–2001*, edited by Dan Berger and Emily K. Hobson, 46–47. Athens: University of Georgia Press, 2020.

Bell, Jonathan. "Rethinking the 'Straight State': Welfare Politics, Health Care, and Public Policy in the Shadow of AIDS." *Journal of American History* 104, no. 4 (2018): 931–52.

Berger, Dan. *Outlaws of America: The Weather Underground and the Politics of Solidarity*. Oakland, CA: AK Press, 2006.

Berger, Dan, and Toussaint Losier. *Rethinking the American Prison Movement*. New York: Routledge, 2018.

Blunk, Timothy. "Cause and Effect." In *The Risks Worth Taking: Poetry and Art from a Decade of Imprisonment*. Teaneck, NJ: Puffin Foundation, 1997.

Bost, Darius. *Evidence of Being: The Black Gay Cultural Renaissance and the Politics of Violence*. Chicago: University of Chicago Press, 2019.

Boudin, Kathy. "The Resilience of the Written Off: Women in Prison as Women of Change." *Women's Rights Law Reporter* 29, no. 1 (2007): 15–22.

Capozzola, Christopher. "A Very American Epidemic: Memory Politics and Identity Politics in the AIDS Memorial Quilt, 1985–1993." *Radical History Review*, no. 82 (2002): 91–109.

Carmichael, Brian. Interview by Kat Cheairs, undated. *Inside/Out: HIV/AIDS Prison Activism and Peer Organizing*, exhibition curated by Kat Cheairs, LGBT Community Center, New York, 2023. https://gaycenter.org/inside-out/ (accessed March 10, 2023).

Clark, Judy, and Kathy Boudin. "Community of Women Organize Themselves to Cope with the AIDS Crisis: A Case Study from Bedford Hills Correctional Facility." *Social Justice* 17, no. 2 (1990): 90–109.

Day, Emma. "The Fire Inside: Women Protesting AIDS in Prison since 1980." *Modern American History* 5, no. 1 (2022): 79–100.

El-Sun White, Moses, and Henry Ramirez. "The Distance from Our Hearts to Our Minds: A Report on Prisoners for AIDS Counseling and Education at Otisville Correctional Facility, 1989 to 2010." *Transformations: The Journal of Inclusive Scholarship and Pedagogy* 21, no. 2 (2010–11): 149–55.

Fleetwood, Nicole R. *Marking Time: Art in the Age of Mass Incarceration*. Cambridge, MA: Harvard University Press, 2020.

Gambill, Sue. "Shawnee: Another Control Unit for Women Prisoners." *Sojourner: The Women's Forum* 18, no. 6 (1993): 11.

Gibson, Jasmine. "Kuwasi Balagoon: On Lineage." *Pinko*, no. 1 (2019). https://pinko.online/pinko-1/kuwasi-balagoon.

Gilbert, David. "The Struggle for AIDS Education in Prison." *New Studies on the Left* 14, nos. 1–2 (1989): 143–44.

Gilbert, David, interviewed and with a prologue by Dan Berger. "Grief and Organizing in the Face of Repression/The Fight against AIDS in Prison." In *Rebellious Mourning: The Collective Work of Grief*, edited by Cindy Milstein, 274–96. Oakland, CA: AK Press, 2017.

Gilmore, Ruth Wilson. "In the Shadow of the Shadow State." In *Abolition Geography: Essays towards Liberation*, by Ruth Wilson Gilmore, edited by Brenna Bhandar and Alberto Toscano, 224–41. New York: Verso, 2022.

Gilmore, Ruth Wilson, with Craig Gilmore. "Restating the Obvious." In *Abolition Geography: Essays towards Liberation*, by Ruth Wilson Gilmore, edited by Brenna Bhandar and Alberto Toscano, 259–87. New York: Verso, 2022.

Gould, Deborah B. *Moving Politics: Emotion and ACT UP's Fight against AIDS*. Chicago: University of Chicago Press, 2009.

Hobson, Emily K. "Fighting HIV/AIDS in Prison." *Sinister Wisdom*, no. 126 (2022): 156–63.

Kaplan, Esther. "Organizing Inside." *Poz*, November 1, 1998. https://www.poz.com/article/Organizing-Inside-1656-9407.

Kramer, Larry. *The Normal Heart*. New York: New American Library, 1985.

Lambert, Bruce. "AIDS in Black Women Seen as Leading Killer." *New York Times*, July 11, 1990.

Law, Victoria. "'Out of Flames and Fear': How People with HIV Forced California to Reform HIV Care in Prisons." *The Body*, May 24, 2017. https://www.thebody.com/article/out-of-flames-and-fear-how-people-with-hiv-forced-.

Levine, Debra. "How to Do Things with Dead Bodies." *Hemispheric Institute* 6, no. 1 (2013). https://hemisphericinstitute.org/en/emisferica-61/6–1-essays/how-to-do-things-with-dead-bodies.html.

Matthiesen, Sara, *Reproduction Reconceived: Family Making and the Limits of Choice after* Roe v. Wade. Oakland: University of California Press, 2021.

Meyer, Matt, and Karl Kersplebedeb, eds. *Kuwasi Balagoon: A Soldier's Story; Revolutionary Writings by a New Afrikan Anarchist*. 3rd ed. Oakland, CA: PM Press, 2019.

Miller, Robin. "Imprisoned by Grief." *Vacaville Reporter*, February 21, 1992.

Rosenberg, Susan. *An American Radical: Political Prisoner in My Own Country*. New York: Citadel, 2011.

Royles, Dan. "Love and Rage." *Nursing Clio*, March 9, 2017. https://nursingclio.org/2017/03/09/love-and-rage/.

Royles, Dan. *To Make the Wounded Whole: The African American Struggle against HIV/AIDS*. Chapel Hill: University of North Carolina Press, 2020.

Samer, Rox. *Lesbian Potentiality and Feminist Media in the 1970s*. Durham, NC: Duke University Press, 2022.

Schulman, Sarah. *Let the Record Show: A Political History of ACT UP New York, 1987–1993*. New York: Farrar, Straus and Giroux, 2021.

Smith, Roslyn. Interview by Kat Cheairs, undated. *Inside/Out: HIV/AIDS Prison Activism and Peer Organizing*, exhibition curated by Kat Cheairs, LGBT Community Center, New York, 2023. https://gaycenter.org/inside-out/ (accessed March 10, 2023).

Sturken, Marita. *Tangled Memories: The Vietnam War, the AIDS Epidemic, and the Politics of Remembering*. Berkeley: University of California Press, 1997.

Testa, Nino. "'If You Are Reading It, I Am Dead': Activism, Local History, and the AIDS Quilt." *Public Historian* 44, no. 3 (2022): 24–57.

Umoja, Akinyele K. "Maroon: Kuwasi Balagoon and the Evolution of Revolutionary New Afrikan Anarchism." *Science and Society* 79, no. 2 (2015): 196–220.

Vider, Stephen. *The Queerness of Home: Gender, Sexuality, and the Politics of Domesticity after World War II*. Chicago: University of Chicago Press, 2021.

Watkins-Hayes, Celeste. *Remaking a Life: How Women Living with HIV/AIDS Confront Inequality*. Oakland: University of California Press, 2019.

Women of ACE (AIDS Counseling and Education). "Voices." In *Women, AIDS, and Activism*, by ACT UP/New York Women and AIDS Book Group, 143–55. Boston: South End, 1990.

Searching for Monse

Mónica A. Jiménez

I am sitting on the floor of my mother's workroom—the place where she sews, binds books, and creates with her hands. I am sewing a small pillow by hand to keep myself occupied while I accompany her. It is just the two of us in the house. My father is at work. My brothers are off being boys in the streets, which is what they are expected to be. I am a girl and so expected to be here, on this floor, with my mother. As a kid I feel resentful of this expectation, that I should stay at home while my brothers are allowed to run the streets. What I don't fully grasp is that my mother is giving me a gift greater than a few hours of unsupervised freedom. She is giving me our family's stories and opening up an entire world for me to explore. There on that floor, my small hands busy with whatever trinket I am making, I am becoming a historian.

Growing up in suburban Houston, where I mostly felt like an outsider, Puerto Rico was my real home. Like many other children of the diaspora, the archipelago was where I felt most free, most able to embrace all parts of myself, and most loved. I wanted to know everything I could about the place we'd left, so I devoured my mother's stories. Later, as I learned more about the history of Puerto Rico, its colonial past and present and its political upheavals, I began to imagine my family members, elders, and ancestors in the milieu of that history. Where would my maternal grandfather have been in 1917, when overnight, he became a US citizen? What, if anything, might that have meant to a boy living in rural poverty? Likewise, in the early 1950s, when political change and revolution were in the air, as Puerto Rico became the Estado Libre Asociado (ELA), or Commonwealth of Puerto Rico, how did things feel in Puerto Viejo, the barrio of Ponce where my paternal

Radical History Review
Issue 148 (January 2024) DOI 10.1215/01636545-10846794

grandparents lived? Was there hope that the ELA would breathe new life into the old Port of Ponce, where my grandfather worked? What did these big political changes, dictated from above, mean for poor and working-class Puerto Ricans like my family members?

During those hours sitting on that floor with my mother, she introduced me to Monserrate del Valle del Toro, my great-aunt, or Titi Monse, as we called her. In the early 1960s my mother joined the great Puerto Rican migration to New York City. She and her sisters stepped off the plane wearing their best dresses and sandals and walked into New York's unforgiving cold and hustle. The girls lived with Monserrate and her family in Williamsburg, Brooklyn. With her husband, Tomás López de Victoria, Monserrate had two daughters, Yvette and Yvonne, my mother's older cousins. Monserrate lied about my mother's age so she could work at a local factory. Titi Monse would walk my mom to her job every day to ensure that she made it there safely because, though my mother passed for working age, she was only twelve years old at the time. To help her stay warm in the cold New York winters, Titi Monse taught my mother how to smoke cigarettes.

Monserrate and her family had been part of a wave of Puerto Ricans who moved to the Williamsburg area of Brooklyn during a period of white flight. After initially working in factories for a time, she and Tomás were able to purchase an old apartment building, which they rented out to other Puerto Rican families. Eventually, they purchased several other small, dilapidated buildings in the area. Despite their growing real estate venture, Monse and her family lived a decidedly working-class existence with the buildings' maintenance costs often outstripping the earnings they made. Over time, owing to inadequate maintenance, my mother tells me, all of Monserrate's buildings burned, a common occurrence at the time.

I begin with this vignette because this is how I first met Monserrate—or at least the Monse of my mother's memories. The aunt who took my mother and her sisters in when their father couldn't care for them. In my mother's memories Monse was a force, with her own small real estate empire. For many years she was a single mother, raising her two young daughters alone, while her husband was imprisoned in Puerto Rico. She herself had been imprisoned for nearly two years for her proximity to the 1950 nationalist uprising in Puerto Rico. Yet she never spoke about prison. What my mother and aunts learned of her life during those years was gleaned from bits and pieces overheard in adults' conversations and their father's recollections about his sister and brother-in-law.

Then there is the Monse I found in the official histories of nationalism and the early 1950s: Monserrate was a Puerto Rican nationalist. She was arrested in Arecibo, Puerto Rico, on October 30, 1950, for participating in an attempt to overthrow the US government in Puerto Rico. She was the wife of a prominent nationalist leader, Tomás López de Victoria, who led the Cadets of the Republic, the youth arm of the Puerto Rican Nationalist Party, and was a devoted acolyte of the nationalist leader Pedro Albizu Campos. Her name appears on a plaque located in Mayagüez, Puerto Rico, that honors nationalist women for "their perseverance, valor, sacrifice, and steadfastness in the battle for [Puerto Rico's] independence." Hers is the last and shortest entry in Olga Jiménez de Wagenheim's 2017 book, *Nationalist Heroines: Puerto Rican Women History Forgot, 1930s–1950s*, which highlights the important role played by women in Puerto Rico's struggle for independence. There she is listed incorrectly as Monserrate Valle de López.

Perhaps because I never met Titi Monse, I have been searching for her all my life—first in my family's stories and later in books and in archives. I have found only whispers of her, echoes and traces of her life—a name on a list of subversives, a mention of her in an account of her husband's life, a name in a legal appeal. To my knowledge, she did not keep a journal. In fact, I am unsure if she was literate. Many Puerto Ricans of her generation were not. There is no archive or collection that I can easily visit to search her out. The government's wide-ranging project of surveillance of the Nationalist Party made it dangerous for members to maintain records of their activities. Much of what we have are government-produced records and the oral histories of a handful of surviving party members. Even finding Monserrate's descendants has been challenging, given the dislocation and displacement of our diasporic family and the deaths of many of our elders. Predictably, as my mother and her sisters have aged, their own memories of Titi Monse have grown hazy.

So it was with great wonder that I found Monserrate's presence in a most unexpected place: the Arecibo District Jail. While she herself never spoke about her time in prison, some of the women with whom she was imprisoned did so in their own oral histories. Through them a clearer picture emerged, not only of Monserrate during those turbulent years but also of the nationalist women with whom she was incarcerated, how they survived, and how they cared for each other and held each other up. The story of their imprisonment is one of sisterhood, collective care, and shared struggle. It allows us a view of the conditions of their incarceration and of what it was to continue to resist deracination by the colonial state while living deep within it.

This article is the start of what I hope will one day be a biography of Monserrate. I begin with the most sensational part of her life—her arrest and incarceration—because it is there that she came into most direct contact with the violence of the colonial state. Though Monserrate's life, like those of every poor or working-class Puerto Rican of her generation, was deeply circumscribed by the US colonial capitalist project, in her incarceration we get an often-ignored view of the story of Puerto Rico's colonization. Through her story, we begin to see a complex picture of the inner workings of the colonial prison, of the ways incarcerated Puerto Ricans navigated that system, and also how those who labored within it contended with their own relationship to the colonial capitalist project. Monserrate's story ultimately illuminates how she and the other nationalist women with whom she was incarcerated asserted their dignity and a praxis of care in the belly of the beast.

In telling Monse's story, fragmented though it is, I hope also to upend certain established narratives of the history of Puerto Rican nationalism, of who fought in the struggle for independence, how they fought, and where. That fight surely took place in political and legal arenas and in the streets of towns all over the archipelago and the continental United States. However, it also took place within the walls of the Arecibo District Jail, where a group of nationalist women, including Monserrate, sheltered, cared for, and fed each other.

The Early Years of US Rule

Monserrate del Valle del Toro was born in 1916 in the rural mountain barrio of Quebradas in the northeastern municipality of Camuy. She was the second daughter and among the oldest in a family of eleven children. Her father, Félix del Valle, worked as an agricultural laborer while her mother, Monserrate del Toro, tended their home and family. Félix's work as a rural laborer was seasonal, and like many families in rural Puerto Rico at the time, they balanced on the edge of poverty. Theirs was a struggle of occasional work in the coffee plantations or sugarcane fields followed by scrambling to make ends meet during the dead months, *el tiempo muerto*. The family survived through subsistence farming, with the elder Monserrate and the children growing the food they needed to survive, in addition to whatever Félix brought in through his work. The youngest children may have attended school for a few years, but once they were able to contribute to the household, their schooling effectively ended. As a result, Monserrate and her ten siblings each had about the equivalent of a first- or second-grade education.

Around 1922 Monserrate's older brother Antonio, my grandfather, left the family home and worked his way to the southern port city of Ponce. There he established himself and made a living at odd jobs, selling various goods, working as a deliveryman, and eventually working in construction. Antonio married and started a family, and as he became more settled, he brought his mother and some of his siblings to Ponce. Monse was one of the siblings who left rural Puerto Rico behind and moved to the city in the late 1920s.

Around the time that Antonio moved to Ponce in search of better opportunities, the Partido Nacionalista de Puerto Rico (Puerto Rican Nationalist Party; PNPR), was coming into existence. In 1930 the attorney Pedro Albizu Campos became the party's president. Albizu Campos's education in the United States and his legal training exposed him to nationalist struggles in other parts of the world. Greatly influenced and moved by the Irish and Indian struggles against British colonialism, he came to see the United States' role in Puerto Rico as parallel to that of Britain in Ireland and India. As a result, upon taking the party's presidency, he quickly set about redefining its platform as one of complete independence for Puerto Rico by any means necessary.[1]

Monserrate's eventual husband, Tomás López de Victoria, became heavily involved with the PNPR in Ponce in the 1930s. That decade was a particularly turbulent one in Puerto Rico.[2] In the throes of the Great Depression and with the collapse of global commodities markets, demand fell for agricultural products such as sugar, Puerto Rico's primary export. The passage of the Sugar Act of 1934 (the Jones-Costigan Amendment), which set quotas on the amount of sugar that could enter the United States and essentially deincentivized the growing of sugar in Puerto Rico, only furthered the difficult conditions in the archipelago. This led to large-scale unemployment among sugar laborers.

With stagnant wages and rampant unemployment, both the political and economic situation in Puerto Rico had become bleak. Political parties struggled to work out a permanent status for Puerto Rico, and infighting among various factions was common. Meanwhile, labor strikes were on the rise in nearly every employment sector in the archipelago, including the important tobacco and sugar sectors. Dissatisfaction and hunger were rampant in Puerto Rico, and Albizu Campos and the PNPR sought to harness Puerto Ricans' growing frustration by traveling around the archipelago delivering passionate anti-imperialist speeches. As a result of this activism, the US government began widespread surveillance of the PNPR.[3] Furthermore, to deal with the growing threat posed by the group, President Franklin Roosevelt appointed the former military leaders E. Francis Riggs as police chief and Blanton Winship as governor of Puerto Rico in 1934.

On February 23, 1936, two members of the PNPR killed Riggs in retaliation for the killings of four party members at the University of Puerto Rico the previous October.[4] The two men were captured and taken to police headquarters, where police later reported that they attempted to escape and were shot. Though Albizu Campos was not directly involved, Riggs's killing led to his first arrest and prosecution for seditious conspiracy. He and several other nationalist leaders were found guilty of conspiring to overthrow the US government and were incarcerated in federal prison in Atlanta, Georgia.

To protest the sentences of the nationalist leaders, a group of nationalists in Ponce organized a peaceful march on March 21, 1937. As the subcommander of the cadets, Tomás helped organize the event. Though it was planned as a peaceful demonstration and procession, the governor pressured Ponce's mayor to revoke the nationalists' permit to hold the march. In defiance, the nationalists moved ahead with the march and the event devolved into chaos when Insular Police officers attempted to break it up.[5] Police and nationalists clashed in the streets. Nineteen people were killed and over two hundred bystanders were injured. These events came to be known as the Ponce Massacre.[6]

Tomás and ten other nationalists were arrested and prosecuted for murder for their participation in the events of March 21, 1937. However, public sentiment ran high against the Insular Police following the massacre. Residents and politicians saw the event as a violent repression of free speech and a curtailment of the PNPR's right to peacefully demonstrate. The eleven nationalists, including Tomás, were eventually acquitted when a jury failed to come to a unanimous verdict on the charges.

A little over a year later, on July 25, 1938, Tomás was again arrested when a group of nationalists attempted to assassinate Winship. Despite public sentiment against him and the Insular Police, Winship insisted on celebrating the fortieth anniversary of the US invasion of Puerto Rico by holding a parade in Ponce. Winship survived the attempt on his life, but a police officer standing near him was shot and killed. Though he was not present at the parade, Tomás was arrested and tried for murder in the first degree. This time he and the others were found guilty and sentenced to life imprisonment. His sentence and those of the other four nationalists convicted with him were commuted eight years later by Governor Rexford G. Tugwell, and in January 1946 they were released from the notorious Oso Blanco, or Puerto Rico Island Penitentiary.[7]

Not long after Tomás's release, Albizu Campos, having completed his sentence in Atlanta, returned to Puerto Rico. He quickly set about refocusing and reinvigorating the party.[8] Though the political status of Puerto Rico had changed little during his incarceration, the political climate had significantly shifted. In 1935, as part of Roosevelt's New Deal policies, the Puerto Rico Reconstruction Administration (PRRA) was created. The agency was charged with improving living conditions in Puerto Rico through development projects, including the electrification of rural areas, the construction of public housing and parks, and the installation of dams for hydroelectric power and flood control.[9] The agency's development projects helped create jobs in Puerto Rico, while the promotion of Puerto Rican migration to the US mainland to supply labor to factories and foundries in Chicago, New York, Philadelphia, and other cities meant that fewer Puerto Ricans were competing for those jobs in the archipelago.[10] As a result of these and other societal changes, the standard of living in Puerto Rico improved as more people moved out of rural poverty and into steady work in urban or urbanizing areas.

These improvements to Puerto Rico's standard of living also helped quiet the political unrest and dissatisfaction of the 1930s. With the formation of the Partido Popular Democrático (Popular Democratic Party; PPD) in 1938, the political mood began to shift.[11] The PPD's initial platform sought independence for the archipelago, but during the 1940s the party turned away from independence and instead focused on liberal economic reform. Prominent PPD members were among those who led the PRRA and Puerto Rico's economic development in the early to mid-twentieth century. As a result, the party was credited with the improved quality of life Puerto Ricans experienced during those crucial decades. PPD leaders were particularly popular with the laboring classes, which most felt the material gains of the PPD's reforms. In 1948 the party's leader, Luis Muñoz Marín, became Puerto Rico's first democratically elected governor, a position he held for sixteen years.

As a result of the PPD's economic and development projects and Muñoz Marín's ability to maneuver and advocate for Puerto Rico in the halls of Congress, popular sentiment had moved away from independence and in favor of the creation of an autonomous state in close association with the US government.[12] Such an arrangement would entail the creation of a government apparatus to handle local affairs, with Congress maintaining ultimate sovereignty over the archipelago and the two engaging in free trade. At the time of Albizu Campos's release, Muñoz Marín was in the final stretch of working with US officials and Puerto Rican politicians to establish the legal-political structure that would become the ELA.[13]

These political changes meant little to Albizu Campos and the PNPR, who saw the arrangement as ultimately colonial in nature despite the creation of a purported local government. In 1950, when the creation of a local constitution and the adoption of the ELA were to be put before the people of Puerto Rico, Albizu Campos urged them to reject the referendum. "In Puerto Rico only the US has jurisdiction," he stated. "That law [Law 600, which enacted the ELA] can be annulled by the US Congress."[14] Given the inevitability of the adoption of the ELA and in a last-ditch effort to disrupt the plebiscite, Albizu Campos and the leaders of the PNPR began to plan a wide-scale uprising and declaration of a free and sovereign Puerto Rico.

The 1950 Nationalist Uprising

In the midst of so much societal change in Puerto Rico, Monserrate del Valle and Tomás López de Victoria were married on May 12, 1949—a little over a year before their participation in the nationalist uprising.[15] Tomás, who only three years before had been released from prison, was a recent widower. His first wife, Fe González, had died at twenty-three during his incarceration. Monserrate and Tomás met and married in Ponce, where he had grown up and she had settled as a young girl. While her involvement with the PNPR preceded her relationship with Tomás, she no doubt had heard of the nationalist hero incarcerated for his role in the attempt to assassinate the hated Winship.

She was nine years his junior, but at thirty-three, Monserrate was no young, impressionable woman. She had lived through the hard years of the Great Depression and Puerto Rico's turbulent 1930s. She had accompanied her mother and siblings from rural Quebradas to Ponce as a young child, leaving her father, Félix, in Camuy. The family had settled in the Playa de Ponce sector of Ponce, a working-class community not far from the Port of Ponce, where in the early twentieth century merchant ships regularly arrived bringing goods from the continental United States and departed laden with sugar, tobacco, and tropical fruit. These merchant ships were often staffed with men from Hawaii, the Philippines, and other parts of the growing US empire—men who had left home in pursuit of opportunities along imperial shipping routes. Often these men disembarked at the Port of Ponce and stayed for a time or became a permanent part of the barrio's racially and ethnically diverse community.

As the second daughter and one of the older children of the family, Monserrate was charged with both helping her mother care for her younger siblings and bringing money into the household. Her mother worked as a laundress, a common job for working Puerto Rican women at that time. Monserrate, too, took in laundry to contribute to the household expenses. Her brother Antonio sold fruit in the Ponce Plaza del Mercado and helped keep his mother and siblings afloat. As the family dynamics changed and the younger siblings grew older, Monserrate joined the ever-expanding group of working-class women employed as domestic workers in the homes of Ponce's well-to-do. As was the custom, she remained a part of her mother's household until she married Tomás.

Although this was Monserrate's first marriage and Tomás's second, their union was one of intellectual and political equals. Despite her lack of romantic experience, Monse knew her mind and her beliefs and was not simply swept away by young love. The two were committed to a cause they were willing to give their lives for: the liberation of Puerto Rico. The newlyweds moved to Arecibo, an area familiar to Monserrate because it was near where she had grown up and where her father still lived on a small farm. There Tomás linked up with Ricardo Díaz and two of his sons, as well as with Juan Jaca, to plan the execution of the Arecibo portion of the uprising.[16] The revolt was to be coordinated across multiple towns in Puerto Rico as well as in the US mainland. Though Monserrate undoubtedly knew about these plans and witnessed the movements of her nationalist comrades, her participation was never proved.

Following Albizu Campos's return to Puerto Rico, and in the lead-up to the plebiscite and adoption of the ELA, US and Puerto Rican officials ramped up their surveillance and intimidation of the group. Infiltrators and special agents were deployed as informants throughout Puerto Rico. The FBI files concerning the 1950 uprising and its aftermath include numerous informants whose names were redacted but who provided information from the most mundane details to thorough descriptions of meetings and discussions about the rebellion. The party members, aware that they were surveilled, took care with what they said and how they spoke in their meetings. Nevertheless, the network of infiltrators was wide, and many of the nationalists' plans became known to government agents.[17]

Despite this surveillance, the PNPR continued their plans, hoping to disrupt the preparations for the adoption of the ELA. However, a series of unforeseen raids and arrests hastened the uprising, and on October 30 at 4:45 a.m. the insurrection began in the southern town of Peñuelas, followed by revolts in ten other towns and cities, including Ponce, Arecibo, Mayagüez, Utuado, and Jayuya. Nationalists led by Blanca Canales bombed the police station in Jayuya and took control of the town for three days.[18] A separate group of nationalists attacked the governor's mansion, La Fortaleza, in an attempt to kill Muñoz Marín. Likewise, on November 1, two members of the party based in New York City traveled to Washington, DC, and attempted to assassinate President Truman.[19]

Given its hasty start, the revolt proceeded in a chaotic manner. Rather than a coordinated start to the uprising, the fighting began at different times in different towns. In Arecibo, Tomás ordered the cadets to attack the police station an hour earlier than initially planned, and as a result the nationalists caught the Insular Police by surprise.[20] In the fray, the nationalists killed four police officers and injured six others before their capture.

In response to the coordinated attacks, Muñoz Marín deployed the National Guard throughout Puerto Rico. Together with the Insular Police, the guardsmen quickly moved to quash the revolts. The fighting ended definitively when the National Guard dropped bombs on Jayuya and Utuado. By November 3 the uprising was over. Twenty-one nationalists were dead and five wounded. And in the next forty-eight hours, all the nationalists involved in the planning and executing of the revolt were arrested, including Tomás and Monserrate.[21]

Incarceration in Arecibo District Jail

Police arrested Tomás, Monserrate, Ricardo Díaz Sr., Juan Jaca, Ricardo Díaz Jr., Ismael Díaz, and Leonides Díaz, the wife of Ricardo Díaz Sr., as the presumed leaders of the attack.[22] They were part of a roundup of nationalists who were taken to Arecibo District Jail, where they remained throughout their legal proceedings. In the days and weeks that followed, the Insular Police and the National Guard initiated a Puerto Rico–wide roundup of hundreds of nationalists and other political undesirables—communists, socialists, and independistas. The newspaper *El Mundo* reported on November 10 that the district attorney of Arecibo, Santiago Porrata Doria, had filed charges against the sixty-one nationalists in that district. Of that group, Porrata Doria charged sixteen individuals thought to have actively participated in the attack on the Arecibo police station, including Monserrate, each with four counts of murder, four counts of attempted murder, and four counts of carrying an illegal firearm.[23]

Monserrate was held in the women's wing of the jail. Initially, she was housed in the general prison population with two other nationalist women, Juanita Ojeda and Leonides Díaz. Ojeda was from Utuado, where she had been arrested for participating in the nationalist attack on that town. There was no evidence to tie her to the Utuado attack; however, she was a close associate of Albizu Campos and had led the Utuado PNPR chapter in the years before the uprising.[24] Leonides Díaz was the wife of Ricardo Díaz Sr., who planned the attack in Arecibo with Tomás, and the mother of Ricardo Jr. and Ángel Ramon, who had participated in the attack on the police station in Arecibo and had been arrested and charged with their parents. Leonides was arrested at her home on November 2, 1950, when police arrived at her farm looking for weapons.[25]

Eventually, the three women were separated from the general prison population and joined five other nationalist women who were brought to the jail from San Juan: Carmín Pérez, Doris Torresola, Olga Viscal, Isabel Rosado, and Ruth Mary Reynolds. Carmín Pérez joined the PNPR in 1949, just a year before the uprising, but she quickly became Albizu Campos's confidant and assistant. She was at the party headquarters in San Juan and arrested on October 30, 1950, when police arrived to arrest Albizu Campos for his role in the attempted assassination of Muñoz Marín. Doris Torresola, another confidant and caretaker of Albizu Campos, was also present at the PNPR headquarters on October 30. When police arrived, a shootout ensued, and Doris was shot in the throat while protecting Albizu Campos.[26] She was taken to the hospital for treatment and later arrested. Olga Viscal first came under government surveillance as a student activist at the University of Puerto Rico (UPR). She later joined the PNPR in San Juan and was seen in the company of prominent nationalist leaders who would play a part in the uprising.[27] Though there was no evidence tying her to the uprising, her proximity to party leaders led to her arrest on November 1, 1950. Isabel Rosado was a teacher and a social worker who devoted herself to improving the living conditions of Puerto Rico's rural poor.[28] Her work with the poor and the events of the Ponce Massacre in 1937 motivated her support for Puerto Rico's independence and ultimately led her to join the PNPR. Though she was at work on the day of the uprising, she was arrested in January 1951 for being a member of the party.

Reynolds, a white North Dakotan, radical pacifist, and member of the Harlem Ashram, had devoted her life's work to the cause of civil rights in the United States. She became interested in Puerto Rico after meeting several nationalists as part of her work with the ashram.[29] Reynolds's commitment to Puerto Rico's liberation from colonialism deepened after she met Albizu Campos in New York in 1944. Eventually, she made her way to Puerto Rico as a leader of the American League for Puerto Rico's Independence. Ostensibly, she was in the archipelago to investigate government suppression of student strikes at the UPR, but she quickly became enmeshed in the work of the PNPR.[30] As a result, she came under the watchful eyes of the government surveillance machine, the FBI, and the Insular Police. In 1950, after the uprising, she too was arrested.

All the women, whether there was evidence tying them directly to the uprising or not, were charged under Puerto Rico's notorious Law 53, an antisedition statute passed in 1948. The law made it a felony to "encourage, defend, counsel or preach, voluntarily or knowingly, the need, desirability, or convenience of overturning, destroying, or paralyzing the Insular Government, or any of its political subdivisions, by way of force or violence."[31] It also made it a felony to publish or distribute any literature advocating for the same or to organize a group or society that encouraged it. Modeled on the US Alien Registration Act (or Smith Act) of 1940, Law 53 was passed during the height of negotiations for the ELA and was seen as necessary to ensure the smooth adoption of a constitution and the creation of the ELA. Dubbed the Ley de la Mordaza, or the Gag Law, the act had an immediate chilling effect on student protest at the UPR and on public support for independence.[32]

Law 53 was said to be a necessary protection against the dangers posed by the PNPR after Albizu Campos's return to Puerto Rico. Ivonne Acosta-Lespier has argued that the law's aim was not to prevent nationalist violence but to cause it. Government officials hoped to "provoke the Nationalists to resort to violence through vigilance and harassment" in order to arrest and detain the leadership for the duration of the legal procedure to create the ELA, thereby silencing their dissent during the most critical part of the process.[33] As a result, while the specter of Law 53 hung over the populace and influenced their speech and activities, it was not used as a prosecutorial tool before 1950.

Following the uprising, in December 1950, the law was amended to make it a crime to belong to any group the government deemed subversive.[34] Not surprisingly, the PNPR was promptly identified as such a group, and membership in it was criminalized. It is estimated that as a result of this amendment, in the months after the uprising, over one thousand nationalists and other political activists were arrested, and up to eight hundred detained and charged with violations of Law 53 for purportedly taking an oath to support the PNPR or for displaying the Puerto Rican flag, then considered a nationalist symbol.[35]

Though initially charged with felony murder and attempted murder, those serious charges against Monserrate were dropped when it became clear that there was not enough evidence to connect her with the attack on the Arecibo police station. Instead, she was charged with violating the Gag Law due to her support of and association with Tomás and the other nationalist organizers. Although those initial charges were made in the days after the uprising, the nationalists were not arraigned until December and January, a delay that clearly violated their civil rights. Furthermore, the government dragged out their prosecutions, so many were detained anywhere from a year to two years before their cases went to trial. Many nationalists spent more time imprisoned than they were eventually sentenced to serve.[36] Monserrate herself spent twenty-two months in prison before a jury found that the evidence was insufficient to prove that she had violated Law 53. She was acquitted and released after nearly two years of unjust imprisonment.

During those twenty-two months Monserrate was held in the Arecibo District Jail's women's wing, with short stints in San Juan's infamous Spanish-era prison, La Princesa. She and several other nationalist women were taken to La Princesa for their arraignments and during their trials. But the bulk of her time was spent in Arecibo, where she, Juanita Ojeda, and Leonides Díaz were housed. The five other nationalist women—Carmín Pérez, Doris Torresola, Olga Viscal, Isabel Rosado, and Ruth Mary Reynolds—were eventually brought to Arecibo but were initially held in a separate section away from Monserrate, Ojeda, and Díaz.[37] During the afternoon siesta, however, Monserrate, Ojeda, and Díaz could visit with the other five through a small hole in the isolation room door and share information about their friends, family members, and comrades.

All the women at the prison were given an initial medical assessment that included a pelvic examination. For decades, poor and disreputable women who

ran afoul of the colonial state were accused of being or were assumed to be prostitutes.[38] As a result, such women were typically subjected to intrusive pelvic exams,
and their incarceration was seen as necessary to protect the American colonial project as well as Puerto Rican morality. Though the nationalists were for the most part
working-class women, they were offended by the procedure and what it implied of
their morals or character so they refused it. Furthermore, according to Reynolds,
the nationalists were "so private that they wouldn't undress in front of anyone."[39]
Indeed, the prison's doctor, Arturo Cadilla, wrote in a report to the superintendent
of prisons that none of the nationalist women had ever consented to any exam in
which they had to undress before the doctor.[40] Perhaps out of embarrassment or
respect for the women's status as political prisoners, or because of his own assumptions about which sorts of women should be subjected to such an invasive procedure, Cadilla desisted and the nationalists were admitted into the prison without
the pelvic exam.

Monserrate was initially held in one of the two open galleries that housed the
general prison population, facing a central patio. According to Reynolds, most
women held in the prison's general population were incarcerated for presumed
prostitution and for having performed or received abortions. Some were there for
having killed abusive husbands. One woman, abandoned by her partner without the
means to feed her children, drowned them to spare them the pain of starvation.
Reynolds described the women as mostly poor and uneducated victims of US
colonialism. Undoubtedly, she was alluding to the colonial capitalist structure
that held countless Puerto Ricans in poverty and to the patriarchal structures
that kept many impoverished women at the mercy of their male partners.

Generally, the nationalist women had a good relationship with the other
inmates. The nationalists treated the others as people worthy of kindness and respect
and not with the scorn and contempt that the guards and warden showed them. As
a result, the women in the general population held the nationalists in high regard and
were sympathetic to them. Reynolds recounts that one young woman told her,
"We're here because we've done wrong. You're here because the things you did
were right."[41] For many of the general prison population, the nationalist women's
efforts to secure Puerto Rico's freedom from colonialism was laudable, and so their
presence in the prison was an injustice. This view, ironically also held by many of the
prison staff, allowed the nationalist women some privileges denied to the general
prison population.

During their first year in the prison, the political prisoners were only allowed
visits with their attorneys and were not allowed to receive any items from outside the
prison. They could receive money through a commissary account to purchase basic
necessities such as sheets, towels, and toiletries, as these were not provided. However, Reynolds acknowledges that the nationalist women were privileged in receiving sheets; other incarcerated women had to purchase all their basic items. Reynolds

also recounts that during that time some of the other inmates shared food with the nationalist women. There were no fruits or vegetables in the prison diet, so these items were prized and difficult to acquire, because they had to be purchased or brought to the women from the outside. The fact that the women in the general prison population were willing to share such items with the nationalists speaks to a level of care and solidarity among all the women.

After some time in isolation, Reynolds and the others were placed among the general population, where they joined Monserrate, Díaz, and Ojeda. Reynolds described the larger of the galleries, where all the nationalist women were housed, as "something like sixty-five by eighteen feet" and made to hold over one hundred women rather than the eighty it was intended to hold. The women slept on "double-decker beds, army leftovers, and under almost every bed was a third person sleeping on the floor. The space between the beds was just wide enough to go through."[42] A single bathroom for all these women was connected to the gallery through an open doorway. It had three toilets, two showers, and two "wash pools." Lacking a door, however, the bathroom was exposed to the gallery, and nothing in the bathroom was enclosed; there were no stalls for the toilets or dividers for the showers.

The lack of privacy was a big concern for some of the younger nationalist women, whom Reynolds described as very modest and offended by having to shower within view of the others. As a result of complaints to the warden, the nationalist women were allowed one hour each day to themselves to shower. They took turns so they could use the bathroom alone during the afternoon siesta, which took place between three and four, when women in the general prison population were required to rest on their beds.

Interestingly, Reynolds describes the warden, J. González Lebrón, as "decent" and not unreasonable. His capitulation to the women's request for privacy was one of several instances in which he allowed them greater freedoms and liberties than the general population. Indeed, Cadilla reported that anytime the women visited his office, they were accompanied by Lebrón's wife, a guard referred to as Doña Segunda, ostensibly to ensure the women's privacy and comfort in his presence.[43] According to Reynolds, the warden thought of them as respectable women because they were not prostitutes, like most of the other incarcerated women, and therefore were considered to be owed greater deference. Though conditions in the prison were grim for all the women, the nationalists' status as political prisoners garnered them greater respect not only from the warden but from the guards.

Moreover, political prisoners were spared the horrors of sexual violence in the prison. "The nationalist women were never bothered in that manner," Carmín Pérez told the historian Olga Jiménez de Wagenheim in 1998.[44] However, "there were cases of inmates, the ones who worked with the prison guards, who were taken out at night by some male guards and brought back in the next morning." But Pérez affirmed that the nationalist women were "always respected by the guards and seen as 'protectors' by the other inmates." She told Jiménez de Wagenheim that the other women would complain to the nationalist women and "we would go to their defense." Isabel Rosado, in particular, was known to defend the women of the general population and was often sought out for help.[45]

These descriptions point to the tension that many Puerto Ricans felt around the prosecution of the nationalists, especially those who worked for the government. According to Reynolds, "The guards, the staff of the prison was sympathetic in general." She describes the warden of the San Juan jail as having been an ex-nationalist who "had the Feds watching him all the time."[46] This is noteworthy given that, as a warden, he was an agent of the colonial state. It also illuminates the complicated relationship that many Puerto Ricans had with US colonialism at the time: holding a desire for independence or an emotional connection to a free Puerto Rico, while needing to eat, feed their families, and survive. Much like today, poverty and need often drove Puerto Ricans to be agents of the colonial state even as they harbored private desires for Puerto Rico's independence or an end to US colonialism.

Sometime after Reynolds and the other nationalist women were reunited in the large gallery, Reynolds managed to send supporters in New York a letter in which she described conditions in the gallery. Reynolds's supporters and her defense committee in the United States used the letter to try to pressure the US government to intervene in her case. These events coincided with Muñoz Marín and his party's work toward getting the ELA finalized and enacted.[47] As a result, his government was keenly interested in making the process go forward as smoothly as possible. It was not a good look to have a respectable, white, US American political prisoner living in an overcrowded, squalid room filled with prostitutes. Shortly after she sent her letter, Reynolds received a visit from an agent of the Department of Justice. Shortly after that, she was taken to a private doctor in Arecibo. The doctor took chest X-rays and blood samples and seemed to be looking for something with which to diagnose Reynolds. He eventually found her to be undernourished and recommended that she be allowed to receive food from outside the prison to supplement the rice, beans, and bread that were staples in the facility.[48]

Moreover, Lebrón informed Reynolds that she would be moved to a large room away from the gallery and would be allowed to purchase a hot plate on which to cook food for herself. Reynolds insisted that all the nationalist women receive the same special treatment. "There are eight of us. . . . I am not going to be in a room, I'm not going to have better food without sharing it. That's all there is to it," she told Lebrón.[49] While agreeing to move all the nationalist women to the large room, Lebrón explained to Reynolds that he could not authorize extra food for them. However, he would not limit how much food she bought or stop her from sharing it. The next day the eight women were moved into a room that Reynolds described as between 100 and 145 square feet. It was not huge, but the women had more space there than they did in the gallery. They also had a window that overlooked the street. Reynolds's insistence that the women all be treated the same made their time in prison a bit easier. They had access to milk, coffee, fresh fruits, even beef and occasionally pork and fish.

Reynolds's account highlights that, generally, all the nationalist women were treated with greater care and respect than the women in the general population. However, it also makes apparent that Reynolds, as a white woman from the United States, had privileges not afforded the Puerto Rican nationalist women, who were largely from rural or working-class backgrounds. Reynolds's politics were such that she insisted on sharing those things that her privilege afforded her with the other women, so they all benefited. But for Reynolds, the others would have remained in the gallery, without access to fresh fruits or better food. Furthermore, Reynolds's supporters and family in the United States regularly sent her small comforts like books, magazines, and funds that she could use to purchase food. Though some of the other women, like Leonides Díaz, whose family owned a farm, received fresh fruits and vegetables that she shared with the group, most of the other women did not have such support that they could rely on. Many, like Monserrate, had nationalist husbands and partners who were also incarcerated. Or they had children, like Monserrate's two young daughters, Yvette and Yvonne, who had been left in the care of family and friends who could not afford to contribute much to the women's commissary accounts.

Reynolds's oral history allows us a view of the bond that the women developed and how it helped them survive their time in prison. Reynolds described it as a sisterhood. "We were happy to be together for the most part, though whenever people are together there are arguments. . . . The bond created by that relationship, however, is firm and cannot be broken. . . . It is one of inseparability."[50] Indeed, Isabel Rosado affirmed this point in an interview with Jiménez de Wagenheim: without each other's company, "we would have died of boredom because we had absolutely nothing to do" but talk and share with each other.[51] Rosado described Monserrate, who came to know most of the women during their incarceration, as particularly amused by the stories the women told.[52] It's clear from their accounts that the sharing of food; of small creature comforts, like books and magazines; of space; and of their stories was a lifeline for the nationalist women and gave them strength throughout the experience of incarceration.

Conclusion (or the Start of Another Chapter . . .)

After waiting twenty-two months for a trial, Monserrate was acquitted of the single charge that remained—violation of the Gag Law. She was released from prison in August 1952. Reynolds and the other women noted that Monserrate seemingly disappeared thereafter.[53] Of course, she didn't disappear. However, the toll of the previous two years had been great—living in a prison for twenty-two months with her husband on the other side of the same prison complex yet completely out of reach from him and separated from her two young daughters. Despite the deep bonds the women developed while incarcerated, when Monserrate left Arecibo, she also left the PNPR behind. Undoubtedly, she always carried her hopes for Puerto Rico's independence in her heart, but her incarceration had so deeply scarred her that she did not speak about it or her time with the PNPR.

For a time, Monserrate moved back to Ponce and reunited with her daughters and siblings. Eventually, she made her way to Williamsburg, where she established a new life for herself far from her nationalist past. Tomás was released early, sometime in the 1960s, and he rejoined his family in Brooklyn. There the couple lived quietly and anonymously, raising their daughters. They ran their business, MyTy Realty, named after the four of them: Monserrate, Yvonne, Tomás, and Yvette. They were members of the Puerto Rican community in Williamsburg. They tried to leave behind the traumas they had endured in their struggle to liberate Puerto Rico from colonial rule. They no longer participated in activism or political organizing for Puerto Rico's independence, even as a new generation of Puerto Rican independistas was coming up.

Despite her turn away from nationalism, Monserrate often told stories of government agents who continued to surveil her and her family. She claimed that for years after her release she was followed and her telephone bugged. On Tomás's death in New York in 1972, the Puerto Rican government initially refused to allow his body to be returned to Ponce for burial. Monserrate had to enlist the help of prominent Puerto Ricans in New York, including several local politicians, to persuade the government to relent. Even many years after her incarceration, Monse continued to resist the strictures of the colonial state, this time to allow her and her family to grieve their loss.

Monserrate lived through and participated in some of Puerto Rico's most tumultuous moments. Her belief in Puerto Rico's right to be independent and free from the bonds of US colonialism led her to the PNPR and eventually to her involvement in the Arecibo revolt. Her time in jail and her relationships with the women with whom she was incarcerated, both nationalists and nonnationalists, illuminate the way the women continued to resist US colonial structures even while being held deeply within them. To care for each other; to hold each other up and, literally, feed each other; and to offer other incarcerated women their humanity were all acts of radical care and of refusal—refusal to allow the colonial state to demean them or their dignity.

Mónica A. Jiménez is a poet and historian. She is an assistant professor in the African and African Diaspora Studies Department at the University of Texas at Austin. Her writing has appeared or is forthcoming in *CENTRO: Journal of the Center for Puerto Rican Studies*, *Latino Studies*, and *sx salon*, among others. Her first book, *Making Never-Never Land: Race and Law in the Creation of Puerto Rico*, is forthcoming.

Notes

1. Rosado, *Las llamas de la aurora*; Jiménez, "Pedro Albizu Campos."
2. See Dietz, *Economic History of Puerto Rico*; Ayala and Bernabe, *Puerto Rico in the American Century*; and Wagenheim and Jiménez de Wagenheim, *The Puerto Ricans*.
3. Bosque-Pérez, "Political Persecution," 20.
4. Jiménez, "Puerto Rico under the Colonial Gaze," 38.
5. National Archives and Record Administration, Record Group 126—Department of the Interior, Office of Territories Classified Files, 1907–1951; 9-8-78: Puerto Rico, Law and Order, General; Box 933, Folder: "Law and Order, Nationalist Party, Ponce Riot of March 21, 1937 (Palm Sunday Massacre), General (Part 1: March 22, 1937–May 1937); "Preliminary Report of the District Attorney of Ponce to the Honorable, The Attorney General of Puerto Rico, dated March 22, 1937."
6. Paralitici, "Imprisonment and Colonial Domination," 72.
7. Paralitici, "Imprisonment and Colonial Domination," 74.
8. Fernandez, *Disenchanted Island*, 151.
9. Burrows, "Rural Hydro-electrification and the Colonial New Deal," 293.
10. Duany, *Puerto Rican Nation on the Move*, 166–84.
11. Maldonado, *Boom and Bust in Puerto Rico*, 16–20; Trías Monge, *Puerto Rico*, 99–106.
12. Maldonado, *Boom and Bust in Puerto Rico*, 16–20.
13. Trías Monge, *Puerto Rico*, 107–18.
14. Quoted in Jiménez, "Looking for a Way Forward in the Past," 266.
15. Puerto Rico, Registro Civil, 1836–2001, Departamento de Salud de Puerto Rico, San Juan.
16. Jiménez de Wagenheim, *Nationalist Heroines*, 293; *El Pueblo de Puerto Rico v. Tomás López de Victoria*, 77 D.P.R. 953, 1955 PR Sup. LEXIS 158 (P.R. 1955).
17. "FBI Files on Puerto Ricans," Center for Puerto Rican Studies, Hunter College, name file: "Nationalist Party of Puerto Rico," no. SJ 100-3, vols. 23, 26–27.
18. Acosta-Lespier, *La Mordaza*, 144; Power, "Puerto Rican Women Nationalists," 465; Jiménez de Wagenheim, *Nationalist Heroines*, 60.
19. "FBI Files on Puerto Ricans," Center for Puerto Rican Studies, Hunter College, name file: "Nationalist Party of Puerto Rico," no. SJ 100-3, vols. 23, 26–27.
20. Seijo Bruno, *La insurrección nacionalista en Puerto Rico*, 110.
21. Acosta-Lespier, *La Mordaza*, 146.
22. *El Pueblo de Puerto Rico v. Tomás López de Victoria*, 77 D.P.R. 953, 1955 PR Sup. LEXIS 158 (P.R. 1955). This section relies heavily on the oral history of Ruth Mary Reynolds, housed in the Ruth M. Reynolds Papers, Series X: Oral Histories, 1985–86, Center for Puerto Rican Studies, Hunter College (hereafter cited as "Reynolds, oral history"). Reynolds's account provides many details about daily life in the prison. Recorded in 1985, over thirty years after the events described, it is told from the perspective of a white, mainland US American woman with a level of privilege Monserrate and the others did not possess. The irony of needing to locate the experiences of a working-class, Puerto Rican woman in the stories told about her by a white, US-born woman is not lost on me. Nonetheless, Reynolds's account is essential to understanding what life was like for Monserrate and the other nationalist women with whom she was incarcerated.
23. Martinez Chapel, "Acusan en la isla más nacionalistas."
24. Jiménez de Wagenheim, *Nationalist Heroines*, 285.
25. Jiménez de Wagenheim, *Nationalist Heroines*, 93.

26. Jiménez de Wagenheim, *Nationalist Heroines*, 182–90.

27. Jiménez de Wagenheim, *Nationalist Heroines*, 203–9.

28. Jiménez de Wagenheim, *Nationalist Heroines*, 161–67.

29. Jiménez de Wagenheim, *Nationalist Heroines*, 129–60; Materson, "Ruth Reynolds," 184.

30. Materson, "Ruth Reynolds," 185.

31. Acosta-Lespier, *La Mordaza*, 77.

32. Acosta-Lespier, "The Smith Act Goes to San Juan," 61.

33. Acosta-Lespier, "The Smith Act Goes to San Juan," 61.

34. Jiménez de Wagenheim, *Nationalist Heroines*, 166.

35. Paralitici, "Imprisonment and Colonial Domination," 77.

36. Helfeld, "Discrimination for Political Beliefs and Associations," 38–39.

37. The following narrative description of prison life is heavily derived from the Reynolds oral history. Where a quote is taken directly from the transcripts, I have given the identification number of the recording where it can be found. Otherwise, the narrative was pieced together from the transcripts of the following audio recordings: tape nos. 42, 47C, 49–51, 55–59.

38. Findlay, *Imposing Decency*, 77–109; Briggs, *Reproducing Empire*, 46–73.

39. Jiménez de Wagenheim, *Nationalist Heroines*, 139.

40. Jiménez de Wagenheim, *Nationalist Heroines*, 139.

41. Reynolds oral history, tape no. 58.

42. Reynolds oral history, tape no. 57.

43. Jiménez de Wagenheim, *Nationalist Heroines*, 139.

44. Quoted in Jiménez de Wagenheim, *Nationalist Heroines*, 116.

45. Jiménez de Wagenheim, *Nationalist Heroines*, 116.

46. Reynolds oral history, tape no. 51.

47. Acosta-Lespier, *La Mordaza*, 90–93.

48. Reynolds oral history, tape no. 51.

49. Reynolds oral history, tape no. 57.

50. Reynolds oral history, tape no. 59.

51. Jiménez de Wagenheim, *Nationalist Heroines*, 169.

52. Jiménez de Wagenheim, *Nationalist Heroines*, 170.

53. Reynolds oral history, tape no. 59; Jiménez de Wagenheim, *Nationalist Heroines*, 294.

References

Acosta-Lespier, Ivonne. *La Mordaza (the Gag Law): The Attempt to Crush the Independence Movement in Puerto Rico (1948–1957).* Rio Piedras, PR: DS Editores, 2018.

Acosta-Lespier, Ivonne. "The Smith Act Goes to San Juan: *La Mordaza*, 1948–1957." In *Puerto Rico under Colonial Rule: Political Persecution and the Quest for Human Rights*, edited by Ramón Bosque-Pérez and José Javier Colón Morera, 59–66. Albany: State University of New York Press, 2006.

Ayala, Cesar, and Rafael Bernabe. *Puerto Rico in the American Century: A History since 1898.* Chapel Hill: University of North Carolina Press, 2007.

Bosque-Pérez, Ramón. "Political Persecution against Puerto Rican Anti-colonial Activists in the Twentieth Century." In *Puerto Rico under Colonial Rule: Political Persecution and the Quest for Human Rights*, edited by Ramón Bosque-Pérez and José Javier Colón Morera, 13–47. Albany: State University of New York Press, 2006.

Briggs, Laura. *Reproducing Empire: Race, Sex Science, and U.S. Imperialism in Puerto Rico.* Berkeley: University of California Press, 2002.

Burrows, Geoff G. "Rural Hydro-electrification and the Colonial New Deal: Modernization, Experts, and Rural Life in Puerto Rico, 1935–1942." *Agricultural History* 91, no. 3 (2017): 293–319.

Dietz, James. *Economic History of Puerto Rico: Institutional Change and Capitalist Development.* Princeton, NJ: Princeton University Press, 1986.

Duany, Jorge. *The Puerto Rican Nation on the Move: Identities on the Island and in the United States.* Chapel Hill: University of North Carolina Press, 2014.

Fernandez, Ronald. *The Disenchanted Island: Puerto Rico and the United States in the Twentieth Century.* 2nd ed. Westport, CT: Praeger, 1996.

Findlay, Eileen. *Imposing Decency: The Politics of Sexuality and Race in Puerto Rico, 1870–1920.* Durham, NC: Duke University Press, 1999.

Helfeld, David M. "Discrimination for Political Beliefs and Associations." *Revista del Colegio de Abogados de Puerto Rico* 25, no. 1 (1964): 5–276.

Jiménez, Mónica A. "Looking for a Way Forward in the Past: Lessons from the Puerto Rican Nationalist Party." In *Aftershocks of Disaster: Puerto Rico before and after the Storm,* 263–70. Chicago: Haymarket Books, 2019.

Jiménez, Mónica A. "Pedro Albizu Campos." In vol. 1 of *Dictionary of Caribbean and Afro-Latin American Biography,* edited by Henry Louis Gates Jr. and Franklin W. Knight. New York: Oxford University Press, 2016.

Jiménez, Mónica A. "Puerto Rico under the Colonial Gaze: Oppression, Resistance, and the Myth of the Nationalist Enemy." *Latino Studies* 18 (2020): 27–44. https://doi.org/10.1057/s41276-019-00238-3.

Jiménez de Wagenheim, Olga. *Nationalist Heroines: Puerto Rican Women History Forgot, 1930s–1950s.* Princeton, NJ: Weiner, 2017.

Maldonado, A. W. *Boom and Bust in Puerto Rico: How Politics Destroyed an Economic Miracle.* Notre Dame, IN: University of Notre Dame Press, 2021.

Martínez Chapel, Juan. "Acusan en la isla más nacionalistas." *El Mundo,* November 10, 1950.

Materson, Lisa. "Ruth Reynolds, Solidarity Activism, and the Struggle against US Colonialism in Puerto Rico." *Modern American History,* no. 2 (2019): 183–87.

Paralitici, José (Ché). "Imprisonment and Colonial Domination, 1898–1958." In *Puerto Rico under Colonial Rule: Political Persecution and the Quest for Human Rights,* edited by Ramón Bosque-Pérez and José Javier Colón Morera, 67–80. Albany: State University of New York Press, 2006.

Power, Margaret. "Puerto Rican Women Nationalists vs. U.S. Colonialism: An Exploration of Their Conditions and Struggles in Jail and Court." *Chicago-Kent Law Review* 87, no. 2 (2012): 463–79.

Rosado, Marisa. *Las llamas de la aurora: Acercamiento a una biografía de Pedro Albizu Campos.* San Juan, PR: Editora Corripio, 1992.

Seijo Bruno, Miñi. *La insurrección nacionalista en Puerto Rico, 1950.* Río Piedras, PR: Editorial Edil, 1989.

Trías Monge, José. *Puerto Rico: The Trials of the Oldest Colony in the World.* New Haven, CT: Yale University Press, 1997.

Wagenheim, Kal, and Olga Jiménez de Wagenheim, eds. *The Puerto Ricans: A Documentary History.* 5th ed. Princeton, NJ: Weiner, 2013.

Feminist Educators against State Neglect

Kaysha Corinealdi

In 1938 Felicia Santizo, then a teacher at the Escuela República de Uruguay in the Panamanian province of Colón, authored a guide for literacy instruction. The guide was intended for teachers, but it was addressed to a broader audience invested in the transformational potential of education. "The primordial task of [the field of literacy]," she explained, "is not just ensuring that a child learns how to read. It has a much bigger and much more notable mission, something elemental: developing thinking skills."[1] This focus on independent thinking, reflection, and knowledge that went beyond skill building connected Santizo to Sara Sotillo and other working women, especially teachers, who understood their role as community leaders. Together they represented a generation of feminist educators who used self-made and popular platforms to center women as agents of change. Their formation as primary school teachers and core organizers of early twentieth-century feminist movements, in particular, provided them with unique insights about the most pressing needs facing working women and children and the need to take action in light of routine state neglect.

State neglect as defined in this essay refers to the lack of proper funding or attention to essential services such as education and full access to civic and political rights. This neglect, to some extent, was by design. The very communities where Santizo and Sotillo spent their time as teachers and organizers—Colón City in the province of Colón and El Chorrillo and Santa Ana in the province of Panama, respectively—were predominantly poor and working-class Black communities. Colón City and El Chorrillo were viewed by the state and members of the elite as

Radical History Review
Issue 148 (January 2024)   DOI 10.1215/01636545-10846808
© 2024 by MARHO: The Radical Historians' Organization, Inc.

foreign Black spaces contaminated by Afro-Caribbean migrants and their descendants. Those in Santa Ana had a long history of being othered. This history extended from the colonial era, when members of Panama City's white elite erected fortifications to keep out their darker and poorer neighbors. Santa Ana became one of the central neighborhoods of the *arrabal*, the area at the periphery of the wealthier city center. Select educated professionals within Santa Ana secured political power, but the vast majority of *arrabaleros* were viewed as impediments to progress. This outsider status persisted after independence and was compounded as elites moved away from the city yet retained their control as landlords. Those living in the *arrabal* had little recourse against these predatory landlords.[2]

The welfare of these communities was not a priority for the state. Colón City, El Chorrillo, and Santa Ana were a microcosm of how state neglect purposefully reflected the economic disparities throughout Panama. A small white and mestizo elite sector controlled commercial and agricultural industries, and most citizens, particularly Afro-descendants and those living in Indigenous communities, faced housing insecurity, unstable and dangerous working environments, and had little to no political representation.[3] That these communities survived and sometimes even thrived was *in spite of* the state, not because of state interest or investment. The women who worked and lived in these communities, like Santizo and Sotillo, fully understood this reality.

In deciding to take a stance against state neglect, feminist educators took on the prospect of state repression and violence. In 1920 workers in the Panama Canal mounted the largest labor strike in the country's history. Their demands included pay increases and gender parity in wages. All strike leaders were fired, arrested, and/or deported.[4] Two major renters' strikes in Colón City and Panama City, in 1925 and 1932, were met with a brutal police response.[5] Teachers who formed part of the Partido Nacional Feminista (National Feminist Party; PNF) in the late 1930s were threatened with dismissal and publicly reprimanded by the president of the country.[6] Adding to this repression, by the late 1940s fear of accusation of communism led progressive parties to go underground.[7] Santizo and Sotillo witnessed and were affected by some of these happenings. Being part of a community of feminist educators allowed both women to operate around the state while also engendering collective action that could not be ignored by the state. This was a result of their experiences as the first generation of teacher educators in an independent Panama, their willingness to test new organizational models, and their ability to garner the respect and support of a dedicated network of fellow conspirators and collaborators.

My assessments of the organizational communities and agendas that Santizo and Sotillo formed part of and developed are drawn largely from newspapers and government reports spanning from 1933 to 1950, correspondence between Santizo and Doris Stevens (in her role as chair of the InterAmerican Commission of Women) in the late 1930s, a literacy teaching guide published by Santizo in 1938, a speech delivered by Sotillo in 1947 in her role as coordinator of the Magisterio Panameño Unido (United Panamanian Teachers; MPU), and the writings of two other MPU members that appeared in national newspapers during the 1940s. These sources allow me to paint a compelling albeit partial picture of what it was like to undertake the work of organizing as feminist educators in the first half of the twentieth century.

Sources in which Santizo, Sotillo, and their friends and collaborators speak in their own terms particularly highlight the scope of what they envisioned and accomplished. I thus examine Santizo and Sotillo not within the lens of exceptionalism but as products of their communities and as advocates for alternative visions of care and protection in the midst of state neglect. These visions primarily entailed creating economic opportunities for one another and their broader communities, securing fair wages and the right to a just retirement, organizing school cafeterias, advocating for the creation of public high schools, teaching night and weekend courses for students unable to enroll in overcrowded public schools, and inaugurating a bank for teachers. Connecting Santizo, Sotillo, and their organizational bases was an understanding of education and advocacy as transformational and the role of feminist educators as instrumental in the growth of progressive communities.

The Power of Education and Feminist Organizing (1914–1925)

Santizo and Sotillo formed part of a small group of young women who between 1909 and 1919 attended and graduated from Panama's Escuela Normal de Institutoras (Teacher's College for Women). Together, they and 378 other trained teachers took on the task of educating the young population of an equally young nation.[8] By the early 1930s forty-two public schools operated in Panama and Colón, the two most densely populated provinces in the country. This number of schools did not meet the demand; fewer than half of all school-aged children five to fifteen years old had access to schooling.[9] Even with this shortage of schools, the focus on women as primary-school educators, first segregated by sex and later as instructors of girls and boys alike, formed a core component of the educational landscape.

Along with being part of this distinct group of educators, Santizo and Sotillo were also among the few women of African descent in their profession. Santizo was born on February 5, 1893, in Portobelo, Colón, on the Atlantic side of the isthmus. Portobelo was home to the descendants of Panama's *cimarrón* (maroon) communities and also a core site for the development of Congo traditions, which drew from cultural practices of Central and West Africa.[10] Congo music and dance, which centered on themes of struggle, freedom, and play, would inform Santizo's love for music and her eventual role as a music teacher. The bustling Afro-diasporic community of Colón City, Colón, where Santizo flourished as a teacher and organizer, would in turn serve as the base of much of her organizational work. As a dark-skinned Black woman from Colón, a province known, and at times derided, as a center of Black life and culture, Santizo had to navigate on a daily basis the anti-Blackness that formed part of social and political discourses of *mestizaje*. Her father's reputation as a leader within the Liberal Party during the independence movement meant that she nevertheless had a model for Black leadership.[11]

Sotillo, a light-skinned Black woman, had a different relationship with race than Santizo. Her skin color meant that her African ancestry did not serve as an immediate identifier for others. Her class standing as poor, for much of her childhood and young adult life, would shape her experience of being othered, especially by members of the elite. Sotillo was born on April 19, 1900, in San Miguel Island, part of an archipelago on the Pacific side of the isthmus. Her parents formed part of a working class that made a living through fishing and farming. Like most of the residents of San Miguel, neither had the opportunity to access or complete formal schooling. Shortly after Panama's independence from Colombia in 1903, her parents moved the family to Panama City. There they lived in the *arrabal*, surrounded by other poor and working-class Afro-descendants seeking better employment and educational opportunities. Sotillo and her siblings Francisco and María del Carmen took advantage of these opportunities. Sotillo, in particular, secured an academic scholarship to the country's only teacher training school for women.[12]

Another factor that shaped the ways that Santizo, Sotillo, and other educators intertwined education, feminism, and organizing corresponded with the economic stability provided by their careers as teachers. For most working women in early twentieth-century Panama, a career as a teacher offered a stable path of employment. Trained teachers by the mid-1920s earned 65 balboas (equivalent to US$65) a month, one of the highest salaries available to women at the time.[13] Most women who worked outside the home did so as domestics, laundresses, and cooks. This was especially the case for poor and working-class women, who, like their counterparts in early twentieth-century Cuba, Brazil, and the United States, often faced additional hurdles securing educational and professional opportunities.[14] The level of economic security provided by the teaching profession correlated with the growth in activism within this space. This took the shape of collective organizing in women-led and feminist-centered movements that called for greater economic, social, and political rights for all girls and women.

Sotillo's first role as a feminist organizer came as the second vice president of the Centro Feminista Renovación (Feminist Renewal Group; CFR) in 1922.[15] At the time she was twenty-two years old and had just begun teaching as an elementary school teacher at the Escuela Manuel José Hurtado in Panama City.[16] The CFR set forth four core goals: educate women culturally, improve the social and moral standing of women, promote women's economic independence, and advocate for equality to men in terms of rights and responsibilities before the law.[17] For the women who formed part of the CFR, a multipronged approach to feminism was paramount. Education, economic and social opportunity, and political guarantees all had an equal role to play in a feminist future.

The Primer Congreso Feminista (First Feminist Congress), held in September 1923, allowed Sotillo and Santizo to cross paths. The congress brought together forty-three women delegates from various Panamanian provinces. Santizo led the writing of a twenty-point platform that would form the basis of the constitution for the PNF. Core goals laid out in the constitution included labor laws protecting women, the creation of homes to help mothers, employment agencies for women, savings accounts for women, and the creation of funds and cooperatives to assist women and children in need.[18] Sotillo then taught for seven years in the Escuela de Cultura Femenina (Women's Cultural School), created by the PNF in June 1924. The school was available for free to young and older women and focused on training in subjects such as reading, writing, and orthography, with all classes taking place at night. Teachers took on this work in addition to their full-time jobs as primary school teachers. They did so without pay and without support from the state. The school also included a donations-based library open to the public.[19]

The ability of feminist educators to make do with funds collected from fellow teachers and members of the community, all while navigating state indifference or neglect, engendered tremendous respect within their communities. These educators, and not state officials, took on the work of providing crucial educational and professional opportunities for the residents of Colón City, El Chorrillo, Santa Ana, and other communities relegated to the margins of the state. The ability of these teachers to work around state neglect would nonetheless be tested by a global depression that debilitated the Panamanian economy. Working around the state remained vital, but feminist educators more forcefully demanded state action to protect those most vulnerable within their communities.

Teaching amid Economic Precarity and State Neglect (1930–1936)

During the global economic depression of the late 1920s and early 1930s, teachers faced the task of educating over fifty thousand young children who arrived at school underfed or not fed at all.[20] As noted by Carlos Smart, a physician who volunteered his time with the Colón City schools, at least 50 percent of the students he examined lacked proper nutrition.[21] On the personal front, teachers had to support their own families amid steep pay cuts. In September 1930 education officials suspended all overtime pay. Two years later this office fixed the monthly base bay of teachers at 50 balboas for teachers in the provinces of Panama and Colón and from 35 to 45 balboas for teachers in other parts of the country. This was a drop in pay of at least 15 balboas a month. By the time of these cuts and into the 1930s, women made up over 80 percent of all teachers.[22] The role of education inspectors and directors, not to mention the secretary of education, nevertheless remained dominated by men.[23] It was these men that teachers found themselves petitioning for recognition of back pay and to negotiate their school placement every year.

Sotillo maintained her placement in the Escuela Hurtado throughout this period of economic instability. She did not have patrons or family members who wrote to the secretary of education or the president on her behalf, a common practice used by elite families at this time.[24] Instead, she made herself an indispensable part of the Hurtado school and by the mid-1930s had taken on the role of writing to education officials on behalf of teachers denied back pay and, once it was reauthorized, overtime pay.[25]

At the same time, Santizo, as a teacher in the Escuela República de Uruguay in Colón City, began to write a guide for the teaching of literacy that combined practical instruction with sociopolitical commentary. She pushed against literacy approaches centered solely on phonics and memorization and instead called for literacy learning that "gave children the truth."[26] Crucial for Santizo was understanding teachers, students, and families as part of a learning team. The state, in turn, had to provide the economic stability needed for this cooperative education. As she wrote in her 1938 guide: "It is households that constitute the greatness of any nation. The virtues of these households determine the well-being of a people. A country where the majority of households live in extreme poverty and where families are illiterate cannot be labeled a happy, much less a progressive, nation."[27] Santizo here did not blame impoverished families, something routinely done by state officials, but instead focused on what the state owed its citizens.

When speaking of teachers and students, government officials expressed some concern about economic struggles and student learning outcomes but focused mostly on the ills of poverty and the failings of educators. Writing in 1934, the secretary of education, Narciso Garay, admitted that most teachers either came from poor economic backgrounds or were themselves the sole earners for an entire family. For Garay, this reality was bleak because such constraints meant that teachers could not "improve their intellectual preparation, nor report to their classes with the correct attire that is expected by their profession and the law." Most disconcerting for Garay was the degree to which this lack of professionalism "lowered the prestige of teachers before the eyes of their students, the parents of their students, and the serviced community at large."[28] Concern for the economic realities faced by teachers was equated with how these realities would affect public perception of the utility and productivity of teachers.

Regarding student outcomes, according to the general inspector of education, C. Arrocha Graell, the true challenge in meeting student learning goals, mainly retention and graduation, directly coincided with the "alarming" proportion of female versus male teachers. He called for more male teachers, especially in the higher grades of primary school.[29] The subsequent secretary of education, Aníbal Ríos, went even farther and suggested that the high index of failure in the first grades were directly connected to the preponderance of women teaching these grades. He also lamented how poverty prevented mothers from properly feeding their children or setting high educational expectations for them.[30]

Mentioned in a brief sentence in Ríos's report was a note on the number of students who had to seek breakfast and lunch from school cafeterias or the Red

Cross. These school cafeterias were not financed by the state. Instead, teachers pooled their money and asked for donations from the surrounding community to create these cafeterias. Domestic education teachers either served as cooks or requested volunteers. Records collected by the Ministry of Education show that by 1937, in one year in Panama City alone, schools with community-funded cafeterias had served over sixty thousand breakfasts and twenty-four thousand lunches.[31] That school officials listed these meal numbers without clarifying that these programs were run entirely on voluntary labor pointed to their desire to take credit for something recognized as a public good, feeding hungry children, while not having to allocate any funding toward this endeavor.

This was the landscape facing teachers like Sotillo and Santizo in the 1930s. School officials asked that teachers do more with less, questioned their ability as educators, and took credit for programs seeking to provide some relief for poor and working-class students. Any educators seeking to question state inefficiency and neglect and offer their own alternatives for change had to contend with these and many other roadblocks, including members of the elite distrustful of their work and qualifications.

Community Organizing and Antifeminist Backlash (1936–1940)

By 1936 Santizo created what would be one of her various communal efforts against state neglect—the Acción Social Femenina (Feminine Social Action; ASF) group. Comprising poor and working-class Black women from the city of Colón, the ASF focused on literacy, housing reform, and women's rights. Santizo, like Sotillo, remained an active member of the PNF, although with the ASF she addressed some of the specific sociopolitical and economic challenges facing Colón. The ASF also built on work Santizo and other teachers had already begun in the province, including the creation of a clothing program for students and several pop-up libraries.[32] Of utmost importance to Santizo, in speaking about the group to those interested in building allegiances or collaborations, was emphasizing that the ASF comprised not women from high society but "honorable working women invested in the well-being of humanity."[33]

As outlined by Santizo, the services provided by the ASF were in dire demand. Within the first year of the organization's existence, she and other volunteer teachers held classes for eighty students who, due to overcrowded schools, were denied entry. "We have children who have been truly abandoned," she affirmed, "because the schools that are supposed to assist them first accept students who can pay, with the end result that the children of the poor become the future citizens of the penitentiaries."[34] Poor students could not even rely on the guarantee of free elementary education as mandated by law. Not surprisingly, the goals of the ASF as laid out in its statutes included increasing access to free and public education through venues like conferences and night courses and spaces like libraries;

advancing hygiene campaigns to assist children facing oppressive conditions at home, school, or in the streets; and creating a school dedicated to addressing childhood delinquency.[35]

Meeting these goals became more difficult with each passing year. As Santizo noted in April 1938, "We have not secured any assistance because those who would like to contribute are without means and the authorities make promises but we never see this help. It is because this organization is composed of working women that there is so little interest in our work."[36] The ASF, rather than being a philanthropic group to which elite men and women could make donations and then champion their own charitable spirit, was made up of women of the community working for the community, and it decried paternalistic donors.

This focus on working women constructing their own agendas contradicted the discourse of the helpless poor who relied on the kindness and charity of wealthy benefactors. Santizo herself was very confident in the ability of the organization to transform the lives of those most in need. One of the programs promoted by the ASF was an intensive literacy course that guaranteed the ability to read after daily thirty-five-minute sessions held over a period of three months. As noted earlier, Santizo published a core literacy guide in 1938, hence her confidence in her ability and that of other teachers familiar with her method to teach children and adults how to read and write. This level of confidence and expertise was respected and supported by her fellow *colonenses* (residents of Colón) but drew the ire of state officials and would-be philanthropists, who saw in her a woman who rejected her societally appointed role.[37]

Another component that complicated the work of Santizo, the ASF, and teachers like Sotillo and other members of the PNF was the adamant antifeminist policies of the government of Juan Demóstenes Arosemena. For these officials, the feminist movement, with its combined calls for political, economic, and social rights, represented a threat to the sanctity of the Panamanian family.[38] Writing on the front page of the national daily *El Panamá América*, President Arosemena made public his opposition to women's suffrage.[39] Adding to the president's open antifeminism was a doubling down on this discourse by the secretary of education, Aníbal Ríos. Speaking to the daily *El Nuevo Diario*, Ríos affirmed that he "detested" feminist activities among teachers and that the Ministry of Education and Agriculture prohibited teachers from participating in party politics or political affairs.[40]

Teachers formed a crucial part of the feminist movement in Panama. With these public statements, Ríos placed all feminist teachers on alert. They could organize, but there would be consequences for this activity. Santizo, reflecting on the aftermath of President Arosemena's and Secretary Río's public statements, admitted to a deep sense of "disillusionment" among the ASF membership. For Panamanian women, she declared, "it will be IMPOSSIBLE" to secure suffrage rights. Furthermore, for a teacher to "participate in feminist propaganda" carried the risk of losing her job.[41]

The backlash against feminists had lasting impacts on the type of organizing that feminist educators would envision. Both Sotillo and Santizo remained invested in the lived realities of working women, with the former playing a leading role in the creation of a teacher's association and the latter running for elected office, but this antifeminism changed them. In their public advocacy they focused on the work of feminism rather than political discourses about feminism. This doubling down on the work of feminism allowed both women to eschew the ire of critics and return to their roots as feminist educators and organizers.

Organizing Teachers (1941–1944)

The creation of the MPU exemplified this feminist legacy of educators. As noted earlier, Sotillo and fellow teachers had in the past taken on the role of writing to education officials regarding back pay or overtime pay owed to teachers. Beginning in 1941 Sotillo and fellow teachers Ana L. de Bellido, Carmen Solé B., and Carmen Sotillo (Sara's sister) began to organize at Escuela Hurtado. Together they were the organizing committee. Because of the number of teachers that these meetings attracted, provincial inspectors denied teachers the right to gather at the school. In response, the committee proposed meeting in the streets and organized a gathering of teachers at Plaza Bolívar on October 14, 1942, to march to the Presidency. The organizing committee also agreed to print circulars to educate teachers throughout the republic on their campaign for economic security for all teachers.[42]

Three core demands animated the October march: a base pay of 75 balboas for all degreed/accredited teachers and 55 balboas for all teachers without degrees, distribution of overtime pay, and a review of the retirement structure under the current social security laws. These changes, they argued, were imperative to prevent teachers from leaving the field in search of higher-paying jobs, or prospective teachers from rejecting the field entirely. They also pointed to the injustice of a retirement system that provided retirees who had served for forty-two years and were sixty years old with benefits totaling 25 balboas a month. Such a system did not account for the taxing nature of the teaching profession and also incorrectly calculated the economic needs of retirees. As the group declared in a public letter addressed to both the Ministry of Education and the Presidency, "Due to prevailing circumstances which we cannot fight, much less escape, we are forced to make these just demands of the Executive, with the expectation of receiving a favorable decision." This framing, in addition to the hundreds of signatures that followed, placed the weight of responsibility on the state to review and address these demands.[43]

Overall, it was a core group of women working collectively, Sara and Carmen Sotillo, Ana L. de Bellido, Carmen Solé, and Elidia Wong de Taylor, who organized and raised public awareness about the need for the MPU. Sara Sotillo served as a spokesperson for the group, a position she earned through the respect of her collaborators, but these feminist educators worked together. Bellido, for example, wrote a public response to the head of the Social Security Department after he criticized teachers' understanding of retirement privileges. Her response provided a robust mathematical breakdown of why the retirement laws were unfair, especially for senior teachers who had been working prior to the establishment of the contemporary Social Security Department. She concluded: "It should now be clear then, that teachers are not confused when they calculate that upon retirement they will only receive 25 balboas. In fact, basic arithmetic puts in evidence that many will receive less." The social security system was not created with teachers in mind, whether it was in accounting for years of labor or for equitably assessing retirement benefits. The degree that officials so readily dismissed the claims made by teachers formed part of a long-standing practice of state neglect.[44]

Success in their campaigns to raise teacher salaries significantly increased national interest in the work of the Escuela Hurtado organizers. By late October 1942, and following direct discussions between Sotillo, the group's spokesperson, and the members of the Education Commission of the National Assembly, teachers received a guarantee of pay increases starting in 1943.[45] Law 110, passed in February 1943, established a pay scale for teachers that included a base pay of 65 balboas for all degreed teachers and 45 balboas for nondegreed teachers. These figures were 10 balboas lower than the teacher advocates had asked for, but they marked the first substantial wage increase for teachers since the 1920s and served as an example of the power of successful organizing. The law also allocated funds for the overtime and back pay owed teachers.[46]

Attending to the low morale among teachers as well the unresolved retirement issue led to the continued work of the Escuela Hurtado organizers and the emergence of the MPU. Law 110 made no mention of retirement and in fact specified that the matter would need to be taken up through other legislation. Following continued meetings at Escuela Hurtado, a nationwide campaign to educate teachers on the benefits of an association, and hundreds of telegrams from teachers congratulating the Hurtado organizers for their work, the MPU became a reality on October 4, 1944. Over two hundred teachers were on hand for this first official meeting, and as was the case before 1944, the organizers took to newspapers to champion their cause and encourage continued support.[47]

Writing as the press secretary for the MPU, Elidia Wong de Taylor informed readers that the organization sought to "liberate teachers from economic concerns!"[48] Teachers, she argued, remained enmeshed in the "política del hambre" (politics of hunger), whereby they routinely had to ask themselves if they should seek other job opportunities with fewer demands that would allow them to live with dignity. "Teachers do not want to be, nor should they be, selfless apostles" who must navigate higher costs of living of "300 percent, which place them in a condition of desperation." The inequities surrounding retirement further exacerbated this unjust condition. Teachers, after arduous years of labor, "bumped into the indifference of those who fail[ed] to remember that they once were students." Wong called on elected and appointed government officials not to forsake the "shapers of future citizens" but instead to pass the necessary retirement laws.[49]

For educators who began their teaching careers in the first two decades of the 1900s, the unjust nature of the retirement system held direct and personal resonance. These teachers had dedicated twenty to forty years of their lives to the public school system, yet because they did not contribute to social security until 1939, they would not be eligible for retirement benefits until 1949, and at 50 percent of their pay. For some, this meant continued labor even as they experienced extreme fatigue and poor health. The MPU succeeded in their demand that the state recognize retirement with full benefits for all teachers who had worked in public service for twenty-eight years. Considering that most of these prospective retirees were women, a number of whom had forgone having children, securing their right to a financially secure and dignified retirement marked an important victory. Other battles would emerge, but this was an important moment in the history of the MPU.[50]

Feminist Work after Suffrage and amid the Rise of Anticommunism

The extension of voting rights to women in 1945, something that Santizo, seven years earlier, had worried would never happen in Panama, generated a boom in the organizational work of the MPU and in political parties such as the Partido del Pueblo (People's Party; PDP) that sought out women like Santizo as leaders. Sotillo, as coordinator of the MPU from 1944 to 1948, was at the helm of the organization's major battles and victories. Santizo, in turn, was a music teacher in Colón's first public high school, Colegio Abel Bravo, and continued to amass the support of the people of Colón, many of whom saw her as a powerful representative of the working classes of the province. It was as a music teacher that she put together plays, comedies, and musicals for her students and their families. Here she also began to brainstorm on how to bring Congo dances and rituals to a wider audience.[51] Politics, music, and community all converged for Santizo in this mid-1940s moment. Propelled by these sentiments, Santizo put herself forward as an independent candidate, backed by the PDP, for the Constituent Assembly in the first nationwide election in which women would have the right to vote and be elected for office.[52] Santizo was not elected, although two women, Esther Neira de Calvo and Gumercinda Páez, both Panama City–based educators, made history in this regard. Páez likewise made history as the first Black woman elected to the National Assembly.[53]

Unlike Santizo and her other teacher peers, Sotillo did not run for political office. Given her nationally recognized work as a teacher organizer she could have proven a serious contender. Instead, Sotillo and the other core organizers of the MPU focused on making their case to fellow teachers and representing them before government officials. The appointment of a new education secretary, José Daniel

Crespo, as part of a party that had shown an interest in centering the needs of teachers and students, offered a new advocacy opportunity. Crespo proposed two new laws, one that set the pay scale for all education employees (Law 36) and another focused on the overall organization and operation of the nation's educational system (Law 47). Sotillo, as MPU coordinator, was a vocal participant in the National Assembly debates over both laws. Regarding Law 36, Sotillo pushed for salary increases for teachers. The result was a salary scale with degreed primary school teachers earning 90 balboas, nondegreed teachers with more than twenty years of service earning 75 balboas, and all other nondegreed teachers earning 60 balboas. An urban-rural divide remained, with degreed teachers from rural teacher training schools earning 75 balboas, but the overall salary increases, particularly those accounting for years of service, finally addressed the dire economic realities that teacher organizers had articulated for at least a decade.[54]

Among the core aspects of Law 47 that the MPU championed were limits on the cause and frequency with which teachers could be transferred from schools, freedom of political thought and activity among teachers, and just sick leave and maternity leave policies. Prior to 1946, education inspectors held absolute transfer powers, with teachers on a yearly basis having to make a case for their continued appointments at a particular school. Inspectors would now only be allowed to transfer teachers with their consent and only if the transfers entailed higher pay. Similarly, Law 47 prevented the transfer, sanctioning, and firing of teachers due to their political affiliations and beliefs. Teachers had in the past faced retribution for their political leanings. This was something that all members of the PNF knew personally. Although Law 47 still prohibited teachers from engaging in party politics in their schools and classrooms, a teacher could theoretically run for political office and join the political party of their choosing. Two other core agendas championed by the MPU that appeared in the new legislation related to the health and stability of teachers. Teachers who became ill during the school year would now be guaranteed full pay for thirty days and 50 percent pay for two subsequent months. On the maternity leave front, the law guaranteed six months of leave with half pay and counted maternity leave toward years of service. Crucially, and at the insistence of the MPU, teachers who gave birth prior to the date certified by their doctors would no longer be fired. Additionally, all teachers returning from maternity leave would be entitled to hold their previous positions.[55]

Another key component of Law 47 that the MPU, with Sotillo as spokesperson, advocated for was the inclusion of teachers in all future conversations about salary scales. The newly passed legislation required the Ministry of Education to name two teachers to a permanent commission on salary scales.[56] This was an important win for teachers, since for much of the history of the education department, all decisions had been top-down and teacher insights and innovations had been often dismissed. Yet, speaking a year after the passage of Law 47, Sotillo, as a

member of the commission, expressed frustration on the lack of any plans or reso-
lutions undertaken by this body. The commission, she reported, had only met once
since its formation.[57] As she implored those gathered for the annual meeting of the
MPU in September 1947, teachers needed to "remember that individual actions are
lost to oblivion, while those based in cooperation live on." Teachers were "no longer
pariahs." They now "knew their rights and were ready to defend them with valor and
energy." This had been the long-term goal of the MPU. Using "a truly democratic
base," the association would lead the way in future actions.[58] This focus on collective
action and democratic organizing reflected the association's cautious engagement
with the state. MPU members did not cast their full hopes on the government to
improve their working conditions. For example, the association inaugurated a
bank to provide low-interest loans to members of the teachers' association. These
loans could be used to address the financial issues that a still mostly working-class
base of teachers might experience. As had been the case with teachers collectively
pooling their money for school cafeterias, with the teacher's bank they now used
their funds to offer economic support to one another.[59]

Santizo, from her vantage point in Colón, took note of the increasingly poor
and dangerous conditions of most schools in the province, something that affected
the well-being of teachers, students, and the community at large. As coordinator of
the ASF she had firsthand knowledge of the hundreds of students who, due to lack of
space or lack of family connections, could not enroll in the city's public schools. By
the 1940s this problem extended to the structural integrity of the schools. All five of
the buildings housing Colón's public schools were deteriorating, with one having
been condemned several times, yet classes continued there because of a lack of
classroom space elsewhere. What is more, most classes remained at fifty students
per teacher, a far cry from the thirty-five-student maximum proposed through
Law 47.[60] Even opening the first public secondary school in Colón, Colegio Abel
Bravo, had been a struggle. Santizo was among those who campaigned for its
opening.[61]

By 1947 Santizo had witnessed the small but fruitful growth of Abel Bravo,
where she held a permanent post as a music teacher. Roughly 140 students formed
part of the first group of *abelistas* (Abel Bravo graduates) in a building intended for
50 students. Plans for a new high school that would accommodate one thousand students were also approved at this time. This would make it the first public school in
Colón to be housed in a newly built campus.[62] For students at Abel Bravo and all
others enrolled or wishing to enroll in public secondary schools, however, tuition
fees were required. Education officials warned school directors against exempting
students from this fee, highlighting that at most 5 percent of all students enrolled
could be offered scholarships.[63] The reliance on fees for a public good such as public
education was further exacerbated by the Ministry of Education's refusal to lead the
building of school cafeterias. Instead, the education officials urged teachers,

parents, and philanthropic organizations to continue with these efforts while nonetheless requiring them to ask for permission to begin such programs.[64]

Private citizens and community leaders like Santizo had long taken on the
task of filling the gaps that emerged from failed or aborted "goodwill" efforts on
the part of the state. Numerous unions, associations, and even select political parties
emerged from this shared frustration. The PDP, which Santizo served as president
of the Colón chapter for part of 1947, was among these groups. The PDP, created in
1943, posited itself as the party of the working and popular sectors and sought to fill
the gap left behind with the dissolution of Panama's Communist Party that same
year. Santizo's leadership of the ASF was directly aligned with the working-class
focus of the PDP, which is why she not only joined the party but served as a leader.[65]
Through the PDP she sought to make changes from within government, using her
long career as a teacher and advocate to make election bids, in 1948 alone, for the
Colón City Municipal Council, the National Assembly, and the vice presidency of
the republic.[66]

In noting her motivations for seeking these offices, Santizo emphasized that
she would protect women and children and center the right to education and recreation. A focus on education is not surprising, given her life's work, but her attention
to providing community members with recreation was also important.[67] By the late
1940s state officials had increased financing for the secret police and the national
police, increased campaigns against vagrancy and other behaviors considered of
"ill repute," and built a detention center for women.[68] No such momentum existed
in the construction of free places of play and relaxation. For Santizo, who spent much
of her life thinking about how to make education accessible and about the value of
music and culture as a site of empowerment, the absence of such spaces required
government attention. Another crucial component of Santizo's campaign was a focus
on addressing the housing crisis and ensuring the land rights of tenant farmers and
farm workers. These two last points were especially controversial. Landlords in the
cities of Panama and Colón rejected calls for affordable and decent housing and
held close connections to a political oligarchy that sought to maintain the status
quo, including by calling on the US military to maintain order.[69] Similarly, in the
realm of farming and agriculture, a handful of landowners, in conjunction with
US-based companies like the United Fruit Company, held vast control over most
of the country's arable land. Calls for land rights for farmers and their families,
and demands that multinational behemoths protect their workers, threatened to
upend a capitalist order that benefited white elites in Panama and the United States
alike.[70]

Santizo was unsuccessful in her bids for elected office. Instead, she and the
PDP had to contend with an anticommunist Panamanian state actively participating
in the US and hemisphere-wide efforts to criminalize communism. Labor leaders,
farmers, and progressive organizers bore the wrath of this policy. Attempts emerged

in the public sphere to distinguish between "healthy" and "unhealthy" communism, but by 1948 the consensus was clear: communism was dangerous and any groups or persons affiliated with this ideology were suspect.[71] As a leader of the PDP, Santizo faced growing scrutiny of her work, including having the Panamanian and US governments actively spy on her and members of the party. By April 1950, an executive decree outlawed Panama's Communist Party. As a result, all organizations viewed as "communist-leaning" came under intense scrutiny. Santizo and the PDP had to operate in secret and under threat of arrests.[72]

The government surveillance and repression that Santizo and the PDP faced by the mid-twentieth century harked back to the very roots of why select officials had so disdained the PNF and the ASF. As a leader in all of these organizations, Santizo had emphasized the rights and protections of working women. In all three spaces she had questioned a status quo that left most of the population to flounder while a select few dictated uneven terms of engagement. Securing the right to vote for women became a reality, but upending an unequal economic order would prove impossible. Adding to this reality was the equating of calls for economic justice with attempts to lead a communist overthrow of the Americas. Communists had now purportedly replaced feminists as the country's and the hemisphere's biggest threat.

Conclusion

For the first half of the twentieth century, feminist educators used their training as teachers and organizers to document, challenge, and offer solutions to problems affecting the poor and working-class Afro-descendant communities where they labored and that they called home. Felicia Santizo and Sara Sotillo are but two examples of feminist educators who engaged in community-centered work and gained the respect and collaboration of their peers. Through her creation and leadership of the ASF, Santizo educated hundreds of children left out of the public education system through state neglect. As a leader of the PDP, she used a national platform to bring attention to the inequities and injustices faced by the residents of Colón— realities faced by all working-class people in Panama exploited by landlords and bosses who viewed them as disposable. Sotillo and the band of organizers of the MPU cemented the role of teachers in the development of policies previously understood as outside the scope of teacher interests: salaries, retirement, and a seat at the legislative table. In doing so, they flipped the assumed logic that teachers, for the love of their profession, would sacrifice their time, health and overall well-being, all while bureaucrats took credit for the unpaid and unrecognized work taken on by teachers.

Sotillo, rather than enjoying the right of retirement after twenty-eight years of service as a teacher, had to work two additional years to secure this benefit. Officials chalked this up to a logistical misunderstanding, but for those who worked with Sotillo during the first decade and a half of the creation of the MPU, this was payback.[73] For every legislative victory championed by the MPU, the governing body, led by Sotillo, fought for more: better pay, greater teacher control, greater transparency. For every shortage in legislation, these feminist educators created their own sources of relief: a teacher's bank and later a housing complex for teachers.[74] The MPU did not merely wait for the government. Women who took matters into their own hands had always faced particular ire on the part of the state.

Santizo also experienced continuous pushback for her work, from members of the elite and political class ignoring the work of the ASF to the anticommunist attacks waged against the PDP and other progressive political outlets. Every victory she won in Colón on behalf of working women and children was due to her resilience amid state indifference and persecution. Yet Santizo ultimately left Colón and died in Cuba. It was in Cuba that state officials finally embraced her literacy methods and used her publications in the literacy campaign that formed a fundamental part of the 1959 Cuban Revolution.[75] Within her lifetime, Santizo was never forgiven for challenging the paternalistic and elite logics of state governance in Panama nor for centering Black working women, and the province of Colón, in her vision of a progressive nation.

Kaysha Corinealdi is a scholar of twentieth-century histories of empire, migration, feminism, and Afro-diasporic activism in the Americas. She is the author of *Panama in Black: Afro-Caribbean World Making in the Twentieth Century* (2022). Her writing can also be found in the *American Historical Review*, *Black Perspectives*, the *Caribbean Review of Gender Studies*, *The Global South*, the *International Journal of Africana Studies*, *Public Books*, *Signs: Journal of Women in Culture and Society*, *Social Text*, and the *Washington Post*.

Notes

1. Santizo, *Método natural*, ii.
2. Corinealdi, *Panama in Black*, 10–11; Lasso, "Nationalism and Immigrant Labor"; Pizzurno, *Memorias e imaginarios*, 17, 164; Westerman, *Urban Housing*.
3. Muñoz and Muñoz Pinzón, *La segunda huelga*, 13–22; Beluche, *Historia agraria*, 131–44.
4. Burnett, "'Unity Is Strength,'" 40.
5. Zumoff, "1925 Tenant's Strike"; Muñoz and Muñoz Pinzón, *La segunda huelga*.
6. Alvarado, Marco, and Vásquez, *Mujeres que cambiaron*, 38.
7. "La legalidad del movimiento comunista," *La Estrella de Panamá* (*LEP*), April 22, 1948.
8. *Memoria (Anexos)* (1938), 206–7.
9. *Memoria* (1933), 1, 89, 109–11.
10. Alexander Craft, *When the Devil Knocks*, 3–4.
11. Martínez et al., *Una maestra ejemplar*, 13–16; Marco Serra, *Clara González Behringer*, 52.
12. Martínez et al., *Una maestra ejemplar*, 13–16; Marco Serra, *Clara González Behringer*, 52.
13. *Memoria* (1935), 14.
14. González, "A mulher negra"; Williams Springer, "La mujer negra"; Brunson, *Black Women*; Flores-Villalobos, "Gender, Race."
15. Alvarado, Marco, and Vásquez, *Mujeres que cambiaron*, 26. In earlier works I have referred to the CFR as the Feminist Renovation Group (Corinealdi, "Being Fully Human").

16. Martínez et al., *Una maestra ejemplar*, 17.
17. Alvarado, Marco, and Vásquez, *Mujeres que cambiaron*, 25.
18. *Recuerdo del Partido*, 28–31.
19. *Recuerdo del Partido*, 4, 54; Alvarado, Marco, and Vásquez, *Mujeres que cambiaron*, 17–18, 54.
20. *Memoria* (1933), 1.
21. *Memoria* (1935), 335. Carlos Smart was the brother of Linda Smart Chubb, a feminist and well-known community organizer in the city of Colón. For more on the history of the Smart family in Colón, see Corinealdi, "Being Fully Human."
22. *Memoria* (1935), lxxv, 7, 15.
23. *Memoria (Anexos)* (1938), 122.
24. One example included the series of letters written by Carlos J. Quintero T. to President J. D. Arosemena requesting placement for his cousin, his daughter, and a daughter-in-law. "Carta de Carlos J. Quintero T. a Presidente Juan Demóstenes Arosemena," April 12, 1939; May 13, 1939; and July 13, 1939, Presidencia de Juan Demóstenes Arosemena, Archivo Nacional de Panamá, 43/67.
25. Martínez et al., *Una maestra ejemplar*, 57.
26. Santizo, *Método natural*, i, 5 (quote), 11.
27. Santizo, *Método natural*, 23.
28. *Memoria* (1935), lxxii.
29. *Memoria* (1936), 7.
30. *Memoria* (1938), 95–98.
31. *Memoria* (1938), 140.
32. Barrera, *Felicia Santizo*, 7–8.
33. "Carta de Felicia Santizo a la Comisión Interamericana de Mujeres," January 11, 1938, 1, Doris Stevens Papers, MC 546, folder 84.5, sequence 82–83, Schlesinger Library on the History of Women in America, Schlesinger Library, Radcliffe Institute, Harvard University, Cambridge, MA, https://nrs.lib.harvard.edu/urn-3:rad.schl:25110112. Citations from this archive are henceforth identified as DSP, with the corresponding sequence information.
34. "Carta de Felicia Santizo a Minerva Bernardino," April 12, 1938, DSP, sequence 88–92.
35. "Estatutos de La Sociedad Acción Social Femenina," n.d., DSP, sequence 93–97.
36. "Carta de Felicia Santizo a Minerva Bernardino."
37. Santizo received the 1939 prize in pedagogy at the Instituto Internacional de Ideales Americanos (International Institute of American Ideals), held at the Public Library of Matanzas, Cuba, and coordinated by the secretary of education of Havana. Marino, "Felicia Santizo," 117.
38. Marino, "Anti-fascist Feminismo," 214.
39. "Soy opuesto al voto femenino," *El Panamá América*, June 14, 1938.
40. "El Srio. Aníbal Ríos D. adversa el voto femenino," *El Nuevo Diario*, June 19, 1938.
41. "Carta de Felicia Santizo a Doris Stevens," July 4, 1938, DSP, sequence 79.
42. Martínez et al., *Una maestra ejemplar*, 57; "Los maestros elevan memorial al Ministro de Educación para pedir aumento de sueldo," *LEP*, October 15, 1942.
43. "Los maestros elevan."
44. Ana L. B. de Bellido, "Los maestros aspiran a una ley especial de jubilación," *LEP*, October 20, 1942.
45. "Aumentarán los sueldos de los maestros," *LEP*, October 21, 1942.
46. "Ley número 110 de febrero 24 de 1943," *Gaceta Oficial*, no. 9053 (1943): 1–2.

47. Martínez et al., *Una maestra ejemplar*, 19.

48. E. W. de Taylor, "El magisterio de la capital se unifica," *LEP*, October 29, 1944.

49. Elidia Wong de Taylor, "Encarando un problema nal.," *LEP*, December 2, 1944.

50. "El Magisterio Panameño Unido se refiere al asunto de la jubilación de los educadores," *LEP*, March 20, 1945; Tomás Gabriel Duque, "Justicia a los educadores," *LEP*, September 23, 1945.

51. Barrera, *Felicia Santizo*, 9.

52. The 1946 constitution would enshrine these rights into law (Staff Wilson, *Reseña histórica*, 6). See "Felicia S. de García de Colón promulgó su candidatura," *LEP*, April 19, 1945.

53. Marco Serra, *Mujeres parlamentarias*, 39; Lowe de Goodin, *Afrodescendientes*, 90.

54. Martínez et al., *Una maestra ejemplar*, 58–59; "Ley 36 de 14 de Septiembre de 1946," *Gaceta Oficial*, no. 10113 (1946): 8–14.

55. "Ley número 47 de 24 de Septiembre de 1946," *Gaceta Oficial*, no. 10113 (1946): 42–56; Martínez et al., *Una maestra ejemplar*, 63; "Decreto número 1891 de 2 de septiembre de 1947 dictado por el Ministerio de Educación," *Gaceta Oficial*, no. 10415 (1947): 2–3.

56. "Ley número 47."

57. MPU, *Concentración*, 67–68; "Decreto número 1950 de 21 de noviembre de 1947 dictado por el Ministerio de Educación," *Gaceta Oficial*, no. 10471 (1947): 3.

58. MPU, *Concentración*, 70.

59. MPU, *Concentración*, 39, 71; Martínez et al., *Una maestra ejemplar*, 39–40.

60. "Es excesiva la matrícula en la ciudad de Colón," *LEP*, May 13, 1945; J. M. Moreno H., "Las escuelas de Colón," *LEP*, October 12, 1945.

61. Barrera, *Felicia Santizo*, 15.

62. "El Colegio Abel Bravo celebró su quinto aniversario," *Colón Al Día*, July 5, 1947; "Discurso de la señorita Ethelyn Edwards, primer puesto de honor de la primera graduación del Colegio Abel Bravo," *LEP*, February 10, 1948.

63. "Decreto número 1892 de 2 de septiembre de 1947 dictado por el Ministerio de Educación," *Gaceta Oficial*, no. 10395 (1947): 3–4.

64. "Ley número 47."

65. Del Vasto Rodríguez, *Historia*, 24, 34.

66. "El Partido del Pueblo escoge sus candidatos a la alcaldía y concejo," *LEP*, February 20, 1948; "Gran concurrencia en la proclamación de la candidatura libre a diputado de Felicia Santizo de García," *LEP*, March 7, 1948; Del Vasto Rodríguez, *Historia*, 37–38.

67. "Gran concurrencia."

68. Pearcy, "Panama's Generation of '31"; "Decreto de Gabinete número 18 de 20 de marzo de 1945," *Gaceta Oficial*, no. 09665 (1945): 1–2.

69. "Gran concurrencia"; "American Troops Patrol Panama to Avert Anti-rent Strike Riots," *Baltimore Sun*, October 13, 1925.

70. Soler, *Panamá*, 34.

71. "La legalidad del movimiento"; "La conferencia interamericana condena la política del comunismo internacional," *LEP*, April 23, 1948; Narciso Navas, "Comunismo Sano," *LEP*, March 26, 1948.

72. "El Partido Del Pueblo, Panama," CREST, General CIA Records, October 17, 1950; "Plans for National Pro-peace Congress in Panama," June 20, 1950, CREST.

73. Alvarado, Marco, and Vásquez, *Mujeres que cambiaron*, 92.

74. Martínez et al., *Una maestra ejemplar*, 43–45.

75. Barrera, *Felicia Santizo*, 13.

References

Alexander Craft, Renée. *When the Devil Knocks: The Congo Tradition and Politics of Blackness in Twentieth-Century Panama*. Columbus: Ohio State University Press, 2016.

Alvarado, Ángela, Yolanda Marco, and Nadya Vásquez. *Mujeres que cambiaron nuestra historia*. Panama City: Universidad de Panamá, Instituto de la Mujer; Fondo de las Naciones Unidas por la Infancia, 1996.

Barrera, Eugenio. *Felicia Santizo: Una educadora al servicio de su pueblo*. Cuadernos Populares. Panama City: CELA "Justo Arosemena," 1980.

Beluche, Olmedo. *Historia agraria y luchas sociales en el campo panameño*. Panama City: Imprenta Articsa, 2017.

Brunson, Takkara. *Black Women, Citizenship, and the Making of Modern Cuba*. Gainesville: University Press of Florida, 2021.

Burnett, Carla. "'Unity Is Strength': Labor, Race, Garveyism, and the 1920 Panama Canal Strike." *The Global South* 6, no. 2 (2013): 39–64.

Corinealdi, Kaysha. "Being Fully Human: Linda Smart Chubb and the Praxis of Black Feminist Internationalism." *Signs* 47, no. 4 (2022): 931–55.

Corinealdi, Kaysha. *Panama in Black: Afro-Caribbean World Making in the Twentieth Century*. Durham, NC: Duke University Press, 2022.

Del Vasto Rodríguez, César Enrique. *Historia del Partido del Pueblo, 1943–1968*. Panama City: Editorial Universitaria Carlos Manuel Gasteazoro, 1999.

Flores-Villalobos, Joan. "Gender, Race, and Migrant Labor in the 'Domestic Frontier' of the Panama Canal Zone." *International Labor and Working-Class History*, no. 99 (2021): 96–121.

González, Lélia. "A mulher negra na sociedade brasileira." In *O lugar da mulher: Estudos sobre a condição feminina na sociedade actual*, edited by Madel T. Luz, 87–106. Rio de Janeiro: Edições Graal, 1982.

Lasso, Marixa. "Nationalism and Immigrant Labor in a Tropical Enclave: The West Indians of Colón City, 1850–1936." *Citizenship Studies* 17, no. 5 (2013): 551–65.

Lowe de Goodin, Melva. *Afrodescendientes en el istmo de Panamá, 1501–2012*. Panama City: Editora Sibauste, 2012.

Marco Serra, Yolanda. *Clara González Behringer: Biografía*. Panama City: n.p., 2007.

Marco Serra, Yolanda. *Mujeres parlamentarias en Panamá, 1945–1995*. Panama City: Universidad de Panamá, Instituto de la Mujer; Fondo de las Naciones Unidas por la Infancia, 1999.

Marino, Katherine M. "Anti-fascist Feminismo: Suffrage, Sovereignty, and Popular-Front Pan-American Feminism in Panama." In *Engendering Transnational Transgressions: From the Intimate to the Global*, edited by Eileen Boris, Sandra Trudgen Dawson, and Barbara Molony, 204–20. London: Routledge, 2020.

Marino, Katherine M. "Felicia Santizo Henríquez, innovadora de la educación." In *Pioneras de la ciencia en Panamá*, edited by Yolanda Marco Serra, 112–23. Panama City: Editora Novo Art, 2022.

Martínez, Emilia Ortega de, Miriam Sarmiento, Brunilda Sierra de Vergara, Auristela E. T. de Muñóz, and Blanca Irene Valdés. *Una maestra ejemplar: Rasgos biográficos de la educadora Sara Sotillo, 1900–1961*. Edited by Aracelly de León de Bernal and Griselda López. Panama City: Impresión Poligráfica, 2000.

Memoria que el Secretario de Estado en el Despacho de Educación y Agricultura presenta a la Asamblea Nacional en sus sesiones ordinarias de 1938. Panama City: Imprenta Nacional, 1938.

Memoria que el Secretario de Estado en el Despacho de Educación y Agricultura presenta a la Asamblea Nacional en sus sesiones ordinarias de 1938 (Anexos). Panama City: Imprenta Nacional, 1938.

Memoria que el Secretario de Estado en el Despacho de Instrucción Pública presenta a la Asamblea Nacional en sus sesiones ordinarias de 1932. Panama City: Imprenta Nacional, 1933.

Memoria que el Secretario de Estado en el Despacho de Instrucción Pública presenta a la Asamblea Nacional en sus sesiones ordinarias de 1934. Panama City: Imprenta Nacional, 1935.

Memoria que el Secretario de Estado en el Despacho de Instrucción Pública presenta a la Asamblea Nacional en sus sesiones ordinarias de 1936. Panama City: Imprenta Nacional, 1936.

MPU (Magisterio Panameño Unido). *Concentración de capítulos del Magisterio Panameño Unido reunida en Chitré, durante los días 26 y 27 de septiembre de 1947.* Panama City: Imprenta Nacional, 1948.

Muñoz, María Rosa de, and Armando Muñoz Pinzón. *La segunda huelga inquilinaria de 1932.* Panama City: Cultural Portobelo, 2006.

Pearcy, Thomas L. "Panama's Generation of '31: Patriots, Praetorians, and a Decade of Discord." *Hispanic American Historical Review* 76, no. 4 (1996): 691–719.

Pizzurno, Patricia. *Memorias e imaginarios de identidad y raza en Panamá siglos XIX y XX.* Panama City: Editorial Mariano Arosemena, 2011.

Recuerdo del Partido Nacional Feminista: A las delegadas al Congreso Inter-Americano de Mujeres. Panama City: Editorial la Moderna, 1926.

Santizo, Felicia. *Método natural de lectura-escritura por combinaciones: Para la enseñanza de la lengua castellana para niños y adultos.* Panama City: La Moderna, 1938.

Soler, Ricaurte. *Panamá: Nación y oligarquía, 1925–1975.* Panama City: Ediciones de la Revista Tareas, 1976.

Staff Wilson, Mariblanca. *Reseña histórica del sufragio femenino en Panamá.* Panama City: Comisión Interamericana de Mujeres, 1996.

Westerman, George. *Urban Housing in Panama and Some of Its Problems.* Panama City: Institute for Economic Development, 1955.

Williams Springer, Agatha. "La mujer negra y su inserción en la sociedad panameña." *Tareas*, no. 57 (1984): 83–91.

Zumoff, J. A. "The 1925 Tenant's Strike in Panama: West Indians, the Left, and the Labor Movement." *Americas* 74, no. 4 (2017): 513–46.

From "Armies of Love" to Demanding Legal Abortion

Piqueteras and Women Workers at the Forefront of Forging New Feminist Politics in Argentina (1990–2005)

Romina A. Green Rioja

This article is a history of how working-class women contributed through social and political action to Argentina's current feminist praxis. It examines how the 1990s neoliberal economic crisis altered the lives of Argentine working-class women, pushing them into the ranks of social movements and politicizing them in the process. As they participated in the union and *piquetero*[1] or unemployed workers' movements, many women realized that they, like their male *compañeros*, were willing to *poner el cuerpo*, or put their bodies on the line, in their confrontations with the factory bosses and the police but remained politically sidelined within their movements.[2] Many women did not have the political language to explain their experiences of gender oppression and marginalization in their homes and organizations. The patriarchal roadblocks to allowing women's full inclusion in social organizations led them to look elsewhere. The *argentinazo*, or nationwide revolts, following the nation's economic collapse in 2001 became the political catalyst not only for the growth and militancy of the social movements but a transformative moment for

Radical History Review
Issue 148 (January 2024)   DOI 10.1215/01636545-10846822
© 2024 by MARHO: The Radical Historians' Organization, Inc.

working-class women who found their way in noticeable numbers to the Encuentro Nacional de Mujeres (National Women's Meeting; ENM).

To highlight shifts and developments in feminist consciousness and praxis, this article uses Maxine Molyneux's methodological approach to analyze women's political formation. She studies how women begin to articulate their "feminist political practice" in moments of social change.[3] She employs a bottom-up approach to analyzing "women's consciousness" by centering women's experiences, actions, and discourse within social movements. To do so, she examines moments of politicization that motivate working-class women to defend or expand their practical gender interests in "response to an immediate perceived need," such as food, housing, and education for their children.[4] Through organizational participation, women identify shared practical interests that develop into a political language of social demands. The shared experience of political action and a common gendered language of demands are transformed "into strategic interests that women can identify with and support which constitutes a central aspect of feminist political practice."[5] Molyneux therefore challenges the idea of singular feminist politics. She instead studies each social movement through its goals and deeds, examining transclass, racial, and ethnic alliances within a specific women's movement. As she affirms, "Such unity has to be constructed, it is never given."[6]

In using Molyneux's approach, this essay historicizes those three stages. The first section centers on the 1990s neoliberal economic crisis that radically changed working-class women's lives. The dismantling of the welfare state and the privatization of nationalized industries left many working-class men without work and, as a result, pushed working-class women to find employment. However, working-class women's entry into the workforce was a catalyst for disrupting family structures, making some women breadwinners and instilling confidence as they learned to control their finances.[7] Nevertheless, underlying the economic crisis was a gendered crisis in which more women sought abortions. Due to its illegality and unsafe conditions, many women died from botched procedures. These experiences functioned as the backdrop of the gendered social crisis when the Argentine economy collapsed in December 2001. Building on that social reality, the next section analyzes the pivotal participation of unemployed women in the 2002 and 2003 meetings of the ENM. Encuentro workshop discussions on abortion rights, lesbianism, and sexuality led piqueteras to question their delegated roles as cooks and caretakers of the movement and motivated them to create *espacios de mujeres* (women's spaces) within their organizations. The third section examines the same period but focuses on the political role of union factory workers at the ENM. They incorporated union politics and social demands in Encuentro discussions and declarations, making those issues feminist concerns. Between 2002 and 2005 a new feminist movement politics and political practice shaped into an abortion rights campaign that brought together seventy organizations, and abortion rights became the movement's earliest strategic gender issue.[8]

To center activist voices, I used feminist activists' posts on *Indymedia Argentina* from 2001 to 2005. *Indymedia* started as an alternative news site to give activists a platform to report on events related to the World Trade Organization protest in 1999 in Seattle, Washington. Its popularity led to its widespread use across the world. *Indymedia* was widely used by social movements, especially after the 2001 crash. Activists posted pictures, videos, and audio recordings of protests, announced upcoming meetings and marches, reported on events, and debated topics in the comments section and forums. *Página 12*, another source, was the only mainstream newspaper that covered the women's movement. Marta Dillon wrote most of the paper's articles, interviewing piqueteras while sitting on a bridge or a picket line. In short, this article seeks to demonstrate that the feminist movement in Argentina took many long, difficult years to build. As the movement took shape, many women died from economic and gender violence and through their direct participation in street protests as they confronted the state's violence. This is their story.

The 1990s: A Gendered Economic Crisis

Argentina in the 1990s was a country in crisis while experiencing an economic boom. The social cost of Argentina's prosperity, like that of other neoliberal "poster child" nations promoted in the 1990s by the International Monetary Fund (IMF), led to the demise of its once-envied Latin American middle class as unemployment numbers soared and growing numbers of children died from malnutrition. If the economic crisis made class positions tenuous and living a daily struggle for survival, it also accentuated the gendered inequalities present in capitalist patriarchal society.[9] In examining that historical moment, this section has two goals: to show how the economic crisis of the 1990s pushed working-class women to enter the labor force, and to demonstrate how the crisis drove more individuals to seek abortions. These two key developments informed shifts in working-class women's political consciousness in the 1990s and were the basis for changes in feminist political practice discussed in the following two sections.

Unlike neighboring Chile, whose military dictatorship (1973–90) dismantled its social democratic state, Argentina went through this process following the return to democracy under the Peronist presidency of Carlos Saúl Menem (1989–99).[10] In Chile open-market reforms led to the collapse of multiple national industries, but it was a crisis managed by a dictatorial regime.[11] Argentina's IMF-led restructuring plan attempted to offset the economic "shock" experienced in Chile. The government instituted the Washington Consensus's ten points, which decreased corporate payroll taxes, weakened labor regulations, allowed capital's free flow to draw investors, and pegged the Argentine peso to the US dollar to secure a "competitive exchange rate."[12] Mass unemployment caused by the privatization of Argentina's once robust nationalized industries (oil, railroads, electricity) led to business closures and an unmanaged decrease in state revenues that affected public sector workers. With the collapse of its homegrown industry, imports increased by 300 percent between 1991 and 1998, and the country solved the resulting trade imbalance with international loans.[13] Argentina's IMF loans reached $142 billion in 2001. Due to the country's inability to make its high-interest payments, the IMF demanded further austerity measures in November 2001 before securing the next loan installment of $1.3 billion.[14] This uncertainty proved too great for many investors and accelerated capital flight, causing a bank freeze to retain the remaining capital. Panic set in as thousands took to the streets, targeting banks and ultimately forcing President Fernando de la Rúa (1999–2001) to resign.

Working-class and poor women experienced a gendered economic crisis throughout the 1990s. The feminist economist Marcela Cerrutti explains that as male unemployment and labor instability increased throughout the decade, more women sought employment to offset their family's financial hardships. The result was an almost 20 percent increase in female labor force participation, primarily among women from marginalized, working-class, and middle-income families, from "38% in 1991 to 46% in 1995."[15] The employment opportunities that these women typically acquired were in the informal economy and usually temporary, low pay, or under the table. In other words, as corporations downsized their labor force, they restructured to create a more "flexible workforce" to increase profits at the cost of lower wages and poorer working conditions. Menem's new labor laws facilitated these shifts.

Cerrutti argues that a gendered analysis of Argentina's employment statistics shows patterns that diverge from the Western hypothesis that 1960s women's radicalization was due to access to higher education, resulting in demands for equal employment.[16] Even though there was a close gender employment parity in Argentina's professional sector, it did not spark feminist activism, since most radicalized youth joined guerrilla movements. Moreover, because Argentina's welfare state economy, which expanded under the presidency of Juan Perón (1946–55), prioritized male employment as heads of household, most working-class women were dissuaded from entering the formal economy. Instead, the rise in female labor force participation took place in low-paying and factory work between 1993 and 1995, at the height of the unemployment crisis.[17] Employment statistics from 2001 underscore that on a national scale, women accounted for 41 percent of professional employment and 49 percent in the technical field but only 28 percent as operatives in factories.[18] On average, most women who entered the workforce in the 1990s held low levels of education and had high turnover rates because of familial obligations and temporary positions. This led to women experiencing higher mobility rates and looking for new employment more frequently than men.[19]

As working-class women entered the workforce, unemployment numbers rose, reaching 60 percent in 2002 accompanied by a significant increase in child hunger.[20] By 2001 at least 25 percent of children under the age of five suffered from malnutrition, and three children died per day nationally.[21] Notably, most children that died from malnutrition were in the northern provinces. Considering that statistics underrepresented the extent of the crisis, about eight children died per week in Tucumán and fifty in 2002 in Misiones.[22] Therefore it is unsurprising that as the economic crisis deepened in Argentina, more individuals sought to terminate their pregnancies.

Between 1995 and 2000 abortion rates increased by 46 percent in Argentina.[23] A 1921 law mandated four years' imprisonment for abortion patients and providers, with legal exceptions for therapeutic abortion and cases of rape. However, the government primarily targeted abortion providers, 80 percent of those arrested from 2002 to 2008.[24] Government abortion data from that time accounted only for women who sought medical attention or died from complications from abortion. The Argentine government estimated half a million pregnancy interruptions in a population of about forty million. In 2000 a woman died every thirteen days in Greater Buenos Aires due to an abortion. However, 72 percent of the women who died due to complications from abortion lived in the northern provinces, the areas hardest hit by the recession. That data correlates with other figures that show that abortion rates increased by 148 percent in San Luis Province, 143 percent in La Rioja Province, and 103 percent in Santiago del Estero Province.[25]

Class and race determined access to abortifacient options. For example, the 2002 Reproductive Health Law made misoprostol (a drug that causes contractions) available, leading to a decrease in maternal deaths.[26] Yet lack of anecdotal knowledge about misoprostol meant that poor women continued to be hospitalized for abortion complications. On the topic of race (see next paragraph for explanation), a 2004 study by the National Gynecological Congress estimated that half of women in Tucumán who interrupted their pregnancies died from home or self-induced abortions. The study calculated regional maternity death figures per 10,000: Greater Buenos Aires, 0.9; Córdoba, 1.3; the Chaco region, 15; and the northeastern region, 20.[27] A few years later the Tucumán provincial legislature voted for nonadherence to the national 2002 Reproductive Health Law and the 2006 Comprehensive Sexual Education Law, approving the latter only in 2022.[28]

Tucumán Province has been historically marked by the sugar industry's boom-and-bust cycle and regional migration by Indigenous and mixed-race workers in the late nineteenth and early twentieth centuries.[29] The national racial imaginary characterizes the province as Indigenous and mestizo within a nation that, as Sandra McGee Deutsch notes, has cloaked "more inhabitants within the mantle of whiteness" while rejecting others.[30] The Argentine film director Fernando Solanas, in *Memoria del Saqueo*, describes the rise of child mortality throughout the 1990s, spotlighting Tucumán as a demonstration of the government's complicity in attempts to "disappear" the *other* Argentina.[31]

While maternal deaths from abortion decreased over the years, pregnancy interruptions rose from 300,000 in 1973 to 385,931 in 1991 and 500,000 in 2005.[32] A 2007 study by the Economic Commission for Latin America and the Caribbean estimated that on a national scale, roughly 55,000 women sought medical treatment in hospitals due to complications from an abortion in 2005.[33] The study deduced that 60.8 to 65.4 of every 1,000 women interrupted their pregnancies, which placed the annual figures between 485,974 to 522,216 on a national scale.[34] Comparing those numbers with recent government figures from 2015 to 2019, during which 368,000 individuals sought abortions of 1,310,000 pregnancies in a population of 44 million, shows a decrease in the abortion rate.[35] These figures highlight two trends. First, the 2019 abortion rates resulted from improved sexual education and resources, producing fewer unintended pregnancies. Second, the high abortion rates between 1990 and 2005 coincided with an economic crisis in which women and pregnant people had to choose between having an illegal abortion that could lead to their death or giving birth to a future starving child.

Espacios de Mujeres: Finding Gender in Class Politics

The women's space or *espacio de mujeres* is a social and political area of analysis with a robust historiography that examines the female private sphere in contrast to the male public sphere.[36] Yet only in the last few decades has social reproduction—as a theory and strategy of political action—expanded as an area of feminist scholarship. This section examines how the women's space transformed from an area of social reproduction to a politicized space within the unemployed movement. It places the economic crisis as a disrupter of female responsibilities as familial food providers, incentivizing working-class women to join the Movimiento de Trabajadores Desocupados (Unemployed Workers' Movement; MTD) and similar organizations. In response to sexism and gender violence in the home and their organizations, MTD women created *espacios de mujeres* to discuss gender-related issues and create sorority. As a result, those spaces became a bridge between the social movements and the burgeoning feminist movement, politically transforming both spaces in the process.

Writing in 1990–91, the Argentine political scientist Elizabeth Jelin framed housework as a form of labor power that embodied the women's space, recognizing social reproduction as a direct contributor to formal production.[37] Jelin described housework and the responsibilities associated with the family unit's reproduction as a measurable social and economic activity. For Jelin, the patriarchal omission of female labor power rationalizes the private/public dichotomy: "As organizers of family consumption, women necessarily enter into contact with institutions in the distribution sector and with the state as the provider of services. There is, in effect, an obvious public dimension to women's role as a housewife because they constantly relate to those offering goods and services and to other consumers."[38] As distributors and organizers of essential services, women collected basic goods, which had become scarce during the 1990s. While the scholarship on social reproduction has evolved since Jelin's text on the topic, she framed the economic activity of working-class and middle-class women as organizers and movers of necessary goods for their families' survival.

In response to the state's 1991 economic restructuring, working-class women demanded state financial support. In 1992 the Buenos Aires provincial government began distributing food baskets (*canastas básicas de alimentación*) consisting of basic subsistence food items for unemployed families. The government mobilized thirty-five thousand women to disperse government aid. According to Laura Mason, one of the plan directors, "Women were chosen because it was unquestionable [to think otherwise and] we knew women would be more honest and would better emanate the resources."[39] Mason's gendered language reiterates a first-wave feminist *politics of difference* that fought for inclusion while maintaining the specified gender roles under patriarchy. Andrea D'Atri and Celeste Escati believe that the government perceived unemployed women as "less combative" and their participation as a form of "vocational solidarity."[40] The government allowed certain levels of militancy, such as fighting for their families' welfare, describing them as "neighborhood armies" or "armies of love."[41] The program reaffirmed women's work as vocational by not paying women for their labor. Nevertheless, working-class women gained experience distributing goods for a state-led program that became network training and the basis for new social organizations.

The piquetero movement emerged from a June 1996 mass rebellion in the southern oil town of Cutral Có in Neuquén following the layoffs of 38,500 employees between 1991 and 1992.[42] The oil industry, Yacimiento Petroliferos Fiscales (YPF), once represented the clientelistic policies implemented during Perón's first presidency that, over the years, had maintained a certain standard of living for its workers. However, that changed after the privatization of the YPF in 1993. While most piqueteros were men, women participated and became central figures, such as Laura Padilla, who signed an agreement with the governor on behalf of protesters.[43] Padilla was not an oil worker but represented the experiences of working-class women politicized by their material and social realities. As the sociologist Javier Auyero notes, "Revolts can also change the life of people, or at least the way in which they understand themselves."[44]

The Cutral Có pickets became neoliberal resistance heroes, motivating workers across the country to mimic their protest methods.[45] Piqueteros typically wear T-shirts to cover their face and burn tires to block the road. Auyero describes these "new forms" of protest as complementary to rather than displacing strikes. The loss of state industries and the deproletarianization of thousands of workers created "new actors (unemployed) and new demands (work) . . . [and] the identities constructed while protesting acquired a specific political character."[46] Auyero underscores that the new movements demanded *trabajo digno* (dignified work or employment) from the state as a solution to the social crisis. The demand became a unifying call, but it did not include unemployed or underemployed working-class women.

As the unemployed movement grew in the 1990s, it also helped shape the new public and political discourse for the working class. These organizations incorporated social issues like housing and food distribution as part of their demands, but these issues were understood as secondary to *trabajo digno*. Employment became the principal contended issue central to the Argentine male's working-class identity as the family provider and head of household. Early on, the piquetero movement replicated the gendered public and private spheres in their organizational work. The social scientist Florencia Partenio describes how limiting women's political participation in the piquetero movement to the perceived female sphere either in the kitchen or in distribution to meet basic needs "impeded their involvement with the realms of representation and the political leadership of the movement."[47] Piquetero male leaders viewed women's roles much like the government officials who described their labor as food distributors as "armies of love." Partenio underscores that even though the piquetero movement had developed a plan of broader social demands, which motivated women's entry into the movement, the central demand remained employment perceived as a male right. The sidelining of women is notable, considering that between 65 and 70 percent of movement members were women.[48] Following the 2001 crash, however, the refusal to acknowledge women's demands and leadership within the piquetero movement proved untenable.

The 2001 *argentinazo* was a moment of social and political rupture that altered the feminist and piquetero movements. These two movements crossed in the streets and coalesced in the ENM's meeting rooms. Argentine feminists founded the yearly ENM in 1986 following the 1975–85 United Nations' Decade on Women and the biannual Encuentros Feministas Latinoamericanas y del Caribe (Latin American and Caribbean Feminist Encuentro) inaugurated in 1981. The ENM gathering fluctuated between six hundred and eight thousand participants during the first decade. A noticeable increase occurred at the 2002 ENM, held in the northern province of Salta, where seventeen thousand women arrived and sizable contingents from the union and piquetero movements participated.[49] The journalist Andrea D'Atri noted, "A different Argentina, a different Encuentro."[50] This development continued in 2003, when fifteen thousand women gathered at the ENM in Rosario.[51]

Piqueteras' participation at the 2002 and 2003 Encuentros ignited gender consciousness, because they envisioned themselves as political actors. A few months after the 2003 ENM, piqueteras organized the First Assembly of Piqueteras on Pueyrredón Bridge in Buenos Aires.[52] The assembly flyer asked: "Do you speak in assembly meetings? Did you decide on your maternity?"[53] Significantly, Pueyrredón Bridge was where the piqueteros Darío Santillán and Maximiliano Kosteki were murdered by police on June 26, 2002; thereafter, for several years, the bridge became a congregation site for piqueteros mobilizing on the twenty-sixth of every month to demand justice and jobs. The piqueteras who attended the assembly had previously met during political actions on that bridge. However, the assembly was the first time that, as Zulema Aguirre recollected, "we recognized ourselves as political subjects."[54] When piqueteras presented their conclusions to the general membership of their respective organizations, the men responded like "stones thrown into an empty tank."[55] Piqueteras were ridiculed by sexist jokes or given the cold shoulder at meetings. Some members described male partners assaulting them in response to their political demands.

As piqueteras prepared for the second assembly in July 2004, male piqueteros described their organizing meetings as a "reunión de tupper" (Tupperware party). Marta Dillon interviewed numerous piqueteras during the second assembly who expressed victory when a piquetera read a declaration on behalf of several social organizations the previous month commemorating the killing of Darío and Maximiliano. Alejandra Giusti, a twenty-five-year-old piquetera, explained: "The moment the act began it became very noticeable when the press was asked to step down from the stage, we [women] resisted or else it would have happened again; a swelling of male presence because they are the accredited ones. We have put our body [on the line], but we must put [forward] our voice."[56] Alejandra had proudly proclaimed herself a journalist representing the piqueteras. In another interview, sixty-two-year-old Elsa Basterra told Dillon that she left her previous organization tied to political interests and joined the MTD. Basterra attended the Rosario Encuentro, explaining: "We went from our neighborhoods because they invited us and we collected the money for the trip. [At the ENM] we became aware that we had not discussed anything beforehand. It could be due to the autonomous nature of our organizations, but [we] also did not view it as a priority. . . . Men would tell us, 'We have to establish our priorities.'"[57] In this reflection, Basterra describes the Rosario Encuentro as a transformative moment in which piqueteras discussed women's issues. It made her question why her organization had never discussed those topics and why men dictated their organization's political work. In an *Indymedia Argentina* interview, Adriana from MTD–Aníbal Verón in Lanús described the development of *espacios de mujeres* to discuss reproductive and bodily autonomy, abortion rights, sexual freedom, and domestic violence. Adriana explained how working-class women experience *double exclusion* due to their double work shifts as social movement militants with expected household and familial responsibilities. She further described the need to distribute labor within the organization better. The *Indymedia* correspondent Zula Lucero asked if she thought women joined piquetero organizations for their children and family. Adriana responded that was probably the case initially; however, she added, "I think they now see it for themselves."[58]

Dillon discerns that following the experience at the Rosario ENM, female MTD members decided to construct their own space. The sisters Zulema and Alejandra Giusti, both members of MTD–Aníbal Verón in Lugano, explained that when they returned from Rosario, they proposed that their assembly participate in the

September 28 demonstration, the Day for the Legalization of Abortion in Latin America and the Caribbean. Alejandra explained: "There were five minutes of silence when we stated that we wanted to march as members of MTD–Aníbal Verón on September 28 for our reproductive health, as discussed in Rosario. It caused confusion and they told us to do whatever we wanted as though what we proposed had little importance."[59] Zulema noted, "Then [the men] asked us if we planned on expanding the kitchen." Further describing the political shift within the piquetero movement, twenty-one-year-old Mónica and MTD–Almirante Brown member explained: "We found it challenging to discuss the things we discussed at the Rosario Encuentro, especially on abortion. In the Rosario workshops, it was beautiful to see women motivated to discuss how they went through such an experience that no one desires [to experience] previously unmentionable because we felt shame or guilt."[60] These quotes capture a political moment in which piqueteras began to articulate their demands, breaking the private/public spheres that functioned to the benefit of patriarchy. Their participation in the ENM gave them a political language to describe and frame issues that affected them and their community, specifically abortion access. The Encuentros motivated the women to form their own women's space to discuss, plan, develop, and grow within the unemployed workers' movement. The confidence they gained through those activities helped them shatter the guilt and shame they once felt about discussing abortion and sexuality openly.

Abortion Rights at Rosario and Beyond

By 2004 over ten thousand workers were involved in the factory recovery movement across Argentina.[61] Like all social movements after 2001, they represented working-class attempts to solve social problems, specifically unemployment and poverty. The word *recovery* was intentional, indicating their action to take over (*tomar*) the factory, an act of recuperating the nation dismantled by neoliberalism. The seamstresses at the Brukman factory in Buenos Aires joined the recovery movement but stood out for two reasons. First, they represented a majority-female and older workforce, between the ages of forty and sixty, whom the capitalist bosses and their managers viewed as disposable. Second, Brukman workers, alongside the Zanón ceramic factory workers in Neuquén, took their battle for recuperation farther by demanding expropriation under workers' control. The gendered and political role of the Brukman struggle elevated these workers as central figures in the ENM and the women's movement.

The Brukman struggle stemmed from the 2001 economic crisis. During the year employees' paychecks became irregular. On December 17 workers did not receive their scheduled paycheck, forcing a couple of workers to sleep over at the factory because they could not afford the public transportation fare home.[62] When workers arrived the next morning and realized what had happened, a group confronted management over their owed wages. In an interview I coconducted in 2002, Nilda Bustamente, a Brukman seamstress originally from Jujuy Province in the north, described how a company manager mocked their grievances: "What do you expect us to do? Withdraw our money from abroad to pay you?"[63] Celia Martí-nez, the union president, explained that the owner, Jacobo Brukman, responded to that confrontation by handing over the factory keys in frustration, "If you think you can run this factory better than we can, then here are the keys."[64] According to Martínez, Brukman had underestimated their organizational capacity. Soon after factory management left the facilities, a group of workers decided to examine the production logs, estimating that the company had maintained a sizable profit margin and had deposited the money in overseas banks. They realized that the owner had used the crisis to slash wages and accumulate wealth.

The day after the takeover, massive protests erupted across Buenos Aires. Martínez explained that they were initially fearful but realized that they needed to act and maintain a permanent presence at the factory. They organized a twenty-four-hour watch to dissuade the owner from sending people to steal the machinery. The workers reorganized their factory and union in more egalitarian terms and connected with workers at other recuperated factories. A solidarity network quickly formed between factory workers, the piquetero movement, and other organizations and individuals supporting social movement causes. That network proved pivotal in resisting a police eviction on March 16, 2002.

A week later, on March 24, Brukman workers participated in a mass rally commemorating the 1976 coup victims. D'Atri and Escati documented the Brukman workers' chants, and in one instance, they yelled, "They killed us in '76 / thousands of comrades / Brukman remembers them / Fighting for workers' control."[65] Their chant placed factory takeovers within the legacy of workers murdered and disappeared by the authoritarian regime. One can also interpret Brukman workers as retaking the historical memory of the nation, which had been scarred by the military state's violence and, once more, by the economic violence of neoliberalism.

During the rally, Brukman workers crossed a feminist column telling them to join their struggle. The feminists responded with a Brukman chant: "Brukman belongs to the female workers / And to those who dislike it / They can go fuck themselves, fuck themselves!"[66] Feminists' reciprocation was a vocal and corporal act of class solidarity and sorority in the streets. The chant describes Brukman's fight as female-led and belonging to the female workers. Brukman workers' presence at the 2002 and 2003 Encuentros showed other working-class women that they now belonged and could lead. Brukman workers also defied feminine convention by exclaiming to those who oppose them—male union leaders, the factory owners, and the state—that "they can go fuck themselves!" Chants are political expressions enacted in the streets that can relay a political program, social issue, or political debate or capture a historical moment. In this case, the chants exchanged between feminists and Brukman workers at a rally commemorating the dictatorship victims encapsulated the nascent moment when feminists and working-class women, including the piqueteras, met at a political crossroads produced by the economic crisis and the social movements that were the working classes' response to that crisis.

Months later Brukman workers attended the 2002 ENM in Salta, the Encuentro that D'Atri described as "a different Argentina, a different Encuentro."[67] In marking their presence at the Encuentro, Brukman and the Pepsico workers' union representatives read a joint declaration to conference participants. The first part focused on rebuilding the union movement by challenging the union bureaucracy. They underscored support for the recuperated factory movement and "our unemployed sisters" who deserve the right to *trabajo digno*. In this declaration, they introduced union battles into the Encuentro arena and positioned themselves as leaders for union democracy. However, more significant for this article was their assertion that working-class women also deserved *trabajo digno*. They spotlighted that battle because it spoke to 2002 Encuentro participants, leveraging their demand for *trabajo digno* for all working-class women as a worthy Encuentro battle flag.

Toward the declaration's end, they explained their panorama of struggle:

Women do not only endure unemployment, misery, [and] exploitation on the job. We have a double work shift because we also do all the housework. We are the ones who are paid less than men, even though we do the same work. We are the ones who experience sexual harassment, rape, abuse, and violence. We are the impoverished within the poor and the ones who . . . have less access to education. We are the ones who die from clandestine abortions or pregnancy and giving birth since we cannot count on basic health care; the most affected by malnutrition and AIDS.[68]

They described grievances that resonated with conference participants, centering the economic crisis as a gendered experience. While the early Encuentros debated double militancy, the declaration highlighted the double work shift and unequal pay as societal problems.[69] They highlighted topics such as gendered violence and abortion as practical gender issues around which to organize. Feminist groups, social organizations, and leftist parties signed the declaration. The 2002 ENM remanded an alliance by working-class women and feminists that was severed when Eva Perón appropriated the women's suffrage struggle to benefit the Peronist party.[70]

If the 2002 ENM marked the moment when working-class women made their political stamp within the Encuentro, the 2003 ENM marked a shift from recognition toward organized resistance. As in the previous year, women workers wore their work uniforms and organizational vests to show their class and political affiliations. The 2003 Encuentro was also emblematic because it was when Catholics for Choice distributed the green kerchief as a symbol for abortion rights.[71] The ENM organized workshops that ran throughout the three-day conference to generate specific action plans. For the first time, a workshop titled "For Free and Legal Abortion" presented abortion as a demand and not as advice or an act of murder.[72] Another workshop, "Strategies for the Right to Abortion," formulated the demand "Sex education to decide, contraceptives to not abort, and legal abortion to not die."[73] Openness to discussing abortion as a right resulted from the experiences of the 1990s.

After the 2003 Encuentro, one can observe its impact on working-class women's political consciousness. In previous years, leftists and feminist organizations mainly observed dates commemorating women's issues: March 8 (International Women's Day), September 28 (Day to Decriminalize Abortion in Latin America and the Caribbean), and November 25 (Day against Gender Violence). Between the 2003 and 2004 Encuentros, social movements transformed these commemorative dates into political action days. September 28 was the first commemorative day after the 2003 Encuentro, when eight thousand people rallied in Buenos Aires, showing the new influx of working-class women into the women's movement.[74] Notably present were members of the MTDs, Partido Obrero (Worker's Party), Movimiento Independiente de Jubilados y Desocupados (Independent Movement of Retirees and Unemployed), and other mass organizations. A rally description in *Página 12* wrote, "At par with decriminalization, they demanded immediate national implementation of the Reproductive Health Law, and at the [presidential house known as the] Casa Rosada a delegation demanded condoms and birth control 'in everyone's pockets.'"[75] The bold demands show that the new women's movement regarded birth control and condoms as social issues and not private matters.

Indymedia posts allow one to visualize rally participants' movements. Activists' posts included rally descriptions accompanied by photographs or audio clips. Zula Lucero reported on the March 8, 2004, activities in Buenos Aires, detailing how activists marched from Plaza de Mayo (in front of the Casa Rosada) to the national court, city legislature, the main Catholic cathedral, and back to the Casa Rosada.[76] Lucero's posts represent the route of the march, which started with a few hundred and ended with a few thousand, mainly from the piquetero movement. In her post on the city legislature protest, Lucero included a picture of two women holding signs that read "Indigenous Women Present."[77] While many piqueteros were and are Indigenous Guaraní and Aymara, they entered the movement as unemployed workers and made Indigenous demands subservient to the movement's broader goals. That Indigenous women presented themselves as Indigenous political actors within the feminist movement underscores the openings made by the movement. As Molyneux notes, even when women participate in movements with broader demands, their lived experiences inform the universal struggle surrounding women's formation as political subjects.[78] Automatic subservience to the universal cause is not a given. The piquetero movement made *trabajo digno* the universal cause, but the ENM had unfurled other demands that, with time, would also become universal for the feminist and labor movements.

Lucero posted an extract from the document read during the rally signed by "MTDs Aníbal Verón and MUP [Movimiento de Unidad Popular]."[79] The extract highlighted another political shift within the new women's movement. While the Brukman-Pepsico declaration captured working-class women's union politics, the MTD-MUP declaration framed social change as the starting point:

> We fight for social change that we are building step by step within our [social] movements and in our neighborhoods. This social change will not be complete if it does not include our rights as piquetera women. We, piquetera women, demand our rights to decide over our bodies in a free and responsible manner. [For the] right to enjoy a free, fulfilling, gratifying sexuality; [For the] rights to receive free quality public care during pregnancy, childbirth, puerperium and menopause in health centers and public hospitals; [For the] right to a life free of violence in both the public and private spheres; [For the] right to be valued and educated in equality with men, we repudiate concepts of inferiority or subordination for the fact of being women; [For the] right to build our autonomy to participate in decisions that affect our personal and social life; The right to pleasure, without discrimination or prejudice; For work, dignity, and social change. Without women, human rights are not human.[80]

While it is challenging to measure the pace of political consciousness, the March 8, 2004, declaration demonstrates piqueteras' political evolution from their first ENM to their assemblies on Pueyrredón Bridge in late 2003 in which they asked, "Do you speak at assembly meetings?" By March 2004 piqueteras were no longer asking but demanding and imagining the social rights and sexual life they desired.

Significantly, twenty thousand women participated in the Mendoza ENM in October 2004.[81] The workshop "Strategies for the Right to Abortion" best captured the Encuentro's momentum. In May 2005 workshop participants met with seventy organizations, including the Central de Trabajadores de la Argentina (Argentine Workers' Central Union), to launch the National Campaign for the Right to Legal, Safe, and Free Abortion.[82] The green kerchief became the movement's unifying symbol, adding to the design the Mothers of the Plaza de Mayo kerchief emblem surrounded by the fighting words, "Sex education to decide, contraceptives to not abort, and legal abortion to not die."[83] The petition campaign ended on November 25, 2005, when thousands of abortion rights supporters in Buenos Aires marched to Congress to deliver the hundred thousand signatures collected.[84] Carrying a banner that stated "Not One More Woman Dead from Clandestine Abortion," the rally embodied the broadening of the movement. There was greater visibility of queer groups and college students, including a student-led *tetazo*.[85] Congress ignored the petition, but the abortion rights movement had just started and demonstrated a willingness to organize offensive actions against the state that would only continue to blossom.

Conclusion

This article describes the transformative years of the social and feminist movements in Argentina from 1990 to 2005. Since 2005 the feminist movement has transformed into a mass movement with regular street protests and clashes with the police. In 2015 the founding of the #NiUnaMenos (#NotOneWomanLess) movement against femicide expanded the movement's reach farther to include those reluctant to support abortion rights, placing greater pressure on the state to enact change. In 2019, in an inclusive move, the ENM changed its name to the Encuento Plurinational de Mujeres, Lesbianas, Trans, Travestis, Bisexuales y No Binaries (Plurinational Meeting of Women, Lesbians, Trans, Bisexual, Intersexual, and Nonbinary). That same year the government created the Ministry of Women, Genders, and Diversity to lead campaigns to confront gender violence, institutionalize more protections for transgender people, and implement the 2006 Integral Sexual Education Law. Finally, after several failed attempts, in December 2021 the Argentine Congress legalized abortion as a sea of green bandanas celebrated in the streets.[86]

The momentum for more feminism has not dissipated, for the struggle against femicide, among other issues, remains at the forefront. As the piquetera Mariana Gerardi Davico reflected on her political transformations since 2003: "Feminism is those purple glasses in which the day you put them on, you cannot see reality any other way. We had to fight for our place, leave behind the everyday, the domestic, to understand that more than the organizational, our role was political and, furthermore, our words had political meaning."[87] As new generations in Argentina put on those purple glasses, new feminist futures continue to be forged. But, most important, if those purple glasses are available to all to speak, think, act, and build feminism, the voices of those most marginalized by the capitalist patriarchal state will continue to be elevated in the movement. Their feminist future can also be ours but, as this article shows, that feminist practice "has to be constructed, it is never given."[88]

Romina A. Green Rioja is an assistant professor of Latin American history at Washington and Lee University. Her book project, provisionally titled *To Govern Is to Educate: Modeling Racial Education in Modern Chile (1879–1920)*, examines the emblematic relationship between state education and immigration policies in former native Mapuche territories that defined Chilean race politics in the twentieth century. In addition to her work on nineteenth-century Chile, she researches contemporary feminism and social movements in Latin America.

Notes

1. *Piquetes* (pickets) refers to picketing as a form of demonstration; the participants are *piqueteros* (male) and *piqueteras* (female). They also use the gender-neutral *piqueterx*. All translations in this article are mine.
2. Sutton, "Poner el Cuerpo," 154.
3. Molyneux, *Women's Movements*, 45.

4.   Molyneux, *Women's Movements*, 44.

5.   Molyneux, *Women's Movements*, 45.

6.   Molyneux, *Women's Movements*, 45.

7.   Tinsman, "Reviving Feminist Materialism."

8.   Argentina's first-wave feminist movement fractured under Juan Perón's presidency (1946–55), rendering women's politics auxiliary to the Partido Justicialista. Once the dictatorship fell in 1983, feminist groups rebuilt with the support of the ENM.

9.   I use Zillah Eisenstein's definition of capitalist patriarchy "to emphasize the mutually reinforcing dialectical relationship between capitalist class structure and hierarchical sexual structuring" (*Capitalist Patriarchy*, 7).

10. Argentina's dictatorship ruled from 1976 to 1983.

11. Winn, *Victims of the Chilean Miracle*.

12. The Washington Consensus was a ten-point neoliberal economic policy by the British economist John Williamson based on discussions with politicians and economists in Washington, DC, in the late 1980s (Féliz, "Note on Argentina," 83; Williamson, "Short History").

13. Féliz, "Note on Argentina," 89.

14. Carranza, "Poster Child," 70.

15. Cerrutti, "Economic Reform," 879.

16. Cerrutti, "Economic Reform," 888.

17. Cerrutti, "Economic Reform," 883.

18. Cerrutti, "Economic Reform," 886–87.

19. Cerrutti, "Economic Reform," 887.

20. ECLAC, *Social Panorama*, 160.

21. Verner, "Rural Poor," 20.

22. Verner, "Rural Poor"; Astudillo, "Child Starvation."

23. Dipierri, "Aborto"; Gogna et al., "Abortion," 128.

24. Finden, "The Law."

25. Dipierri, "Aborto."

26. Steele and Chiarotti, "With Everything Exposed," 40.

27. *La Gaceta*, "Los abortos."

28. Petracci and Ramos, *La política pública*, 63–65; ANRed, "Tucumán"; *El Tucumano*, "Tras 16 años."

29. Juarez-Dappe, *When Sugar Ruled*.

30. McGee Deutsch, "Insecure Whiteness," 27; Chamosa, "Indigenous or Criollo"; Edwards, *Hiding in Plain Sight*.

31. See *Memoria del Saqueo* (dir. Fernando Solanas, Argentina, 2004). The disappeared also include those who were murdered during the dictatorship and whose bodies were never found.

32. Mario and Pantelides, "Estimación," 96.

33. Mario and Pantelides, "Estimación," 103; Ministerio de Salud, "Mortalidad materna en Argentina."

34. Mario and Pantelides, "Estimación," 111.

35. Guttmacher Institute, "Country Profile."

36. Lavrin, *Women, Feminism*; Craske, *Women and Politics*; Twinam, *Private Lives*; Dore and Molyneux, *Hidden Histories*.

37. Benson, "Political Economy"; Dalla Costa and James, *Power of Women*; Vogel, *Marxism*; Bhattacharya, *Social Reproduction Theory*.

38. Jelin, *Family*, 187.
39. D'Atri and Escati, "Movimiento piquetero," 7.
40. D'Atri and Escati, "Movimiento piquetero," 7.
41. D'Atri and Escati, "Movimiento piquetero," 7; Masson, "Una red feminista," 104.
42. Auyero, *Contentious Lives*, 43.
43. Auyero, *Contentious Lives*, 16–17.
44. Auyero, *Contentious Lives*, 191.
45. Auyero, "Los cambios," 193.
46. Auyero, "Los cambios," 196.
47. Partenio, "Género y participación política," 5.
48. Dillon, "Rebelión en el piquete"; Trionga, "Argentine Social Movements."
49. Alma and Lorenzo, *Mujeres que se encuentran*, 72.
50. D'Atri, "XVII Encuentro Nacional de Mujeres."
51. Alma and Lorenzo, *Mujeres que se encuentran*, 144.
52. Dillon, "Rebelión en el piquete"; D'Atri, "XVII Encuentro Nacional de Mujeres"; Parodi and Canteros, "Que en todos lados"; ANRed, "La primera asamblea de mujeres."
53. ANRed, "La primera asamblea de mujeres."
54. ANRed, "La primera asamblea de mujeres."
55. Dillon, "Rebelión en el piquete."
56. Dillon, "Rebelión en el piquete."
57. Dillon, "Rebelión en el piquete."
58. Lucero, "Mas voces en el Dia de la Mujer."
59. Dillon, "Rebelión en el piquete."
60. Dillon, "Rebelión en el piquete."
61. See *The Take* (dir. Avi Lewis, Canada, Argentina, 2004).
62. Celia Martínez and Liliana Torale (Brukman workers), interview by author, April 23, 2002; Koppel and Green, "Workers in Buenos Aires."
63. Koppel and Green, "Workers in Buenos Aires."
64. Koppel and Green, "Workers in Buenos Aires."
65. D'Atri and Escati, "Movimiento piquetero," 9.
66. D'Atri and Escati, "Movimiento piquetero," 9.
67. D'Atri, "XVII Encuentro Nacional de Mujeres."
68. CEPRODH, "Declaración de las obreras."
69. Craske, *Women and Politics*; Jaquette, *Women's Movement*; Maffía, *Mujeres pariendo historia*.
70. Carlson, *Feminismo!*; James, *Doña María's Story*; Perón, "Women's Suffrage."
71. Carbajal, "El pañuelo verde."
72. Indyná, "XVIII Encuentro Nacional de Mujeres"; Alma and Lorenzo, *Mujeres que se encuentran*, 115, 124.
73. Hernández, "Olga Cristiano."
74. Dandan, "Para tener el derecho a decidir."
75. Dandan, "Para tener el derecho a decidir."
76. Lucero, "Dia de la Mujer/Anibal Veron"; Lucero, "Dia de la Mujer en las Tribunales"; Lucero, "Dia de la Mujer/Escrache"; Lucero, "Mujeres en la Legislatura"; Lucero, "Mujeres en Plaza de Mayo."
77. Lucero, "Mujeres en la Legislatura."
78. Molyneux, *Women's Movements*, 39.

79. Lucero, "Extracto del documento."
80. Lucero, "Extracto del documento."
81. Dillon, "Mujeres en llamas."
82. Rosenberg and Gutiérrez, "Evita no usa pañuelo"; Hernández, "Olga Cristiano."
83. Dillon, "Mujeres en llamas."
84. Lipcovich, "Multitudinaria marcha"; Campaña por el Derecho al Aborto Legal, "BsAs"; CMI, "Marcha por el derecho."
85. *Tetazos* are confrontational protests in which people exhibit their breasts to challenge prudish social mores.
86. Marcus-Delgado, *Politics of Abortion*.
87. ANRed, "La primera asamblea de mujeres."
88. Molyneux, *Women's Movements*, 45; Sutton and Vacarezza, *Abortion and Democracy*.

References

Alma, Amanda, and Paula Lorenzo. *Mujeres que se encuentran: Una recuperación histórica de los Encuentros Nacionales de Mujeres en Argentina (1986–2005)*. Buenos Aires: Feminaria Editora, 2009.

ANRed. "La primera asamblea de mujeres en el Puente Pueyrredón, en la voz de sus protagonistas." June 25, 2020. https://www.anred.org/2020/06/25/somos-mujeres-piqueteras-las-brujas-que-no-pudiste-quemar/.

ANRed. "Tucumán: Sin leyes que reconozcan los derechos de salud sexual y reproductiva." May 28, 2009. https://www.anred.org/2009/05/28/tucuman-sin-leyes-que-reconozcan-los-derechos-de-salud-sexual-y-reproductiva/.

Astudillo, Perla. "Child Starvation Stalks Argentina's Northern Provinces." World Socialist Web Site, February 25, 2003. https://www.wsws.org/en/articles/2003/02/arge-f22.html.

Auyero, Javier. *Contentious Lives: Two Argentine Women, Two Protests, and the Quest for Recognition*. Durham, NC: Duke University Press, 2003.

Auyero, Javier. "Los cambios en el repertorio de la protesta social en la Argentina." *Desarrollo Económico*, no. 166 (2002): 187–210.

Benson, Margaret. "The Political Economy of Women's Liberation." *Monthly Review* 21, no. 4 (1969): 13–27.

Bhattacharya, Tithi. *Social Reproduction Theory: Remapping Class, Recentering Oppression*. London: Pluto, 2017.

Campaña por el Derecho al Aborto Legal. "BsAs: Marcha por el derecho al aborto legal." *Indymedia Argentina*, November 24, 2005. https://archivo.argentina.indymedia.org/print.php?id=352055.

Carbajal, Mariana. "El pañuelo verde, el símbolo." *Página 12*, June 14, 2018. https://www.pagina12.com.ar/121322-el-panuelo-verde-el-simbolo.

Carlson, Marifran. *Feminismo! The Women's Movement in Argentina*. Chicago: Academy Chicago, 1988.

Carranza, Mario. "Poster Child or Victim of Imperialist Globalization? Explaining Argentina's December 2001 Political Crisis and Economic Collapse." *Latin American Perspective* 32, no. 6 (2005): 65–89.

CEPRODH (Centro de Profesionales por los Derechos Humanos). "Declaración de las obreras de Brukman y las trabajadoras despedidas de Pepsico." XVII Encuentro Nacional de Mujeres en Salta, Argentina, August 21, 2002. https://www.ceprodh.org.ar/Declaracion-de-las-trabajadoras-de-Brukman-y-las-obreras-despedidas-de-Pepsico.

Cerrutti, Manuela. "Economic Reform, Structural Adjustment, and Female Labor Force Participation in Buenos Aires, Argentina." *World Development* 28, no. 5 (2000): 879–91.

Chamosa, Oscar. "Indigenous or Criollo: The Myth of White Argentina in Tucumán's Calchaquí Valley." *Hispanic American Historical Review* 8, no. 1 (2008): 71–106.

CMI. "Marcha por el derecho al aborto." *Indymedia Argentina*, November 26, 2005. http:// argentina.indymedia.org/news/2005/11/352732.php?theme=2.

Craske, Nikki. *Women and Politics in Latin America*. Cambridge: Polity, 1999.

Dalla Costa, Mariarosa, and Selma James. *The Power of Women and the Subversion of the Community*. 3rd ed. Bristol: Falling Wall, 1975.

Dandan, Alejandra. "Para tener el derecho a decidir." *Página 12*, September 27, 2003. https:// www.pagina12.com.ar/diario/elpais/1-26039-2003-09-27.html.

D'Atri, Andrea. "XVII Encuentro Nacional de Mujeres." *La verdad obrera*, no. 107 (2002). http://www.pts.org.ar/spip.php?article2925.

D'Atri, Andrea, and Celeste Escati. "Movimiento piquetero/a en Argentina." In *Cambiando el mundo: Movimiento piquetero/a en Argentina*. Buenos Aires: Asociación para los Derechos de la Mujer y el Desarrollo, 2008.

Dillon, Marta. "Mujeres en llamas." *Página 12*, October 15, 2004. https://www.pagina12.com.ar /diario/suplementos/las12/13-1527-2004-10-15.html.

Dillon, Marta. "Rebelión en el piquete." *Página 12*, July 2, 2004. https://www.pagina12.com.ar /diario/suplementos/las12/13-1297-2004-07-02.html.

Dipierri, Pablo. "Aborto: Mujeres en peligro." *Defiendense.com*, August 14, 2014. https://web .archive.org/web/20140814115630/http://www.defiendase.com/muestranota.asp ?id=805&ant=.

Dore, Elizabeth, and Maxine Molyneux, eds. *Hidden Histories of Gender and the State in Latin America*. Durham, NC: Duke University Press, 2000.

ECLAC (Economic Commission for Latin America and the Caribbean). *Social Panorama of Latin America, 2002–2003*. United Nations ECLAC, May 2004. https://www.cepal.org/en /publications/1218-social-panorama-latin-america-2002-2003.

Edwards, Erika. *Hiding in Plain Sight: Black Women, the Law, and the Making of White Argentina*. Tuscaloosa: University of Alabama Press, 2020.

Eisenstein, Zillah. *Capitalist Patriarchy and the Case for Socialist Feminism*. New York: Monthly Review Press, 1979.

El Tucumano. "Tras 16 años, la Legislatura de Tucumán aprobó la adhesión a la Ley de Educación Sexual Integral." August 30, 2022.

Féliz, Mariano. "A Note on Argentina, Its Crisis, and the Theory of Exchange Rate Determination." *Review of Radical Political Economics*, no. 80 (2007): 80–99.

Finden, Alice. "The Law, Trials, and Imprisonment for Abortion in Argentina." International Campaign for Women's Right to Safe Abortion, November 8, 2016. https://www.safe abortionwomensright.org/news/the-law-trials-and-imprisonment-for-abortion-in-argentina/.

Gogna, Mónica, Mariana Romero, Silvina Ramos, Mónica Petracci, and Dalia Szulik. "Abortion in a Restrictive Legal Context: The Views of Obstetrician-Gynaecologists in Buenos Aires, Argentina." *Reproductive Health Matters*, no. 19 (2002): 128–37.

Guttmacher Institute. "Country Profile: Argentina. Unintended Pregnancy and Abortion." https://www.guttmacher.org/regions/latin-america-caribbean/argentina.

Hernández, Mario. "Olga Cristiano, la lucha por el aborto legal desde sus inicios." *Marcha*, April 12, 2018. https://marcha.org.ar/olga-cristiano-la-lucha-por-el-aborto-legal-desde-sus-inicios/.

Indyná. "XVIII Encuentro Nacional de Mujeres: Agenda." *Indymedia Argentina*, August 10, 2003. https://archivo.argentina.indymedia.org/print.php?id=125257.

James, Daniel. *Doña María's Story: Life History, Memory, and Political Identity*. Durham, NC: Duke University Press, 2003.

Jaquette, Jane. *The Women's Movement in Latin America: Participation and Democracy*. London: Unwin Hyman, 1989.

Jelin, Elizabeth, ed. *Family, Household, and Gender Relations in Latin America*. London: Kegan Paul International in association with UNESCO, 1991.

Juarez-Dappe, Patricia. *When Sugar Ruled: Economy and Society in Northwestern Argentina, Tucumán, 1876–1916*. Athens: Ohio University Press, 2010.

Koppel, Martin, and Romina Green. "Workers in Buenos Aires Occupy Garment Factory in Fights for Jobs." *Militant*, August 26, 2002. https://www.themilitant.com/2002/6632/663203.html.

La Gaceta. "Los abortos caseros son causantes del 46% de las muertes maternas." September 16, 2004. https://www.lagaceta.com.ar/nota/89013/informacion-general/abortos-caseros-son-causantes-46-porciento-muertes-maternas.html.

Lavrin, Asunción. *Women, Feminism, and Social Change in Argentina, Chile, and Uruguay, 1890–1940*. Lincoln: University of Nebraska Press, 1995.

Lipcovich, Pedro. "Multitudinaria marcha en reclamo de la despenalización del aborto." *Página 12*, November 12, 2005. https://www.pagina12.com.ar/diario/sociedad/3-59683-2005-11-26.html.

Lucero, Zula. "Dia de la Mujer/Anibal Veron en la Plaza de Mayo y el MUP." *Indymedia Argentina*, March 9, 2004. https://archivo.argentina.indymedia.org/news/2004/03/180867.php.

Lucero, Zula. "Dia de la Mujer en las Tribunales." https://archivo.argentina.indymedia.org/news/2004/03/180872.php.

Lucero, Zula. "Dia de la Mujer/Escrache a la catedral." https://archivo.argentina.indymedia.org/news/2004/03/180906.php.

Lucero, Zula. "Extracto del documento." https://archivo.argentina.indymedia.org/news/2004/03/180867_comment.php#180879.

Lucero, Zula. "Mas voces en el Dia de la Mujer: Adriana del MTD de Lanús." *Indymedia Argentina*, March 11, 2004. https://archivo.argentina.indymedia.org/news/2004/03/181841.php.

Lucero, Zula. "Mujeres en la Legislatura." https://archivo.argentina.indymedia.org/news/2004/03/180969.php.

Lucero, Zula. "Mujeres en Plaza de Mayo." https://archivo.argentina.indymedia.org/news/2004/03/180978.php.

Maffía, Diana. *Mujeres pariendo historia: Cómo se gestó el Primero Encuentro Nacional de Mujeres*. Buenos Aires: Dirección General de Impresiones y Ediciones, 2013.

Marcus-Delgado, Jane. *The Politics of Abortion in Latin America: Public Debates, Private Lives*. Boulder, CO: Rienner, 2020.

Mario, Silvia, and Edith Alejandra Pantelides. "Estimación de la magnitud del aborto inducido en la Argentina." Presented at the Unión Internacional para el Estudio Científico de la Población, Paris, November 7–9, 2007.

Masson, Laura. *La política en femenino, Género y poder en la provincia de Buenos Aires*. Buenos Aires: Antropología Social, 2004.

McGee Deutsch, Sandra. "Insecure Whiteness: Jews between Civilization and Barbarism, 1880s–1940s." In *Rethinking Race in Modern Argentina*, edited by Paulina Alberto and Eduard Elena, 25–52. Cambridge: Cambridge University Press, 2016.

Ministerio de Salud. "Mortalidad materna en Argentina." Dirección Nacional de Maternidad e Infancia, Estudio 2008.

Molyneux, Maxine. *Women's Movements in International Perspective: Latin America and Beyond*. New York: Palgrave Macmillan, 2001.

Parodi, Camila, and Laura Salomé Canteros. "Que en todos lados se vea el poder de las piqueteras." *Marcha*, June 25, 2015. https://marcha.org.ar/queen-todos-lados-se-vea-el -poder-de-las-piqueteras/.

Partenio, Florencia. "Género y participación política: Los desafíos de la organización de las mujeres dentro de los movimientos piqueteros en Argentina." Presented at Las Deudas Abiertas en América Latina y el Caribe. Programa Regional de Becas CLACSO, 2008.

Perón, Eva. "Women's Suffrage Speech." September 23, 1947. https://college.cengage.com /history/world/keen/latin_america/8e/assets/students/sources/pdfs/73_eva_peron_suffrage_ speech.pdf.

Petracci, Mónica, and Silvina Ramos. *La política pública de salud y derechos sexuales y reproductivas en la Argentina: Aportes para comprender su historia*. Buenos Aires: CEDES, 2006.

Rosenberg, Martha I., and María Alicia Gutiérrez. "Evita no usa pañuelo." *Anfibia*, February 19, 2018. https://www.revistaanfibia.com/evita-no-usa-panuelo/.

Steele, Cynthia, and Susana Chiarotti. "With Everything Exposed: Cruelty in Post-abortion Care in Rosario, Argentina." *Reproductive Health Matters*, no. 24 (2004): 39–46.

Sutton, Barbara. "Poner el Cuerpo: Women's Embodiment and Political Resistance in Argentina." *Latin American Politics and Society* 49, no. 3 (2007): 129–62.

Sutton, Barbara, and Nayla Luz Vacarezza, eds. *Abortion and Democracy: Contentious Body Politics in Argentina, Chile, and Uruguay*. London: Routledge, 2021.

Tinsman, Heidi. "Reviving Feminist Materialism: Gender and Neoliberalism in Pinochet's Chile." *Signs* 26, no. 1 (2000): 145–88.

Trionga, Marie. "Argentine Social Movements: Taking Matters into Their Own Hands." *Americas Program*, November 7, 2002. https://www.americas.org/1679/.

Twinam, Ann. *Private Lives, Public Secrets: Gender, Honor, Sexuality, and Illegitimacy in Colonial Spanish America*. Stanford, CA: Stanford University Press, 1999.

Verner, Dorte. "Rural Poor in Rich Rural Areas: Poverty in Rural Argentina." World Bank Policy Research Working Paper 4096, December 2006. https://elibrary.worldbank.org/doi/abs/10 .1596/1813-9450-4096.

Vogel, Lise. *Marxism and the Oppression of Women: Toward a Unitary Theory*. New Brunswick, NJ: Rutgers University Press, 1983.

Williamson, John. "A Short History of the Washington Consensus." Fundación Centro de Investigaciones de Relaciones Internacionales y Desarrollo. Paper commissioned for the conference "From the Washington Consensus towards a New Global Governance." Barcelona, September 24–25, 2004.

Winn, Peter, ed. *Victims of the Chilean Miracle: Workers and Neoliberalism in the Pinochet Era, 1973–2002*. Durham, NC: Duke University Press, 2004.

"To Repulse the State from Our Uteri"

Anarcha-feminism, Reproductive Freedom, and Dual Power

Spencer Beswick

Anarcha-feminists declared that "our choice is revolution" as they fought for reproductive freedom and women's liberation in the 1990s. The US Supreme Court's ruling in *Roe v. Wade*, which protected abortion under the guise of privacy, had been under attack from the Christian Right and the US government since it was passed in 1973. By the 1990s the mainstream feminist movement had been on the defensive for years. Unlike the combative women's liberation movement of the 1960s and 1970s, much of the feminist movement consigned itself to fight on the terrain of the state: legal battles, electoralism, and individual "freedom of choice." As the state and the Christian Right increased their attacks on abortion, it became increasingly clear to many activists that this strategy was insufficient.

Anarcha-feminists went on the offensive in the fight for reproductive freedom in the 1990s. Women in the Love and Rage Revolutionary Anarchist Federation (1989–98), the leading US anarchist organization of the period, advanced sharp critiques of the liberal abortion strategy that had ceded so much ground to the Right. Anarchists offered radical alternatives for women to take back control of their lives and bodies. Rather than petition the state for reforms, they mobilized to defend abortion clinics from the Far Right and taught themselves how to perform reproductive care at the grassroots level. They maintained that abortion restrictions were a form of state violence, especially as they corresponded with the structural

Radical History Review

Issue 148 (January 2024) DOI 10.1215/01636545-10846837

© 2024 by MARHO: The Radical Historians' Organization, Inc.

violence of white supremacy, patriarchy, and capitalism. Anarchists argued that feminists must oppose the state itself as the ultimate patriarchal institution and the source of much of the violence they faced. Thus, rather than the slogan "We're prochoice and we vote," anarchists often marched behind a banner reading "We're prochoice and we riot!"

This article analyzes how anarcha-feminists critiqued the state and attempted to build feminist dual power—through institutions that challenge the dominance of the state and provide the foundation for a new world—in response to the New Right's attacks on reproductive freedom. The first part gives historical context by laying out a brief account of abortion struggles in the 1960s–1970s women's liberation movement. This section analyzes both how *Roe v. Wade* was won and the implications of protecting *Roe* through a liberal state-centric strategy as abortion came under sustained attack. The second part analyzes the critique of state power developed by anarcha-feminists in the 1970s. Building on the classic anarchist analysis of the state, they argued that it was an inherently patriarchal institution that could only ever be the enemy of women. The third part turns to anarcha-feminist abortion struggles in the 1990s. It uses primary source materials from Love and Rage's newspaper, internal discussion documents, and oral history interviews to explore how the organization's intersectional critique of the state influenced its political practice.[1] Anarcha-feminists argued that women must organize themselves from below "to repulse the state from our uteri" by defending abortion infrastructure, forming self-help groups in which they learned to perform reproductive care, and building dual power institutions. In their conception of dual power—influenced more by the 1994 Zapatista uprising in Mexico than by the 1917 Russian Revolution—it was strategically necessary to build autonomous institutions such as alternative health clinics and workers councils that challenged the hegemony of the state and capitalism and concretely prefigured a new world. Ultimately, Love and Rage argued, the only way to guarantee reproductive freedom and women's liberation is the revolutionary construction of a libertarian socialist society.

The Women's Liberation Movement and the Historical Struggle for Abortion

A growing body of scholarly literature recognizes the central role of the radical feminist movement in the struggle for abortion rights in the 1960s and 1970s. Feminist historians have challenged the popular narrative seen in accounts like David J. Garrow's *Liberty and Sexuality* that focus primarily on legal battles and internal Supreme Court deliberations.[2] The feminist scholar Mary Ziegler argues in *After Roe* that although "conventionally, historians and legal scholars suggest that the interference of the courts transformed the abortion wars," they have greatly inflated the importance of the Supreme Court's legal decision. Instead, Ziegler situates *Roe* and the broader abortion debate within major social developments of the postwar period, including the key role played by feminists who challenged abortion restrictions and "created new constituencies in favor of reproductive rights."[3] The feminist historian Leslie J. Reagan argues in *When Abortion Was a Crime* that although doctors and lawyers initiated early efforts to reform abortion laws, "ultimately, women's pressing need for abortion fueled a mass movement that succeeded in reversing public policy toward abortion in the late 1960s and early 1970s."[4] In her classic history of the radical feminist movement *Daring to Be Bad*, Alice Echols details the growth and power of the movement as feminists fought for the repeal of all abortion laws as a foundational component of women's liberation.[5] Militant mass struggle by a new generation of radical feminists transformed society and produced an opening for legal strategies to succeed.

Reproductive rights were won by grassroots feminist movements working in conjunction with electoral and legal strategies. Doctors, lawyers, and even many clergy spent decades fighting legal battles to lift restrictions on abortion and birth control. As they do today, they often limited their focus to cases based on health concerns or rape rather than arguing for the fundamental right to bodily autonomy and reproductive freedom. These tactics laid the legal foundation for *Roe v. Wade*, with the Supreme Court's 1965 decision in *Griswold v. Connecticut*, which legalized birth control for married couples on the basis of the right to privacy, playing an especially important role. Yet the reliance on the framework of privacy limited the scope of reforms by obscuring the actual fight for reproductive freedom and bodily autonomy. It was only with the birth of a militant feminist movement that fought to repeal all laws restricting abortion that there was substantive progress regarding abortion access at the level of the state.

Radical feminists in the late 1960s and 1970s employed new strategies for building power and effecting change. Feminists in the women's liberation movement, many of whom were veterans of the antiwar movement and New Left organizations like Students for a Democratic Society, began forming autonomous women's groups in the late 1960s. They organized consciousness-raising groups across the country in which women discussed their shared experiences.[6] This provided the foundation for women to speak out publicly about their abortions and to fight openly for the repeal of all abortion restrictions. Feminists began disrupting male-dominated medical spaces and challenging men's supposed expertise. The Redstockings led the way when they spoke out at a 1969 New York State joint legislative committee hearing and proclaimed that "the only real experts on abortion are women!"[7] In addition to speak-outs and demonstrations, feminists also built grassroots women's infrastructure including underground abortion networks. Women across the country took reproductive care into their own hands, including through the new at-home abortion technique of menstrual extraction developed in 1971. Feminists were inspired to put into practice what they learned from the Boston Women's Health Book Collective's landmark text *Our Bodies, Ourselves*.[8] The Chicago Jane Collective, for instance, performed over ten thousand illegal abortions between 1969 and 1973. Feminists demanded the repeal of all abortion laws and advocated for women themselves—not the state or the male-dominated medical system—to control their bodies. The feminist scholar-activist Jenny Brown argues that it was these "massive feminist mobilizations" that "brought hundreds of thousands into the streets," alongside consciousness-raising and underground abortion provision, that "in just four years forced a reluctant Supreme Court to legalize most abortions across the country."[9] Militant mobilization and widespread public disobedience, in combination with ongoing legal cases, pressured the court into granting limited abortion rights via the 1973 *Roe v. Wade* ruling.

Immediately after *Roe*, however, the antifeminist New Right commenced what became a decades-long attempt to overturn the ruling and restrict abortion provision. The 1976 Hyde Amendment prevented federal funds from being used for abortion, thus limiting access for poor people.[10] The antiabortion movement continued to grow within the broader backlash against feminism, buoyed by the official stance of President Reagan and the New Right condemning abortion.[11] Yet the radical wing of the movement was unsatisfied that Reagan did not push hard enough to end abortion at the federal level. They resolved to go on the attack, and extremists began bombing clinics and murdering doctors who provided abortions. In 1986 Randall Terry founded Operation Rescue, which tacitly endorsed violence while presenting itself as a more respectable "mainstream" organization that regularly picketed and blockaded clinics in an effort to prevent abortion. Many mainstream feminists, discouraged by the defeat of the Equal Rights Amendment in 1982 and the broader attack on the women's movement, ceded ground to the Right by embracing a limited framework of "prochoice" activism instead of openly fighting for abortion and women's liberation.[12] Bodily autonomy and reproductive freedom were increasingly replaced by more abstract notions of individual rights for the state to protect, even as those rights were further whittled away through legal rulings like *Planned Parenthood v. Casey* (1992) that allowed states to impose restrictions on the procedure as long as they did not constitute an "undue burden." Yet many feminists rejected the mainstream movement's retreat into liberal prochoice advocacy.

Anarcha-feminism and the Patriarchal State

In the 1970s a growing current within the women's liberation movement began to embrace a conscious anarchist orientation. These activists rejected the liberal turn of the mainstream wing of the movement as well as the state socialism of Marxist feminists. Small groups of women "rediscovered" Emma Goldman and began to theorize a synthesis of feminist and anarchist politics. The feminist historian Julia Tanenbaum explains that "most anarcha-feminists were initially radicalized by the political and cultural milieu of the antiwar movement, but it was their experiences in the women's liberation movement combined with the influence of Emma Goldman that led them to develop anarcha-feminism as a strategy."[13] Although self-identified anarchists formed only a relatively small portion of the women's liberation movement, their political impact stretched far beyond their small groups and publications.

The feminist movement generally practiced what Helen Ellenbogen called an "intuitive anarchism": they organized in decentralized groups, rejected hierarchy, and embraced horizontal notions of sisterhood.[14]

Anarcha-feminists built on the classic anarchist principle that the state is an institution of hierarchy and domination. Anarchists agree with Marxists that the state is a tool of class rule; thus, in a capitalist society, the state generally represents the interests of capital. Unlike Marxists, however, anarchists do not believe that it is possible to seize the state and wield it in the interests of liberation. The state does not simply represent a certain class's interests but stands above all of society to rule over it from its own privileged position. Thus the state in any form, whether under supposedly bourgeois or proletarian dictatorship, necessarily promotes inequality and injustice. As the Russian anarchist Mikhail Bakunin put it in 1873, "Since every state power, every government, by its nature and by its position stands outside the people and above them, and must invariably try to subject them to rules and objectives which are alien to them, we declare ourselves the enemies of every government and every state power, the enemies of state organization of any kind."[15] This applies equally to the possibility of a socialist state. Indeed, the Italian anarchist Errico Malatesta cautions even more strongly against an ostensibly revolutionary state, arguing that it "would end up as usual, in an *oligarchy*," for "what an all-powerful, oppressive, all-absorbing oligarchy must one be . . . that has at its disposal, all social wealth, all public services, from food to the manufacture of matches, from the universities to the music-halls!"[16] Anarchists thus distrust any strategy for liberation that passes through the state.

Anarchists maintain that the only path toward a socialist society is nonhierarchical, voluntary federation from below. Peter Kropotkin, the foremost nineteenth-century theorist of anarchist communism, supports social movements that build federated structures from below, for "modern progress is really towards the free aggregation of free individuals so as to supplant government in all those functions which formerly were entrusted to it, and which it mostly performed so badly."[17] Bakunin concurs, explaining that anarchists "believe that the people can be happy and free only when they create their own life, organizing themselves from below upward by means of independent and completely free associations."[18] Today most anarchists contend that the experience of the twentieth century, from the Soviet gulag to the disappointments of social democracy, has proved the classical anarchist analysis of the state correct.[19] Yet whatever their prescience in some areas, these nineteenth-century anarchist theorists generally failed to consider the role of patriarchy—as a hierarchical social system rather than interpersonal prejudice—in relation to their understanding of state power.

A crucial innovation of anarcha-feminists within the 1960s–1970s women's liberation movement was their analysis of the patriarchal nature of state power. As Arlene Wilson of the Chicago Anarcho-Feminists put it in a manifesto published in the *Siren* newsletter in 1971, "The intelligence of womankind has at last been brought to bear on such oppressive male inventions as the church and the legal family; it must now be brought to reevaluate the ultimate stronghold of male domination, the State," which she describes as "rule by gangs of armed males." Indeed, the manifesto declares that

we believe that a Woman's Revolutionary Movement must not mimic, but destroy, all vestiges of the male-dominated power structure, the State itself— with its whole ancient and dismal apparatus of jails, armies, and armed robbery (taxation); with all its murder; with all of its grotesque and repressive legislation and military attempts, internal and external, to interfere with people's private lives and freely-chosen cooperative ventures.[20]

The state was inherently patriarchal because it replicated the paternal rule of the father over society. As Love and Rage later put it in its 1997 "Draft Political Statement," patriarchy "operates as a foundation of state power, used to justify a paternalistic relationship between the rulers and the ruled." The state reproduces at a higher scale the father's rule over the family, which is "disguised as protection and support" but is "often enforced through violence and sexual terrorism."[21] Thus the state could only be the enemy of all women. Simply electing women to the top of the government could never change the basic patriarchal structure of its hierarchical power. Anarcha-feminists brought their antistate socialist analysis to various social movements from the late 1970s through the 1980s. They played an important role in the growing direct-action movement that began with antinuclear activism—most famously in the Clamshell Alliance, which helped introduce the concept of decentralized, consensus-based affinity groups.[22] A new generation of radicals in the 1990s took up the torch of anarcha-feminism, expanded its analysis, and applied it to contemporary struggles for reproductive freedom.

"Our Choice Is Revolution": Dual Power and Reproductive Freedom in the 1990s

Although its role has often been overlooked, the Love and Rage Revolutionary Anarchist Federation made significant contributions to the grassroots feminist movement in the 1990s.[23] The federation was the foremost American anarchist organization of the late twentieth century.[24] Founded in 1989 after a series of continental anarchist convergences that revitalized the North American anarchist movement, Love and Rage had major chapters in New York City, Minneapolis, and Mexico City as well as smaller groups across the United States and Canada.[25] Although it never claimed more than a couple hundred members—and usually had a core of only a few dozen active cadres—Love and Rage exercised an outsized influence within social movements because of its relatively strong organization, its widely distributed newspaper (typically with a bimonthly print run of close to ten thousand copies), and its commitment to making strategic interventions in key social struggles.[26] Beginning in 1994, Love and Rage had three main working groups: antifascism, antiprison struggle, and Zapatista solidarity. It attempted, with some success, to infuse each struggle with feminist and antiracist principles. Much of its feminist activism took place in the antifascist working group because of its analysis of how the antiabortion movement had become a key component of contemporary fascism.[27] Love and Rage's revolutionary strategy rested on building dual power institutions that would challenge the dominance of the state and lay the foundation for a libertarian socialist world.

Chris Day, a cofounder and leading theorist of Love and Rage, reimagined dual power through a Zapatista-tinted grassroots anarchism. Dual power is typically associated with a period of the 1917 Russian Revolution in which workers' soviets established parallel power structures that provided the basis to seize the state and establish a dictatorship of the proletariat. Day argues that building anarchist dual power means establishing nonhierarchical institutions and organizations that combat and eventually supplant the state without ever "seizing" it.[28] This approach draws on the Industrial Workers of the World's attempt to "build the new world in the shell of the old"; this nascent world would contest the political and cultural dominance of the state without attempting to conquer it. This radical infrastructure serves two purposes. First, to begin to meet needs outside of the state and capitalism to lessen people's dependence on the system and free up their time and energy for revolutionary activity. Second, to build genuine democratic institutions at the grassroots level that directly challenge the hegemony of bourgeois institutions. Women's self-help groups and other grassroots feminist infrastructure were meant to do exactly that: to challenge the power of the patriarchal state and medical establishment and help lay the foundation for a revolutionary movement.

Beginning in 1994, Love and Rage looked to the Zapatistas for models of how to build revolutionary feminist dual power. After a difficult first year of open struggle, the Zapatistas announced the creation of thirty-two "autonomous municipalities"—self-determined, self-governing, autonomous communities. Day describes them as "democratically chosen, independent governments based on popular assemblies that would exist parallel to the 'official' municipal governments of Chiapas." This is a classic case of dual power in which parallel institutions compete for real power and authority. Day goes on to say that "the autonomous municipal governments were to take on all the functions of governance, including many that had been largely neglected by the 'official' PRI-dominated municipalities: public health, settling land disputes, education and so on."[29] Since then this system has been greatly expanded and formalized. Crucially for women in Love and Rage, the Zapatistas challenged patriarchal power structures as they built revolutionary dual power. Subcomandante Marcos recounts that one Zapatista woman declared: "We aren't going to ask the government to give us freedom, nor are we going to ask you male fools. We are going to ensure our freedom, our respect, and our dignity as women and as human beings."[30] Marcos also famously described the struggle for the 1993 Women's Revolutionary Law (which recognized women's rights to self-determination, dignity, and equality) as "the EZLN's first uprising . . . led by Zapatista women. There were no casualties, and they won."[31] For feminists in Love and Rage, this was how to win women's liberation: through grassroots struggles and as part of a broader revolutionary movement, not through elections, legal battles, and liberal reforms.

Feminists in Love and Rage refused to appeal to the state to protect abortion. As anarchists, they rejected the state's patriarchal power and argued that it could only be an enemy of reproductive justice and women's liberation. Thus Love and Rage argued in its draft political statement that "our freedom will not come through the passage of yet more laws but through the building of communities strong enough to defend themselves against antichoice and antiqueer terror, rape, battery, child abuse and police harassment."[32] They did not ignore struggles to maintain legal abortion—and warned of the negative impact of its potential criminalization—but argued that women must develop their own capacity for bodily autonomy and self-determination. Anarcha-feminists argued that establishing autonomous reproductive health care infrastructure was key to building feminist dual power.

Love and Rage members looked to the experience of the women's liberation movement for lessons in feminist struggle. As one anonymous older member of Love and Rage who had been involved in these struggles wrote in a letter to the newspaper, women discovered that their personal issues, including reproduction, were deeply political. She ends her letter on a hopeful note of intergenerational connection and solidarity, observing that "over the years, the Women's Liberation Movement has not died but has changed forms many times, based on the current status of women."[33] Anarcha-feminists in Love and Rage attempted this very transformation by expanding on the earlier generation's understanding of the patriarchal state as necessarily shaped by white supremacy and capitalism.

The US state attempted to control women and their bodies—particularly poor women and women of color—through a series of attacks on their ability to access safe and affordable reproductive care. In an article in Love and Rage's newspaper reflecting on the twenty-fifth anniversary of *Roe v. Wade*, the anarcha-feminist Laura W. emphasizes that activists cannot blame only the Christian Right for denying reproductive freedom. Rather, "the US state has controlled women's reproductive lives through policies of sterilization abuse and population control, within and across US borders. In government policies institutionalized racism and sexism are most apparent. The feds will not pay for Medicaid abortions, but they will pay for sterilization."[34] Given this context, it is not surprising that the legal right to abortion that was ostensibly guaranteed by *Roe v. Wade* was de facto severely curtailed. Liberal rights often meant little in practice, particularly for poor women and women of color. Indeed, Laura W. argues that despite the legal rights laid out in *Roe v. Wade*, "the ability to control our reproductive lives is not a reality for most women" due to a range of issues including cutbacks on welfare and social services, lack of health care, and the harassment and violence that women face inside and outside their homes. These obstacles take away women's ability to control their reproduction, which

Laura W. deems the "critical aspect of women's freedom."[35] Recent work by feminist scholars including Laura Briggs and Sara Matthiesen has further underscored how the New Right's dismantling of social support for raising children and caring for families in the 1980s limited true "choice" in reproductive labor.[36]

Love and Rage was almost all white, yet this argument drew on the experience of the reproductive justice movement led by women of color. Reproductive justice groups like SisterSong criticized the "prochoice" movement for ignoring the particular struggles of women of color. The issue, they maintained, was not solely individuals' legal access to abortion but the substantive right either to have or not to have children as well as the necessary social support to raise children.[37] Anarcha-feminists were influenced by this framework but, as the former Love and Rage member Suzy Subways explains, they generally used the phrase "reproductive freedom" instead of "reproductive justice." "Justice," she argues, "implies that we could have that under the current system. We wanted to abolish the current system and create something better."[38] Perhaps the difference was mostly semantic. Still, it underlines that anarcha-feminists fought not for reform but for revolutionary transformation into a society that their predecessor Emma Goldman described as "free communism, actuated by a solidarity of interests."[39]

Focusing on legal access to abortion was a losing strategy if it was not part of a comprehensive effort to transform society. Framing abortion as an individual right based on privacy—not a universally provided aspect of routine health care—set the stage for state violence targeted at poor women and women of color. Indeed, Laura W. argues, it was not just what came after *Roe* that was the problem. The initial Supreme Court ruling itself "was never enough. *Roe v. Wade* itself was a compromise, an effort to co-opt the powerful women's movement that was demanding an end to all laws that regulate abortion. *Roe* made abortion a matter of privacy rather than an essential human right."[40] *Roe* was an important reform, but in hindsight anarchists argued that it worked to co-opt and neutralize the militant feminist struggle for bodily autonomy and antipatriarchal revolution. This is the danger, they maintained, of orienting toward winning legal reforms through the state.

Love and Rage criticized the mainstream feminist approach that continued to cede ground to both the state and the Far Right. Despite the major threats to abortion and reproductive care more broadly, Laura W. predicted in 1998 that "the tepid 'pro-choice' response, which the mainstream feminist leadership will broadcast at press conferences, will most likely focus on the need for more laws on the single issue of abortion." This is problematic, she argues, because single-issue focus on legal access

does not speak to the reality of most women's lives. While abortion is one of many significant issues women deal with, it is lack of access to all health services. Racism, inability to control fertility, a discriminatory, dead-end labor market and poverty are some of the real issues restricting women's free exercise of choice in their lives—not simply the legal status of abortion. "Choice" is a middle-class construct that presumes women have the economic ability to "choose."[41]

True "choice" would thus never be possible under capitalism. Faced with violent state repression, anarcha-feminists argued that working within the state for reforms was counterproductive. *Roe v. Wade* provided an example of the danger of co-optation that would defang movements and open them up to state repression. Instead, reproductive justice movements needed to operate outside the state to build autonomy and power from the ground up. What was needed, Laura W. argued, was "a clear vision of what we are fighting for. We are fighting for women's freedom. 'Choice' just doesn't cut it."[42]

These debates revealed important strategic differences within the broader feminist movement. While they criticized mainstream feminism, anarchists in Love and Rage often joined forces with other left-wing feminists. They worked with a growing network of radical groups that regularly collaborated in the fight to protect abortion clinics and develop autonomous reproductive care infrastructure, including Women's Health Action and Mobilization (WHAM!), the Bay Area Coalition for Our Reproductive Rights (BACORR), the Fight Back Network, and Refuse & Resist! Each of these groups recognized the need to organize at the grassroots level and fight back against both the Far Right and the state itself. On the other side of the divide, mainstream feminists, like the Fund for the Feminist Majority (now the Feminist Majority Foundation), oriented themselves toward reforms and legal battles. These strategies clashed at a major mobilization to defend abortion clinics in Los Angeles in 1995. Anarchists and their allies attempted to physically protect clinics from Operation Rescue and the Missionaries to the Preborn. They were opposed by members of the Feminist Majority, who argued that confrontations were unhelpful and could cause harm to patients seeking care. Instead, the Feminist Majority called on activists to trust in the police and the legal system. President Clinton had recently signed into law the Freedom of Access to Clinic Entrances Act (FACE Act), which made it a federal crime to block clinic doors. This mobilization was a test case for the law.[43] The antiabortionists blockaded multiple clinics and were eventually arrested, but they were quickly released and in fact were never charged under the new law. Meanwhile, several anarcha-feminists were beaten and arrested by the police.[44] For the anarchists, the lessons were clear: the state would never protect them, and liberal feminists could not be trusted as allies.

Anarcha-feminists in Love and Rage argued for a multipronged strategy to build autonomy and power from the bottom up. First, it was important to fight some defensive battles to protect abortion. In particular, the struggle to defend abortion clinics was an important fight against the Far Right.[45] Influenced by feminists within Anti-Racist Action, a segment of the anarchist movement began to see antiabortion activism as central to contemporary fascism.[46] Anarchists brought antifascist tactics to the struggle around abortion clinics, including the practice of disrupting their opponents' meetings and using black bloc tactics in street fights against the likes of Operation Rescue. This was often very successful, such as when a coalition of anarchists, leftists, and feminists of many stripes ran Operation Rescue out of Minneapolis in 1993. Operation Rescue had attempted to hold a major summer training camp for antiabortion activists there as a follow-up to its successful "Summer of Mercy" action in Wichita in 1991.[47] Love and Rage helped organize the leftist-feminist Action Coalition for Reproductive Freedom to defend clinics from Operation Rescue. Rather than solely defend clinics from antiabortion activists, however, anarchists went on the offensive. They blocked access to the church that was hosting Operation Rescue members, disrupted their meetings, vandalized their posters and other materials, and physically prevented them from carrying out both their planned clinic blockades and the trainings.[48] But defending existing clinics was not enough, particularly when anarchists worried that the government seemed poised to outlaw abortion.

Anarchist women thus took it upon themselves to build autonomous institutions and learn to care for their own bodies. As Love and Rage member Liz Highleyman put it, the possibility of abortion being outlawed meant that "we must be ready to take our bodies and our lives into our own hands."[49] In the issue of the Love and Rage newspaper dedicated to the twenty-fifth anniversary of *Roe v. Wade*, Scarlet Os wrote what she called a "Public Cervix Announcement: Learn Self-Help Menstrual Extraction!" After briefly discussing the scope of the abortion access challenge—including the fact that 85 percent of US counties had no abortion provider—she argued that "while movements for liberation need to step up our battle for reproductive rights in the streets, women can also learn how to provide basic gynecological care, including how to end early term pregnancies safely with a group of friends."[50] This meant revisiting traditional methods developed across generations—including herbal and holistic approaches—while also focusing on the technique of menstrual extraction that was first developed in the early 1970s but had fallen out of use after *Roe v. Wade* was won. The key step was to get organized: "Getting involved in a self-help group rather than waiting to see what awful things the antiwomen/antiabortion forces come up with next is a potent offensive move in the battle for women's freedom."[51] Building on the example of consciousness-raising groups and self-help groups in the 1960s–1970s, anarcha-feminist self-help groups were small groups of women who committed themselves to collective study to develop their capacity to take care of their bodies. Unlike many study groups focused on theory, these were largely oriented toward practice: "Women teach each other how to check their cervixes for irregularities (potentially detecting precancerous cells), study and practice identification and treatment of basic infections and STDs, do self–breast exams, check ovaries and uteruses for growths or cysts."[52] All of this laid the foundation for learning to provide abortions.

In the 1990s many feminist self-help groups (anarchist and otherwise) embraced the technique of menstrual extraction.[53] Rebecca Chalker and Carol

Downer (one of the original creators of the technique) published *A Woman's Book of Choices: Abortion, Menstrual Extraction, RU-486* in 1992, which helped revive its use for a new generation. Feminists pointed out that abortion through menstrual extraction—removing the contents of the uterus around the time of an expected period—is a safe home health care technique that puts women in control of their own bodies. It cannot be performed by oneself but relies on a group of lay practitioners who have studied and practiced together. Unlike official medical settings, a small group of close friends could be in control of the entire process. As Os notes: "The woman having the procedure gets to be at home, or a safe place of her choice. Unlike a clinical setting, she is in control. If she wants to put in her speculum or needs to take a break, she can. What a difference from any clinical medical procedure!"[54] This individual and collective sense of empowerment was a key outcome of self-help groups. Anarchists in Love and Rage organized a "Wimmin's Health Tour" in 1993 that spread the technique and encouraged women to get organized. In part due to this effort, feminist self-help groups proliferated across the United States in the 1990s. Although their underground nature means that we have little idea just how many abortions were performed in this manner, they made a real difference in people's lives. Beyond the benefits to individual people seeking abortion, the ability to perform reproductive care without having to deal with the state or the medical system has significant political implications.

Love and Rage members argued that women's capacity to care for their own bodies and reproduction materially lessens state power. Establishing grassroots reproductive health care infrastructure is a key component of building autonomy and feminist dual power that challenges the rule of the state and capitalism. Inspired in part by the Zapatistas, anarchists began to build and defend new institutions as part of a broader project challenging the patriarchal violence of the capitalist state.[55] Grassroots reproductive infrastructure laid the foundation for further revolutionary action. As Love and Rage member Sunshine Smith remarked in 1990, forming self-help medical groups and abortion infrastructure in the Bay Area

has, in very concrete ways, made our struggle against the antiabortion group Operation "Rescue" and the "Supreme" Court stronger and more effective. We have learned that if the time comes, we can and will do home abortions. We are becoming physically aware of the invasion the government is conducting into our bodies. We are now able to repulse the state from our uteri because we are gaining the knowledge that enables us to control our own bodies.[56]

Expelling the state and capital from the process of reproduction provided a model for doing so in other areas of life ranging from the workplace to community safety. This strategy provided a tangible example of the new world for which anarchists fought.

Conclusion

After decades of right-wing activism, in June 2022 the Supreme Court finally overturned *Roe v. Wade*. In response, feminists mobilized to defend abortion both in the street and at the ballot box. When the question has been put on the ballot—even in conservative states like Kansas and Kentucky—voters have enacted stronger protections on abortion.[57] But it has become clear that voting is not enough. Feminists originally won *Roe v. Wade* by organizing mass movements and grassroots reproductive care infrastructure in conjunction with legal and electoral struggles. Even in the 1970s, however, anarcha-feminists cautioned against orienting toward legal reforms and other state-centric strategies. They argued that anything the state gives—including *Roe v. Wade*—can be taken away, for it is ultimately a tool of sexual and class violence in the hands of the patriarchal, capitalist ruling class.

In the 1990s anarcha-feminists in Love and Rage picked up the torch of radical feminism and analyzed how state violence intersected with patriarchy, white supremacy, and capitalism. Rather than fight legal battles to protect abortion, they defended abortion clinics in the streets and built autonomous feminist infrastructure from below. Inspired by the Zapatistas, they believed that this was an important step in building feminist dual power that would eventually overthrow the state and capitalism. Love and Rage collapsed in 1998 after several years of acrimonious ideological debates in which several leading members repudiated anarchism. But the grassroots fight for reproductive freedom continues. Today we bear witness to the failures of the "prochoice" framing and of the liberal belief in the state. Movements today have much to learn from Love and Rage's analysis of the intersection of the state, capitalism, patriarchy, and white supremacy—and its commitment to building autonomy and feminist dual power from below.

Spencer Beswick holds a PhD in history from Cornell University. His dissertation, "Love and Rage: Revolutionary Anarchism in the Late Twentieth Century," explores the transformation and revitalization of the US anarchist movement in the 1980s and 1990s. His writing on anarchist theory and history has appeared in *Anarchist Studies*, *Coils of the Serpent*, *Hard Crackers*, *It's Going Down*, *Left History*, *Perspectives on Anarchist Theory*, *Truthout*, and the *Washington Post*.

Notes

1. The entire run of the newspaper is online in the *Arm the Spirit* collection at https://issuu .com/RandallJayKay. The newspaper as well as various internal documents were accessed in print at the Interference Archive in Brooklyn, New York. The article also draws on oral history interviews that I conducted as well as on documents from the personal collections of former Love and Rage members who generously agreed to share them.
2. Garrow, *Liberty and Sexuality*.
3. Ziegler, *After Roe*, 9, 8.
4. Reagan, *When Abortion Was a Crime*, 1.
5. Echols, *Daring to Be Bad*.

6.   See the essays on consciousness-raising in Firestone and Koedt, *Notes from the Second Year*, including Carol Hanisch's influential piece "The Personal Is Political" as well as multiple essays on abortion. For a classic history of radical feminism and the women's liberation movement, see Echols, *Daring to Be Bad*.

7.   *Hard Crackers*, "Who Are the Experts?"

8.   Boston Women's Health Book Collective, *Our Bodies, Ourselves*.

9.   Brown, *Without Apology*, 2.

10.   For more on the rise of the post-*Roe* antiabortion movement, see Ziegler, *Abortion and the Law in America*; and Schoen, *Abortion after* Roe.

11.   See Susan Faludi's classic *Backlash*.

12.   See Ziegler, *After* Roe, chap. 4 ("The Rise of Choice").

13.   Tanenbaum, "To Destroy Domination in All Forms."

14.   Quoted in Tanenbaum, "To Destroy Domination in All Forms," 19.

15.   Bakunin, *Statism and Anarchy*, 136.

16.   Malatesta, "Anarchy."

17.   Kropotkin, "Anarchist Communism," 67.

18.   Bakunin, *Statism and Anarchy*, 136.

19.   See, e.g., Grubačić and Graeber, "Anarchism."

20.   Chicago Anarcho-Feminists, "Who We Are."

21.   Love and Rage Revolutionary Anarchist Federation, "Love and Rage Draft Political Statement."

22.   See Barbara Epstein's classic history of the movement in *Political Protest and Cultural Revolution*. For a broader history of the development of direct-action tactics and movements in this period, see Kauffman, *Direct Action*.

23.   Its role has been neglected in the emerging historical scholarship on feminism in the 1990s, such as Lisa Levenstein's book *They Didn't See Us Coming*, which—despite its claim to uncovering a "hidden history"—focuses much more on the world of mainstream feminist nongovernmental organizations, nonprofits, and foundations.

24.   See Beswick, "From the Ashes of the Old."

25.   For more on these convergences, see Wood, "Anarchist Gatherings."

26.   Relatively little has been written about Love and Rage. See San Filippo, *A New World in Our Hearts*. For a broad account of anarcha-feminism in Love and Rage, including internal struggles against "anarchist patriarchy," the organization's role in the student movement at the City University of New York, and members' interventions in queer and trans liberation movements, see Beswick, "'We're Pro-choice and We Riot!'" For more on Love and Rage's antiracist activism, see Beswick, "Smashing Whiteness."

27.   See Beswick, "Smashing Whiteness"; and Katrina Knutson, interview by author, February 10, 2022.

28.   Day, "Dual Power in the Selva Lacandon."

29.   Day, "Dual Power in the Selva Lacandon," 17. PRI is the Partido Revolucionario Institucional (Institutional Revolutionary Party).

30.   Jessica, "Women in Zapatista Territory," 4.

31.   Quoted in Klein, *Compañeras*, 73. EZLN is the Ejército Zapatista de Liberación Nacional (Zapatista Army of National Liberation).

32.   Love and Rage Revolutionary Anarchist Federation, "Love and Rage Draft Political Statement."

33.   LM, "Women's Liberation Movement," 19.

34. Laura W., "Twenty-Fifth Anniversary of Roe v. Wade," 13.
35. Laura W., "Twenty-Fifth Anniversary of Roe v. Wade," 1.
36. See Briggs, *How All Politics Became Reproductive Politics*; and Matthiesen, *Reproduction Reconceived*.
37. See Luna, *Reproductive Rights as Human Rights*.
38. Suzy Subways, interview by author, November 2, 2021.
39. Goldman, "What I Believe."
40. Laura W., "Twenty-Fifth Anniversary of Roe v. Wade," 13.
41. Laura W., "Twenty-Fifth Anniversary of Roe v. Wade," 1, 13.
42. Laura W., "Twenty-Fifth Anniversary of Roe v. Wade," 13.
43. See the US Department of Justice's description of the law in "Protecting Patients and Health Care Providers."
44. For two accounts of this action and its fallout, see Subways, "Clinic Defense in the Era of Operation Rescue"; and Laura [W.], "Liberal Attack on Choice."
45. For a broader history of the fight over abortion clinics, with a focus on how clinic escorts have volunteered to help people receive care in the face of the antiabortion attack, see Rankin, *Bodies on the Line*.
46. Knutson, interview. See also Clay, Schwartz, and Staudenmaier, *We Go Where They Go*, chap. 6 ("Our Bodies, Our Choice").
47. See Toner, "Minneapolis Clinics Brace for Siege."
48. See one participant's account of this mobilization in Liza, "Minnesota Not Nice to Operation Rescue."
49. Highleyman, "Reproductive Freedom in Everyday Life," 6.
50. Os, "Public Cervix Announcement," 5.
51. Os, "Public Cervix Announcement," 5.
52. Os, "Public Cervix Announcement," 5.
53. See Cindy Pearson's contemporary account in "Self Help Clinic Celebrates Twenty-Five Years."
54. Os, "Public Cervix Announcement," 5.
55. Jessica, "Women in Zapatista Territory." For more on Zapatista women, see Klein, *Compañeras*.
56. Smith, "East Bay Women's Community Gets Rolling," 10–11.
57. Lysen, Ziegler, and Mesa, "Voters in Kansas Decide"; Kimball, "Kentucky Rejects Antiabortion Constitutional Amendment."

References

Bakunin, Mikhail. *Statism and Anarchy*. Edited by Marshall Shatz. Cambridge: Cambridge University Press, 1990.

Beswick, Spencer. "From the Ashes of the Old: Anarchism Reborn in a Counterrevolutionary Age (1970s–1990s)." *Anarchist Studies* 30, no. 2 (2022): 31–54.

Beswick, Spencer. "Smashing Whiteness: Race, Class, and Punk Culture in the Love and Rage Revolutionary Anarchist Federation (1989–98)." In *DIY or Die! Do-It-Yourself, Do-It-Together, and Punk Anarchism*, edited by Jim Donaghey, Will Boisseau, and Caroline Kaltefleiter. Karlovac: Active Distribution, forthcoming.

Beswick, Spencer. "'We're Pro-choice and We Riot!': Anarcha-feminism in Love and Rage (1989–98)." *Coils of the Serpent: Journal for the Study of Contemporary Power*, no. 11 (2023): 148–71.

Boston Women's Health Book Collective. *Our Bodies, Ourselves*. Cambridge, MA: New England Free Press, 1970.

Briggs, Laura. *How All Politics Became Reproductive Politics: From Welfare Reform to Foreclosure to Trump*. Oakland: University of California Press, 2018.

Brown, Jenny. *Without Apology: The Abortion Struggle Now*. New York: Verso, 2019.

Carolyn. "Pro-choice Revolution or Reform?" *Love and Rage* 6, no. 2 (1995): 1, 3, 26.

Chalker, Rebecca, and Carol Downer. *A Woman's Book of Choices: Abortion, Menstrual Extraction, RU-486*. New York: Four Walls Eight Windows, 1992.

Chicago Anarcho-Feminists. "Who We Are: An Anarcho-feminist Manifesto." In *Quiet Rumours: An Anarcha-feminist Reader*, edited by Dark Star Collective, 15–16. Expanded ed. Oakland, CA: AK Press, 2012.

Clay, Shannon, Lady, Kristin Schwartz, and Michael Staudenmaier. *We Go Where They Go: The Story of Anti-racist Action*. Oakland, CA: PM Press, 2023.

Day, Christopher. "Dual Power in the Selva Lacandon." In *A New World in Our Hearts*, edited by Roy San Filippo, 17–31. Oakland, CA: AK Press, 2002.

Echols, Alice. *Daring to Be Bad: Radical Feminism in America, 1967–1975*. 30th anniv. ed. Minneapolis: University of Minnesota Press, 2019.

Epstein, Barbara. *Political Protest and Cultural Revolution: Nonviolent Direct Action in the 1970s and 1980s*. Berkeley: University of California Press, 1993.

Faludi, Susan. *Backlash: The Undeclared War against American Women*. New York: Crown, 1991.

Firestone, Shulamith, and Anne Koedt, eds. *Notes from the Second Year: Women's Liberation*. New York: Radical Feminism, 1970. https://repository.duke.edu/dc/wlmpc/wlmms01039.

Garrow, David J. *Liberty and Sexuality: The Right to Privacy and the Making of* Roe v. Wade. Berkeley: University of California Press, 1998.

Goldman, Emma. "What I Believe." *New York World*, July 19, 1908. http://dwardmac.pitzer.edu /Anarchist_Archives/goldman/whatibelieve.html.

Grubačić, Andrej, and David Graeber. "Anarchism; or, The Revolutionary Movement of the Twenty-First Century." ZNet, 2004. https://theanarchistlibrary.org/library/andrej-grubacic -david-graeber-anarchism-or-the-revolutionary-movement-of-the-twenty-first-centu.

Hard Crackers. "Who Are the Experts? An Archival Glimpse at 1969 Abortion Rights Actions." *Hard Crackers: Chronicles of Everyday Life*, July 24, 2022. https://hardcrackers.com/who -are-the-experts-an-archival-glimpse-at-1969-abortion-rights-actions/.

Highleyman, Liz. "Reproductive Freedom in Everyday Life." *Love and Rage* 3, no. 2 (1992): 6, 10.

Jessica. "Women in Zapatista Territory." *Love and Rage* 8, no. 2 (1997): 4, 16.

Kauffman, L. A. *Direct Action: Protest and the Reinvention of American Radicalism*. New York: Verso, 2017.

Kimball, Spencer. "Kentucky Rejects Anti-abortion Constitutional Amendment in Surprise Victory for Reproductive Rights." *CNBC*, November 9, 2022. https://www.cnbc.com/2022 /11/09/midterm-elections-kentucky-rejects-anti-abortion-constitutional-amendment.html.

Klein, Hilary. *Compañeras: Zapatista Women's Stories*. New York: Seven Stories, 2015.

Kropotkin, Peter. "Anarchist Communism." In *Anarchism: A Collection of Revolutionary Writings*, edited by Roger N. Baldwin, 46–78. Mineola, NY: Dover, 2002.

Laura [W]. "Liberal Attack on Choice." *Love and Rage* 6, no. 4 (1995): 3, 24.

Laura W. "Twenty-Fifth Anniversary of Roe v. Wade." *Love and Rage* 8, no. 5 (1997): 1, 13.

Levenstein, Lisa. *They Didn't See Us Coming: The Hidden History of Feminism in the Nineties*. New York: Basic Books, 2020.

Liza. "Minnesota Not Nice to Operation Rescue." *Love and Rage* 4, no. 4 (1993): 1, 3, 19.

LM. "Women's Liberation Movement: Remembered and Continuing [Letter]." *Love and Rage* 6, no. 5 (1995): 19.

Love and Rage Revolutionary Anarchist Federation. "Love and Rage Draft Political Statement." In *Love and Rage Revolutionary Anarchist Federation (New York Local) Member Handbook*, 1997. https://theanarchistlibrary.org/library/love-and-rage-revolutionary -anarchist-federation-l-r-draft-political-statement.

Luna, Zakiya. *Reproductive Rights as Human Rights: Women of Color and the Fight for Reproductive Justice*. New York: New York University Press, 2020.

Lysen, Dylan, Laura Ziegler, and Blaise Mesa. "Voters in Kansas Decide to Keep Abortion Legal in the State, Rejecting an Amendment." *NPR*, August 3, 2022. https://www.npr.org /sections/2022-live-primary-election-race-results/2022/08/02/1115317596/kansas-voters -abortion-legal-reject-constitutional-amendment.

Malatesta, Errico. "Anarchy." *Freedom Press*, 1974. https://theanarchistlibrary.org/library/errico -malatesta-anarchy.

Matthiesen, Sara. *Reproduction Reconceived: Family Making and the Limits of Choice after* Roe v. Wade. Oakland: University of California Press, 2021.

Os, Scarlet. "Public Cervix Announcement: Learn Self-Help Menstrual Extraction!" *Love and Rage* 8, no. 5 (1997): 5.

Pearson, Cindy. "Self Help Clinic Celebrates Twenty-Five Years." *Network News*, March–April 1996. https://www.fwhc.org/selfhelp.htm.

Rankin, Lauren. *Bodies on the Line: At the Front Lines of the Fight to Protect Abortion in America*. Berkeley, CA: Counterpoint, 2022.

Reagan, Leslie J. *When Abortion Was a Crime: Women, Medicine, and Law in the United States, 1867–1973*. Oakland: University of California Press, 2022.

San Filippo, Roy, ed. *A New World in Our Hearts: Eight Years of Writings from the Love and Rage Revolutionary Anarchist Federation*. Oakland, CA: AK Press, 2003.

Schoen, Johanna. *Abortion after* Roe. Chapel Hill: University of North Carolina Press, 2015.

Smith, Sunshine. "East Bay Women's Community Gets Rolling: Smashing Scales, Wielding Speculums, and Demanding Much More than Our Rights." *Love and Rage* 1, no. 1 (1990): 10–11.

Subways, Suzy. "Clinic Defense in the Era of Operation Rescue." *Hard Crackers: Chronicles of Everyday Life*, July 28, 2022. https://hardcrackers.com/clinic-defense-in-the-era-of -operation-rescue/.

Tanenbaum, Julia. "To Destroy Domination in All Forms: Anarcha-feminist Theory, Organization, and Action, 1970–1978." *Perspectives on Anarchist Theory*, no. 29 (2016): 13–32.

Toner, Robin. "Minneapolis Clinics Brace for Siege: Operation Rescue's on the Way." *New York Times*, July 6, 1993.

US Department of Justice. "Protecting Patients and Health Care Providers." *United States Department of Justice*, September 15, 2022. https://www.justice.gov/crt/protecting-patients -and-health-care-providers.

Wood, Lesley. "Anarchist Gatherings, 1986–2017." *ACME: An International Journal for Critical Geographies* 18, no. 4 (2019): 892–908.

Ziegler, Mary. *Abortion and the Law in America:* Roe v. Wade *to the Present*. Cambridge: Cambridge University Press, 2020.

Ziegler, Mary. *After* Roe: *The Lost History of the Abortion Debate*. Cambridge, MA: Harvard University Press, 2015.

Taking Over, Living-In

Black Feminist Geometry and the Radical Politics of Repair

Randi Gill-Sadler and Erica R. Edwards

In 1988, the Black feminist culture worker Toni Cade Bambara imagined a film that would document a radical response to state violence, one that demanded of the state not repair but abdication: a self-renunciation. In Bambara's vision, the film would end with a motley crew of poor, unhoused Philadelphians taking over a luxury apartment building and taking over, too, the technology through which their "living-in," as they called it, would become known. Turning away from the state and its corporate welfare partnership with real estate developers, the characters commandeer the camera and turn it on themselves in a militant act of self-recording. What Bambara imagines in her unfinished film is a reorientation of *care*, a communal rising that refuses the state care offered through social workers, the housing authority, welfare agencies, and the police. In place of a reparative appeal, the unfinished film stages a refusal—what Tina Campt refers to as a cultural practice whose "power lies in its ability to engage negation as generative."[1] In a cultural context of American film in which, as Bambara suggested, "there is no revolutionary alternative ever conceived," and in a political context that likewise outlawed revolutionary refusals of reform, Bambara's project, like many narratives by Black feminist writers, filmmakers, and intellectuals of the late twentieth century, visualized what might happen when those who are normally seen as objects of state repair establish and enact improper and incomplete remedies to state violence.

Radical History Review

Issue 148 (January 2024)   DOI 10.1215/01636545-10846851

© 2024 by MARHO: The Radical Historians' Organization, Inc.

We begin here with Bambara's speculative filmmaking practice because the reorientation of care effected in her treatment for a film titled *Come as You Are* is a turn that leftist Black feminist activists, collectives, theories, and forms have performed often over the past five decades. If we consider radical Black feminism as an emphatic turn away from state-mediated repair, we can understand how feminist scholarship's capacity to effectively theorize and resist state violence rests on such a turn—the turn, that is, against the warfare that governance wraps in care. As the Kānaka Maoli scholar Hiʻilei Julia Kawehipuaakahaopulani Hobart and Tamara Kneese suggest, the "kind of care that can radically remake worlds that exceed those offered by the neoliberal or postneoliberal state" is the kind of care that emphasizes mutual aid and structural critique rather than "moralized self-management," which "produces the body as a site in which idealized citizenship coalesces as an unachievable goal" and "glosses over the political, economic, and ideological structures that do the work of marginalization."[2] To historicize and theorize the *radical care* that Hobart and Kneese write of is to recognize second-wave feminism's limited imagination with respect to state violence. As Emily Thuma documents, feminists of color who took on militant self-defense as a "grassroots alternative to abusive men and an unresponsive state" in the 1970s registered a critique of carceral feminism's commitment to incarceration as a tool of justice and care.[3] As the sociologist Elizabeth Bernstein explains, carceral feminism is a concept that allows us to understand how feminist activists, especially in the context of antitrafficking work, "have relied upon strategies of incarceration as their chief tool of 'justice.'" Importantly, this reliance on policing effects a "drift," as Bernstein puts it, "from the welfare state to the carceral state as the enforcement apparatus for feminist goals," trading one model of state care for another.[4] Put simply, the relationship between feminism and state violence at times relies on and reproduces the desire for the very violence against women it purports to reject.

If one of the legacies of second-wave feminism is an uninterrogated reliance on state-based forms of care, including policing and incarceration, feminists of color have imagined and enacted radicalized forms of care throughout the post–civil rights era. Late twentieth-century feminist-of-color formations were forged in a moment when the US state was not only strategically aiming its violent strategies of care and repair at minority populations—strategies it draped in lexical cloaks such as "urban renewal" and "war on poverty"—but also attempting a dramatic project of *self*-repair. As Erica Edwards suggests, the global rebellion of the 1960s challenged the state's authority, and its attempts to recover what policymakers such as Samuel Huntington and Daniel Patrick Moynihan called *governability* were based on a strategic shift from exclusion to inclusion.[5] It was through practices of care, that is, of opening and inclusion, that the state recovered its damaged legitimacy. And these practices of care-as-invitation—what Sylvia Wynter refers to as the "sanitization" of the 1960s rupture—have not only fortified class inequality and defanged radicalism but also occluded Black feminism's radical histories by stabilizing versions of Black and women-of-color feminism that are legible within and useful to neoliberal institutions of education and commerce.[6] We situate Bambara in the history of what Edwards calls "insurgent care," the radicalized forms of safety that Black feminists imagined in scenes of watchfulness, internationalist coalition, and mutual tending.[7]

This article offers a cultural history of Black feminist negations of state repair by analyzing Bambara's work as a filmmaker. We analyze Black feminist representations of state violence and contra-state forms of repair that complicate how feminist theory encounters the problem of reparative appeal. Following Bambara's filmic arguments about the generative refusal of state care, we argue that if the state *over-determines* care, the unfinished projects of radical Black feminist culture stubbornly undermine that overdetermination. Bambara's speculative figuration of living-in offers a radical Black feminist geometry of power: a theory of state power's vertical application of various forms of surveillance, a critique of capitalism's promise of upward mobility, and a utopian vision of horizontal power that privileges radical collective care. Here we mean *horizontal* in the way that Christina Sharpe suggests when she distinguishes between caring "laterally," as in the intramural care for the dead, and the vertical "care from state-imposed regimes of surveillance."[8] The forms of living-in that Bambara stages throughout her work, especially in her films, imagine this lateral care as a taking over of state-controlled space and resources, not as a move underground or out of sight but as a collective *surrounding* in the very spaces of containment, deprivation, and surveillance. The living-in staged by the characters in her film treatment, for example, horizontalizes the lines of care, turning the characters into "creative combatants"—as Bambara describes radical feminists in her foreword to *This Bridge Called My Back*—who "mutually care and cure each other into wholeness" and, in doing so, "make revolution irresistible."[9]

Bambara's work emerged when Black and women-of-color feminists were developing critical theories of violence, that is, in a historical moment when the formal granting of citizenship rights to Black Americans and the victories of second-wave feminism laid bare how metanarratives of freedom and equality obscured the realities of ongoing state violence. The neoliberal turn "held out the promise of protection from premature death and precarity," as Grace Hong powerfully argues, while depending on the "selective protection and proliferation of minoritized life *as the very mechanism* for the brutal exacerbation of minoritized death."[10] Some minoritized subjects and populations became "recognized as protectable life for the first time," Hong suggests, and BIPOC feminisms of the post-1960s decades wrestled with what state recognition meant for feminism's capacity to unmask and challenge state violence in the crucible of inclusive liberal democracy.[11] Kimberlé Crenshaw's now-canonical theorization of intersectionality, for example, began with the observation that forms of violence considered private had to be "recognized as part of a broadscale system of domination that affects women as a class."[12] BIPOC feminists also exposed how state policy and praxis have been designed to destroy the lives of women of color under the guise of care. According to Dorothy Roberts, for example, the surveillance, control, and extraction of Black women's reproductive capacity has been a crucial motive of the US state; at the same time, American child welfare agencies remove Black children from their homes and place them under state supervision, using narratives of Black mothers' carelessness to justify the state's intrusion into Black communities and families.[13] Other Black feminist theorists, such as Patricia Williams, Crenshaw, Andrea Ritchie, and LaShawn Harris, have likewise exposed how the state's monopolization of violence has particularly damaging effects on those who identify (or those it identifies) as women or femmes; more important still, they have questioned whether the state can be imagined to remedy the violence that secures its authority.[14] Research on policing and incarceration has been key to thinking beyond reform, beyond appeal-oriented solutions to state violence. In her work on anti-Black police terror in the Americas, Christen Smith points out that police terror affects Black women at a higher frequency than Black men, where *frequency* refers not only to statistical occurrence but also to the "multiple wavelengths"—the *frequencies*—on which everyday harm operates. As Smith suggests, "Police terror sickens, maims, and kills slowly": the state distributes death not only in bullets and tasers and chokeholds but also in the "physical aftereffects of being wounded . . . or the psychological effects of watching someone be killed."[15] Borrowing the medical term used to describe the morbid infections that are caused by sudden injuries, Smith uses the term *sequelae* to refer to the slow violence of contemporary state terror. Given the frequency of police terror and the larger culture of carcerality in a self-consciously postracist society, political appeals for repair are limited in their usefulness. "There are too many lives at peril to recycle the forms of appeal that, at best, have delivered the limited emancipation against which we now struggle," Saidiya V. Hartman writes.[16] If state violence is articulated as policy that *cares* and protection that *kills*, how do we imagine the care that, as Hobart and Kneese urge, *radically remakes worlds*?

Abolitionist Black feminist theorists have exposed the limits of the *reparative appeal*, that is, the limits of seeking redress from a state whose authority rests on its right to be the sole arbiter of violence (and justice) while absolving itself from its own violence via discourses of care, protection, and security. As Ruth Wilson Gilmore explains, the building of the neoliberal order depended on "the ascendance of antistate actors: peoples and parties who gain state power by denouncing state power." The withdrawal of the state from social welfare, these actors suggest, "will enhance rather than destroy the lives of those abandoned," and, importantly, "where the market fails, the voluntary, nonprofit sector can pick up any stray pieces because the extent to which extra economic values (such as kindness or generosity or decency) come into play is the extent to which abandonment produces its own socially strengthening rewards."[17] Reparative appeals to a state that is actively "shrinking" are shuttled into the nonprofit industrial complex, Gilmore suggests, which privileges "projects rather than core operations."[18] Moreover, radical Black feminists of the post–civil rights era have shown how class often functions to cloak resistance to the state's *care*. The 1973 anthology *Lessons from the Damned*, for example, explains how the state leverages middle-class Black people's desire for inclusion and acceptance in the imperial state to neutralize contra-state forms of repair within Black, working-class communities. Edited by a collective of Black women in Mount Vernon calling themselves "the damned," *Lessons from the Damned* is a collection of poor and working-class Black people's analyses of their conditions. "This book may be the first time," the authors assert, "that poor and petit-bourgeois Black people have described the full reality of our oppression and our struggle."[19] It is founded in an unflinching appraisal of how the Black middle class often facilitates and provides cover for state violence. The authors suggest that the Black petit bourgeoisie "are assigned as caretakers and slave foremen over the black slums."[20] Tasked with surveilling, disciplining, and neutralizing the potential of Black radical organizing, the Black middle class establishes the conditions by which the state's and the corporate class's capitalist designs might be realized within the Black community. As the caretaker class, the Black American petit bourgeoisie oversees the dissemination and persistence of US imperial cultural narratives of self-help and personal responsibility in Black working-class communities and encourages working-class Black people to aspire to inclusion rather than revolution.

The Black Women's Revolutionary Council (BWRC), established in 1980 in Oakland, California, also identified the new valences of state violence in the post–civil rights era. Established by the Black lesbian poet Pat Parker, the BWRC aimed to "educate people about the effects of this imperialist system and how it manifests in our lives in the form of racism, classism, and sexism" and to "make revolution in this country."[21] Consistent with the authors of *Lessons from the Damned*, the BWRC pointed out that post-1960s incorporation recruited Black people's participation in state violence. "Imperialist forces in the world are finding themselves backed against the wall," the BWRC suggested, "no longer able to control the world with the threat of force." The BWRC exposed the state's turn to (and eventual overdetermination of) care to neutralize radical political and social movements. The BWRC also identified how Hollywood's misrepresentation of revolution and the corporate media's military propaganda would facilitate more state violence. On the one hand, the BWRC writes, Hollywood films depicted revolution as "the revolutionary man [who] kills his enemies and walks off into the sunset with his revolutionary woman who has been waiting for his return and that's the end of the tale," effectively reducing the scale and complexity of revolutionary collectives and efforts to heteronormative relationships with patriarchal gender roles. On the other hand, the BWRC described the media's incessant invitations to viewers to join the military: "The media is bombarding us with patriotic declarations about 'our' hostages and 'our embassy.' . . . Ads inviting us to become the few, the chosen, the marine or fly with the air force, etc. are filling our television screens." Given Hollywood's mis-representations of revolution and the media's calls for collectivity only in service to state violence, radical Black feminist cultural workers were tasked with both outlin-ing the mechanisms through which the media made state violence appear as care and reconceptualizing care toward radical ends.

Bambara was not alone, then, in using cultural means—writing and filmmaking—to expose and challenge the state's manipulation of vertical forms of care. These vertical forms of care, which included surveillance and policing from above and enticements into upward mobility, reinforced the authority of the state to monopolize violence and then to correct, justify, and repair its incursions into wom-en's lives. Bambara's capacious body of fiction, essays, and film horizontalizes care, refusing reparative appeals to the state or its arbiters and insisting, instead, on the living-in of those who dwell on the edges of capitalist development, such as those who take over the luxury building in *Come as You Are*. As Avery Gordon suggests, Bambara does not offer perfect utopian scenarios, only "stories of living otherwise with the degradations and contradictions of exploitation, racism, and authoritarian-ism."[22] This living-in/living-otherwise takes on a new geometry of power.

Toni Cade Bambara and the Cultural Work of Radical Repair

Black feminist cultural workers served as archivists for existing social movements and imagined new possibilities for Black social life during the post–civil rights era, when such possibilities were tightly constrained by the twin forces of brute repres-sion and co-optation. Their experiments with form—which ranged from the gener-ation of new genres like the choreopoem and the biomythography, the use of invented languages, the use of music and performance to frustrate distinctions between "high" and "low" culture and to advance an "intellectual revolution," and, most important for us, the use of experimental film to preserve Black radical history—were experiments with radical care.[23] Black feminist cultural workers drafted cultural collectives and cultural texts that situated *care* not as the surveillant, ordering work that government agencies were undertaking toward enhancing the stability and resources of a "Negro American family" that was seen as aberrant, but as the collectively generated pro-cesses of supporting health (including medical, mental, and dietary health), increas-ing food security, generating material resources for communities that were targeted by US imperial invasions, and creating shelter. While our focus in the remainder of this article is on Bambara's experiments with radical care, it is important to see her experiments not as exceptional but as representative of a larger culture of Black rad-ical feminist refusal.[24]

A self-proclaimed Pan-African socialist feminist, cultural worker, and media activist, Bambara is one of the most recognizable figures of the Black women's liter-ary renaissance of the 1970s and 1980s and among radical Black feminism's staunch-est critics of the state. Though especially adept at the short story, Bambara's entire oeuvre—which includes anthologies, novels, screenplays, and films—is comparable to a musical "obligato," according to the literary scholar and cultural critic Cheryl A. Wall, as it is "an essential component of the composition of the era."[25] Indeed, Bambara's literary works proved invaluable to various feminist groups throughout the post–civil rights period. Farah Jasmine Griffin notes that Bambara's anthology *The Black Woman* (1970), for which Bambara was a contributor and the editor, was a "foundational text in the then emerging field of Black women's studies."[26] Contributors to *The Black Woman* included teachers and students from the City University of New York's Search for Education, Elevation, and Knowledge (SEEK) Program, Black women's study groups, and feminist activists like Frances Beal, who went on to be an integral member of the Third World Women's Alliance. In addition to its importance to Black women readers and Black feminists, *The Black Woman* garnered attention from other radical feminist circles. After having read *The Black Woman* in the spring of 1975, the activist and teacher Arlene Eisen invited Bambara to be part of a women's delegation called the North American Academic Marxist-Leninist Anti-Imperialist Feminist Women, which visited the Women's Union of Hanoi. For Bambara, international travel to places like Vietnam and Cuba, where she went to meet with the Federation of Cuban Women two years earlier, both informed her literary work and affirmed writing as a significant mode of political struggle against the state.

Bambara's own fiction attended to various scales and iterations of state violence. Bambara described the stories in her second short story collection, *The Sea Birds Are Still Alive* (1977), as " both on-the-block and larger-world-of-struggle pieces" that were concerned with how people would sustain themselves in the post–civil rights era.[27] Her first novel, *The Salt Eaters*, charts violence on a similar scale, "from the intimate and bodily . . . to the terrorist threat and planet level nuclear devastation that is imminent."[28] Rather than present an appeal to the state for rescue or protection as the solution, *The Salt Eaters* prompts readers to view the scales of state violence as both material and metaphysical, to resist the rigid bifurcation of the spiritual and political, and to rejoin political struggle and African-descended cosmologies. In her posthumous novel on the Atlanta missing and murdered children's case, *Those Bones Are Not My Child* (1999), Bambara fictionalizes the real efforts of Black families and communities to protect and rescue their children in the face of state neglect and "official narratives" that blamed Black mothers and "phantom killers" for the missing and murdered children. The novel itself, according to Jodi Melamed, becomes a survival guide "in the face of neoconservative repression and possibilities for dissociation and misrecognition that liberal multiculturalism enabled."[29]

While most of the scholarship on Bambara's critiques of state violence privileges her literary oeuvre, we contend that Bambara's cinematic work is invaluable to her critique of state violence and reimagining of care. Our careful attention to her film activism becomes even more critical when we consider that Bambara turned away from literature to participate more fully in activist work and to resist the pressures from a liberal-leaning literature industry that was rapidly canonizing Black women writers. Only three years after publishing *The Salt Eaters*, Bambara believed that she had exhausted her passion and curiosity for literary forms. "There's not much more I want to experiment with in terms of writing," she declared to Claudia Tate in a 1983 interview.[30] While Bambara admits that she still derives pleasure, insight, and a sense of sanity from writing, she cites the solitude of writing as well as the formal demands of the publishing industry as catalysts for her turn away from writing. Bambara concedes her growing impatience with sitting in her back room, all alone, knocking out books. Describing novel writing as "a lonely business," Bambara described herself as "more sociable and street-based-work committed than noveling permits."[31] Furthermore, she recognized that the publishing industry as well as the academy has privileged the novel as the most profitable form in the 1980s:

> The major publishing industry, the academic establishment, reviewers, and
> critics favor the novel. And the independent press journals can rarely afford to
> print a ten-page piece. Murder for the gene-deep loyalist who readily admits in
> interviews that the move to the novel was not occasioned by a recognition of
> having reached the limits of the genre or the practitioner's disillusion with it,
> but rather Career. Economics. Critical attention.[32]

Bambara not only described the material, economic conditions that have made the novel more viable across literary and scholarly institutions but also highlighted the culture of silence surrounding the inculcation of the novel as the mark of writerly distinction—a culture of silence that traded transparency about the dictates of the publishing and academic industry for the promise of stability, salary, and stature. Bambara even admitted that these promises were "a major motive behind the production of *Salt*."[33]

    Although Bambara turned to film in part to circumvent the fetishization of the novel by the academy and publishing houses, she was under no illusions about the film industry's desire to conceal its ideological imperatives and suppress the spread of radical political values via hegemonic standards around cinematic conventions. Bambara often showed and circulated independent Black and Third World Cinema films well before her explicit turn to filmmaking in the 1980s. During her tenure as a writer in residence at Spelman College, for example, Bambara taught a course titled Images of Black Women in Lit and Film that included domestic and international independent films like *Lucia*, *La luta continua*, *Bush Mama*, and *The Battle of Algiers*.[34] Bambara circulated flyers about the course in community centers and senior citizens' homes and prepared press releases in local newspapers that advertised it to the entire community.[35] In addition to opening up her classroom to the community, Bambara opened her home film viewings to the community and, in doing so, contributed to the development of the Atlanta Third World Film Festival:

Then I moved to Atlanta in 1974. Louis Bilaggi Bailey and Richard Hudlin (kin to the Hudlin brothers) were programming independent black films, and every once in a while a filmmaker would come through and we would show films at my house because I had a big old sloppy house and I didn't care if you moved things around and dropped things. Bailey founded the Atlanta Annual [*sic*] Third World Film Festival and attempted to program films from around the world. The Festival became a genuinely international event when Cheryl Chisolm took over as director.[36]

Bambara's interest in independent cinema tied her to the Atlanta arts community. Bambara saw the promise of independent cinema, particularly the works of filmmakers in the LA Film Rebellion and Third World Cinema movements, for producing films that contested the legitimacy of American imperialism in the world and on the screen.

In "Why Black Cinema?" (1987), which serves as her Black independent film manifesto, Bambara explained that the real products of the entertainment industry were ideas of inferiority, hierarchy, and stasis.[37] "Hollyweird," as she termed it, would "annex the global mind by annexing the global screen, maintaining control over the production, distribution and exhibition."[38] To confront this annexing of the global mind, Bambara not only outlined the cinematic conventions that conceal this takeover—the advancement of individualism and other bourgeois values, visual opulence, and so on—but also pointed out that the "flat, dull/normal propagandizing images pleading 'We, too, are clean,' 'We deserve the vote'" were not up to the tasks of decolonizing the global mind or the global screen.[39] Thus, for Bambara, exploring alternative film conventions, aesthetics, and language was an opportunity to reimagine care and design liberatory practices.

Bambara's explicit turn to filmmaking coincided with her move to Philadelphia in 1985. The move, a crucial turning point in her career as a cultural worker, brought Bambara into new cinematic and activist circles. She started working at Louis Massiah's Scribe Video Center shortly after her arrival. Working as a production facilitator for Massiah's Community Visions, Bambara taught script-writing classes and held workshops for the community.[40] Through her work at the Scribe Center, she connected with activist groups mobilizing around homelessness in Philadelphia at the time, including the Committee for Dignity and Fairness for the Homeless, the National Union of the Homeless, and the Have Nots, a homeless theater group. These groups often collaborated with the Scribe Center on various activist projects, so Bambara gained intimate knowledge of these activist works and local political strategies, including building takeovers.

A significant outcome of Bambara's work at Scribe was *The Bombing of Osage Avenue* (dir. Louis J. Massiah, 1987), a film that chronicled the 1985 bombing of Philadelphia's MOVE organization. When Philadelphia police bombed the Osage

Avenue residence of MOVE, a Black radical organization originally known as the Christian Movement for Life, they claimed to be responding to complaints from residents of Philadelphia's Cobbs Creek neighborhood that the MOVE house was unsanitary and that its residents habitually disturbed the neighborhood's peace with their use of a loudspeaker to call attention to the state's anti-Black violence. The police emptied ten thousand rounds of ammunition at the home, used tear gas to drive the residents out, and dropped bombs on the house, starting a fire that killed eleven people, displaced over two hundred more, and destroyed sixty-one homes. Recognizing that "official versions" of the bombing obscured state surveillance, and nurturing her desire to profile the state's manipulation of discourses of protection and safety, Bambara suggested that she and Massiah produce a film that would be a "community voice video" that detailed the perspectives of residents from that community.

Bambara wrote and narrated the film. Her narration, importantly, forecasts the living-in that she thematized in her later film work. Rather than portray the state violence of MOVE as exceptional, Bambara narrates the bombing as the continuation of the violence of settler colonialism, white vigilante violence, and police brutality. As her biographer Linda Holmes writes: "Bambara approached the subject as an integral part of the community whose story she was telling, serving in the role of community scribe. She eschewed the third-person authoritarian, uninvolved voice that was standard for documentaries of the period." Instead, she spoke in the voice of "a mother and neighbor living in the community under siege."[41] Her voice-over emphasizes that Cobbs Creek was built on Lenape land, and the film's interview footage gives narrative power to elderly residents and children; both of these tactics train viewers of the film to value the community members' situated knowledge and, through their eyes, to understand the state as the arbiter of violence.

In *The Bombing of Osage Avenue* Bambara's narration emphasizes that the impact of state violence is not simply felt in the moment of its occurrence but unfolds in its long aftermath: the physical displacement of Cobbs Creek residents and the fracturing of communal values such as trust and friendship. When the film pictures scenes of living-in, it is this displacement and fracturing that it addresses: not simply the *event* of the bombing but the bombing's *sequelae*, to use Smith's term. Near the end of the film, an interview shot outdoors shows a middle-aged Cobbs Creek resident struggling with his guilt. The resident admits that he feels guilty for asking the police to do something about the MOVE home: "I was agonizing because that's not what I asked for, that's not what I expected." In response, Bambara's voice-over narrates a scene of communal care. The camera shows survivors of the bombing coming together to grieve and move forward. Elders gather in what appears to be a church fellowship hall around tables covered with cloths. One table holds construction paper signs with handwritten words: CARE, PEACE, PATIENCE. While the camera zooms in on those words, Bambara's voice-over calls attention to the state's—rather than the residents'—responsibility for its violent assistance, reframing the interviewee's "agonizing" as an irrational response to the state's vertical care: "Irrational guilt, the therapists say. For it wasn't the residents who requisitioned the powerful military explosive from the FBI. No resident transported the plastique to Osage in a bomb squad vehicle. No resident picked up a Thompson automatic or an Uzi machine gun, on loan from the federal bureau. Or ordered up that helicopter borrowed from the state patrol." As the film visualizes care *from among* rather than care *from above*, its audible narrative exposes the gratuitous violence that the state wraps in care. As Hobart and Kneese suggest, radical care comprises forms of mutual aid that helps those who are neglected or actively abandoned by the state and other institutions. Radical care, *The Bombing of Osage Avenue* suggests, also provides material and affective mutual aid in the aftermath of the state's violent intrusions into the worlds and lives of those populations most often called on to supply its care work. The fellowship hall in the film is a site of what Bambara came to imagine more fully as living-in.

Bambara's work in culture, specifically film, offered radical Black feminist aesthetics as a rejoinder to state ideologies of care that situated Black communities as reservoirs of care labor while making them subject to the state's violent incursions, which themselves were articulated as acts of care. In this way, Bambara joined other Black feminists in theorizing state violence and imagining workable ways of regenerating life in its aftermath. In Bambara's speculative film work, this regeneration was imagined as living-in, a fuller inhabitation of the fellowship-hall practices of horizontal care.

Living-In and the Black Feminist Geography of Care

On the same day that the Philadelphia police bombed MOVE and leveled sixty-one homes in Cobbs Creek, construction workers in downtown Philadelphia broke ground on One Liberty Place, the luxury skyscraper that became the city's tallest structure the following year. The simultaneity of these two events brings into sharp relief the vertical geometry of power that we have outlined: the promise and possibility of upward mobility was linked to the state's gratuitous aerial assault on Black life. While the MOVE bombing was the catalyst for Bambara and Massiah's first cinematic collaboration, the occupation and takeover of One Liberty Place in 1987 by members of the National Union of the Homeless would be one of the catalysts for another cinematic collaboration, *Come as You Are*.

We have argued that Bambara's culture work articulated a Black feminist geometry that theorized the state's violent care as violence, critiqued bourgeois upward mobility, and offered horizontal modes of care, particularly living-in, as vertical power's utopian alternative. In this last section, we turn to Bambara's treatment for *Come as You Are*. We chose this text not only because of what its narrative reveals about feminist theories of state violence but also because Bambara's decolonizing film language *aestheticizes* and clarifies Black feminist critiques of state violence's pretense of care. *Come as You Are* is a treatment for a film that Bambara hoped would be her first feature film. As Holmes explains, Bambara conceived of the film when she organized with unhoused people in Philadelphia alongside her longtime collaborator and friend Louis Massiah. Working together at Scribe, Bambara and Massiah shared their cinematic expertise and resources with the National Union of the Homeless and Dignity Housing as the latter mounted takeovers of luxury, high-rise buildings. "In the late 1980s," Massiah explains, "very few people had access to cameras, editing, or the knowledge of how to make a film." Therefore organizations would call the Scribe Center and ask them to come out and record the building takeovers. "We were their media," Massiah says.[42] Rather than appeal to the state to solve the problem of houselessness, the National Union used takeovers to mark the withholding of shelter as an example of state violence and to "embarrass the city, embarrass the developers, etc."[43] The outcome of these collaborations between Scribe and the housing organizations were short documentaries like *The Taking of One Liberty Place* and *Mayday Takeover* as well as the Community Visions workshop designed to pair experienced filmmakers with community organizations to share cinematic resources and knowledge.[44]

Come as You Are* was designed to reflect and distribute the kinds of guerrilla actions Scribe was documenting. "Focused on the growing insurgency of the homeless movement," Holmes writes, Bambara "wanted to include stories emanating from the homeless that included ceremonies narrated in Spanish, Haitian Creole, Lakota, and Greek."[45] Crafted as a heteroglossic, polyglot collection of stories about housing resistance, the film was to offer a moving picture of Bambara's theory of how state violence operates on a vertical axis of care. While Bambara never secured adequate funding to produce the film, the treatment she wrote allows us to imagine what might have been and to embrace her own belief in the utopian power of what might have been. This is to follow the film theorist Allyson Field's suggestion that feminist film history is necessarily speculative. Indeed, Field not only suggests that film history's positivist tendencies have narrowed the field's focus to extant film and its surviving evidence, but she also argues that film historians' speculative research on "nonextant film" could follow Black filmmakers' own engagement with archival absence as an invitation to collaborative, creative engagement. Of invented archives in films such as Cheryl Dunye's 1996 *The Watermelon Woman*, Julie Dash's 1982 *Illusions*, Zeinabu Davis's 1999 *Compensation*, and Garret Bradley's 2019 *America*, Field writes, "In replacing the nonextant with the reimagined, these filmmakers arguably create a speculative archive of images and ephemera that serve as visible evidence for an otherwise inaccessible history."[46] In this case, we consider *Come as You Are*'s status as a nonextant film—nonextant because it was never filmed or screened—as an invitation to find "innovative ways of working with absence, erasure, silences and loss," a utopian training in "what can't be seen."[47] We view the treatment as the reality Bambara imagined it to be, not only to extend the capacious body of work on her radical uses of narrative forms but also to suggest that attention to her decolonizing film language expands our understanding of how radical Black feminism theorizes state violence.

The treatment for *Come as You Are* conforms to the expectations of film treatments: it is a dynamic summary of a film meant to sway those with the means to produce it. But, in a way that recalls L. H. Stallings's suggestion that Black feminist treatments are both practical and curative—"portals into the interior worlds of those attempting to create or speculate about alternative realities," as Stallings describes them—Bambara's treatment visualizes utopian alternatives to state violence.[48] These alternatives, importantly, do not depend on citizens' reparative appeals. Rather, they are called into being by decolonizing forces that *horizontalize* the power that the state asserts vertically. Indeed, Bambara's film treatment exposes a *geometry of state power* characterized by a hierarchical architecture of care and protocols of vertical ascent. We argue that to combat this geometry of state power and scale its architecture, Bambara visualizes what Sharpe describes as *lateral care* in various forms throughout the treatment. The film follows several characters "in varying states of homelessness" who move errantly throughout the city. During a citywide power outage, when the main characters are all trapped in a subway car, the unhoused organize to take over a luxury high-rise that is temporarily vacant because its developers are awaiting a court decision.[49] They then commandeer the camera, documenting their live-in, and, in an act of radical Third Cinema pedagogy, record a "How-To Primer" (2).

While the collective might be said, in the idiom of Black culture, to have "moved on up," we suggest that in the context of the film treatment's geometry of state power, the live-in sketches power horizontally, replacing vertical forms of repair with radical care. The "welfare-hotel syndicate" erects its policy from above, temporizing as its "200 houses for the homeless program" languishes, and the middle-class and wealthy Philadelphians in the film ascend to thirty-story sky-rises and move along "'escalator' type skywalks" (13a). But the unhoused in Bambara's treatment—a jilted twenty-seven-year-old mother of three with no potential for upward mobility at her fast-food-restaurant job, a plumber who works odd jobs and falls behind on his rent, an "elderly white guy, three-time rehabilitated drunk" (2), a woman in professional wear who wanders from bench to bench in search of a place to read, and Burma Road, an elderly nonbinary character who lives underground and leads the group through the subway channels—move through the city on, around, and under its horizontal grid. Jenelle Tillinghast, the fast-food worker, and the professional-looking "Woman in Gray" board a bus to a shelter, which ends up taking them on an "endless roundabout ride to nowhere, since the shelters are filled" (13); Burma Road nurtures a daily ritual of wandering to the river; and they agonize in lines for shelter and services. The main characters experience precarity as a consignment to horizontality, a life "on the slide" (6); they also *live in*, or live into, this horizontality. We might see Burma Road's wanderings, for example, as ramblings in which "free black worlds become possible."[50] But we also might note that before the collective takes over the luxury condo complex, Bambara previews the lateral care of the live-in. When Jenelle is evicted with her children, and her husband, Cordell, has left with another woman, she finds shelter at her coworker's temporary home, the house of her uncle who is away at sea: "Night Time. Jenelle is put up by Alysha. It's a warm and noisy household. A sewing machine being gunned. A card game. Someone in the kitchen fixing dinners to sell to barber shop and beauty parlor people. Teenagers coming and going, delivering the foil-covered plastic plates. Boom box going, TV's going" (10). The scene imagines characters crisscrossing each other's paths, cross-talking one another, saturating the horizontal grid with noise, play, food, and underground commerce. This is perhaps what Stefano Harney and Fred Moten mean by "planning" when they refer to "those who plan together," who participate "without fully entering this dim enlightenment, without fully functioning families and financial responsibility, without respect for the rule of law, without distance and irony, without submission to the rule of expertise." Their participation is "too loud, too fat, too loving, too full, too flowing, too dread; this leads to crisis."[51] The planners in Alysha's household lack the aerial perspective of the developers. They are understood by policymakers, to quote Harney and Moten again, as "out of joint—instead of positing their position in contingency, they seek solidity in a mobile place from which to plan, some hold in which to imagine, some love on which to count."[52] Alysha's home pictures Bambara's Black feminist geometry of power, her radical deverticalization of care.

While Bambara previews the lateral care of the live-in in the scene in Alysha's home, she also previews the corporate media's commitment to disrupting horizontality and perpetuating a vertical logic of care. As the people in Alysha's home plan together, the television in the background is playing commentary from the Iran-Contra hearings. Rather than analyze Oliver North's testimony critically, Bambara notes that the "network folks . . . act like performance art critics, speaking on the charisma, voice pitch, and telegenic nature of Oliver North" (10). In this seemingly fleeting detail, Bambara highlights how the corporate media functions in this vertical logic of care, especially following the radical breaches of the state in the 1960s and 1970s. By deemphasizing the illegal sale of weapons during the Iran-Contra affair, which led to state violence against the Sandinistas in Nicaragua, and characterizing North as desirable and aesthetically pleasing, the "network folks" attempt to repair any damage to North's reputation and, by extension, to restore viewers' faith in the state and the project of neoliberal democracy writ large. Within this vertical logic of care, not only is the state the sole arbiter of legitimate forms of care—justifying waging hemispheric war as a means of "caring" for American citizenry—but it is the only political formation worthy of citizens' care. That care is to be demonstrated via total acquiescence to state power, unconditional support of its officials, and the condemnation of anyone who would challenge, critique, and/or attack the state. With trust in the state and neoliberal democracy restored, viewers will redirect their care away from anti-imperialist, transnational solidarities and bestow it back onto the state. The network commentary and the hearings are not representations of justice or truth finding but preliminary steps in the process of sanitizing and rebranding war criminals into media personalities and endearing them to American viewers. It should come as no surprise, then, that North went on to have his own nationally syndicated radio show, the *Oliver North Radio Show*, from 1995 to 2003 and hosted a television show from 2001 to 2016 called *War Stories with Oliver North*. One could speculate that the aestheticizing commentary on the Iran-Contra hearings was a precursor to his transition into a conservative media personality. While the observation of the aestheticizing commentary is not attributed to a specific character in Bambara's treatment, the observation introduces the corporate media's reparative function in this vertical logic of care into the film while also gesturing toward the "second sight" required to withhold one's care for and trust in the state.[53]

The film treatment does not focus on a single protagonist; this is important, given its interest in narrative horizontality. Still, much of the narrative revolves around Jenelle and her search for home. Effectively a single parent, Jenelle finds her livelihood and shelter precarious. Her subplot makes the family a smaller model of Bambara's geometry of state power: just as the welfare-hotel syndicate's care from above reproduces conditions of precarity that lock the characters of the film into a horizontality that they come to claim as a radical prompting, the bourgeois family's fallacy of protection shatters, and this pushes Jenelle into a horizontality that she will turn to radical ends. While Jenelle dreams of "becoming a makeup artist to Patti LaBelle" (1), her trajectory in the treatment is downward or, at best, lateral rather than upward. Early in the text, when Jenelle leaves her apartment to take her children to school, she sees an eviction notice on her door. Bambara specifies that the eviction be filmed in a way that captures the fracturing effect of unhousing: "Disparate images are caught in the mirror of [Jenelle's] wardrobe being set on the sidewalk with her other belongings. We view the children's things through the triangular frame of the ironing board upended. Logic sprung by the surreal nature of reflected objects topsy-turvy, we then begin to view the 'economy'" (9). The camera would then capture what Bambara refers to as "'economy' images" (9) through a triangular frame created by a hanging scale. It is through a depersonalized view through a dispossessed mirror, then, that viewers come to apprehend Jenelle's crisis. With things unmoored from possession and personhood unmoored from place, the film tracks Jenelle's quest to make a life without home.

The eviction dislodges the desire for upward mobility and household stability suggested by Jenelle's dream of becoming a cosmetologist and her former life with

Cordell. The prologue of the film shows Jenelle in a salon, "demonstrating cosmetics and taking orders" to supplement her income (6). At her fast-food job, Jenelle works with a manager whose "prerogative and bluster" disallow opportunities for advancement (8). When the cash register breaks, Jenelle is shot "showing off her ability to add, subtract, make change without the benefit of the computer register" (8). The manager is not impressed, and Jenelle attempts to "show her managerial stuff" by throwing Burma Road out of the restaurant (8). Unable to advance at work and left without the protections and seductions of the bourgeois family ideal, Jenelle is "on the slide" into the lateral life. After the eviction, she leaves the children with Cordell and his lover for the night and stays with Alysha in the "warm and noisy" workup of the live-in (10). Next she visits a social service center and is defeated by the "lines at every counter" (11).[54] The social services office gathers a striking image of horizontal gridding: children sleep on counters and desks, and mothers gather in stairwells to breastfeed. Spatiotemporally suspended in government care, mothers and children layer on top of one another and crowd into and around the horizontal lines that are "everywhere" (11). At her fast-food job later, Jenelle works at the cash register while watching her kids in the booth. When another worker gives her children free milk—we have learned earlier that their school ended its free milk program—Jenelle is fired. She is then pictured on a bus, on an "endless roundabout ride to nowhere, since shelters are filled" (13).

Importantly, the characters' relationship to the camera projects the degree to which they value horizontality; interactions with the camera come to mark the characters' cultivation of lateral care. Jenelle's addresses to the camera exemplify this relation. When she watches Cordell drive off in the film's prologue, for example, she ignores the camera. Bambara writes, "To the degree that Jenelle and others disacknowledge street folks, is the degree that they are not aware of the camera" (6). Jenelle later disdains the camera and, by extension, the *street folks*. At the women's shelter where Hector, a nineteen-year-old Latinx man and a central figure in the treatment, works security, she "confronts Camera, 'What the hell are you looking at?'" (12). But eventually, when the power goes out at the film's climax, Jenelle repositions herself in relation to, in relationship with, the camera. During the power outage, Jenelle exits the subway car with her children and enters the underground city. In this underground space, Jenelle follows the underground dwellers to Burma Road's living space and looks at "the newsclippings and magazine tear sheets Burma Road has used to wallpaper her dwelling." She is "drawn to a particular building. Unfinished in actuality, the sketches of what it will look like attract her" (16). Here it is through Jenelle's perspective that the film displays the speculative promise of the horizontal: the long look at Burma Road's underground living room decor gives way to the fugitive planning session in which the stranded, unhoused characters "seriously [begin] to make out what would be involved in a take over [*sic*]" (16). Here, crucially, they "adjust their bodies to let the Camera join the circle" (16). As the camera enters the planning circle, its capacity to distribute attention laterally, around the circle, corresponds to the group's growing sense of lateral affectivity. At the end of the film, the group's practice of horizontal care—joined by the camera, a jovial participant in the live-in—culminates in the group's "getting together and directing the Camera to move here, there" (17). As the group drafts press releases and issues calls to the press, "Jenelle and a few others take a good, long look into the lens and then take over the camera as people move into the luxury [*sic*] building for a live-in. etc." (17). Jenelle and the other characters take over the means of storytelling, and caring, as they take over the building. But the takeover, again, must be understood not as an antagonistic staking claim to bourgeois property and home but as a staging of a life in common, in horizontality. Jenelle's subplot makes this orientation to bourgeois notions of family clear: while she is in the subway tunnel going horizontal, Cordell is shown desperately trying to acquire the means to get back to Philadelphia from Atlantic City, where he has gone with his lover. But his attempt to restore the family, to assert his vertical care, fails. Jenelle's recourse—her resource—is the turn to horizontality exemplified by the embracing turn to the camera.

While Jenelle explores horizontality underground, Hector engages the speculative promise of horizontality above ground. Hector's trajectory in the treatment, like Jenelle's, is downward, quite literally; while bartending at an art show in a loft gallery in the prologue of the treatment, he descends to navigate the city's horizontal grid and limited economic opportunities that range from the blood bank to the army recruiting center and the pawn shop before "choosing" to work as a security guard at the women's shelter. Having decided against seeking employment in the army recruiting center, Hector looks laterally, toward the women in the shelter, to participate in the building takeover during the power outage.

Before we explore the lateral army that Hector and the women in the shelter form at the end of the treatment, it is important to note the means by which Hector becomes involved in the building takeover. During the power outage, members of the welfare-hotel syndicate attack an organizer of the "Street Forces." Students who are participating in a shantytown protest to encourage their university to divest from South Africa witness the attack and rush to help the organizer. Though Bambara had been part of radical movements on university campuses—during her time as an instructor for the SEEK program at City College alongside figures like Addison Gayle, Larry Neal, June Jordan, Barbara Christian, and Audre Lorde, for example—and had published her vision for a Black university in the 1970s, the university depicted in *Come as You Are* has extinguished the radical potential cultivated on college campuses in the previous decade. On this university campus, the administration orders physical plant workers to destroy the shantytown, and when they refuse, "the administration has gotten hold of some student government reps to testify that whenever they pass the maintenance office, they smell marijuana" (14–15).

The university administration functions as another node in the vertical construction of power, not only in its surveillance from the top but also in the ways it seeks to disrupt and foreclose horizontality between students and university staff. The administration incentivizes and deputizes student government members to surveil and accuse the physical plant workers of drug use while wielding the threat of carcerality to force physical plant workers to destroy students' attempts at practicing a transnational, anti-imperialist solidarity. In the background of the campus conflict, on a portable Sony television in the campus security booth, President Reagan is shaking the hand of "a local white boy of Philly who used his allowance to purchase blankets and sandwiches for the homeless" (15). Analogous to North's presence being invoked in the Iran-Contra hearings commentary playing in the background of Alysha's home earlier in the treatment, Bambara inserts this image of Reagan in the treatment both to invite readers to consider connections between domestic state violence and imperial violence abroad and to critique the media for insulating state officials from critique by presenting them as arbiters of care and generosity. In this scene, Reagan celebrates the "generosity" and "philanthropy" of the white child even though his policies have produced and exacerbated hunger and homelessness both domestically and abroad. While the media clip depicts Reagan as a generous, caring, paternal figure, Bambara's cinematic vision positions him as a central antagonist to lateral practices of care and solidarity.

As the conflict between the supporters of the organizer and the welfare-hotel syndicate escalates and spills out into a courtyard and the streets, Hector is rushed by people telling him about the attack on the organizer and the welfare-hotel syndicate's threats of violence against anyone participating in a building takeover. When Hector proceeds to call his boys to join him in fighting, they respond that their "throw down days are over" (16). Without support from his boys, Hector turns to the women in the shelter:

Hector motions for the Camera to follow him. The women are on cots
discussing what kitchens would be like if women designed homes. This carries
then into a discussion of what homes would be like if women designed them.
Then what buildings and streets would be like if homeless designed them.
One woman says, they'd be so hip, everybody would copy. . . . They make
room on the cot for Camera, turning to invite Hector to join the circle too.
He's a good guy. (17)

While it is Jenelle's long look at Burma Road's living room decor that gives way to fugitive planning underground, in the shelter, it is the continuous unfurling of "what would be" questions that create the conditions of horizontality and lateral care. With each question, the scale of the women's designs enlarges, leading to the literal and lateral expanding of their circle to make room for Hector and the camera. This "roundabout" geometry imagines a way to live into the horizontal grid of the city and to refuse the verticality of the state. Moreover, while the treatment suggests that the women compose the only army or navy that Hector could "raise," he is not invited into their designing because of his position in a gendered hierarchy, as he might have been had he chosen to go into the army recruiting center at the opening of the treatment. Instead, he is invited to join for his goodness—perhaps, his lateral care. In both the underground and aboveground scenes, Bambara's characters realize the potential of living-in through a rejection of state-sanctioned notions of care, domesticity, and security.

Though *Come as You Are* never made it to screens, its invitation to live on the slide remains urgent. As Black women are rapidly ascending vertical lines of power in the government and the academy, the media encourages us to embrace, not critique, their ascensions, consigning us all to verticality in the name of "Black excellence," "Black feminism," and "Black girl magic." The unfinished works of Toni Cade Bambara and other radical Black feminist cultural workers, however, offer a geometric reorientation and a cultural history of contra-state forms of care and repair.

Randi Gill-Sadler is an assistant professor of English and Africana studies at Davidson College. Her work has been published in *Feminist Formations*, *Small Axe*, and the edited volume *Digital Humanities, Libraries, and Partnerships: A Critical Examination of Labor, Networks, and Community* (2018). Her research interests include Black women's literary history, Black feminist literature, and US cultures of imperialism.

Erica R. Edwards is a professor of African American studies and English at Yale University. She is the author of *The Other Side of Terror: Black Women and the Culture of US Empire* (2021), which was awarded the John Hope Franklin Prize from the American Studies Association. Her first book, *Charisma and the Fictions of Black Leadership* (2012), was awarded the Modern Language Association's William Sanders Scarborough Prize. She is the editor, with Roderick A. Ferguson and Jeffrey O. G. Ogbar, of *Keywords for African American Studies* (2018).

Notes

1. Campt, "Black Visuality and the Practice of Refusal."
2. Hobart and Kneese, "Radical Care," 2, 4.
3. Thuma, *All Our Trials*, 46.
4. Bernstein, "Sexual Politics of the 'New Abolitionism,'" 143.
5. See Edwards, *Other Side of Terror*. Cathy Cohen theorizes this pattern of inclusion as "advanced marginalization," the "symbolic opening of dominant society," a "model of inclusion premised on the idea that formal rights are to be granted only to those who demonstrate adherence to dominant norms of work, love, and social interaction" (*Boundaries of Blackness*, 63–64).
6. Wynter, "Unsettling the Coloniality of Being/Power/Truth/Freedom."
7. Edwards, *Other Side of Terror*, 216.
8. Sharpe, *In the Wake*, 20.
9. See Bambara, foreword, xlii–xliii.
10. Hong, *Death beyond Disavowal*, 7.
11. Hong, *Death beyond Disavowal*, 9.

12. Crenshaw, "Mapping the Margins," 1241.

13. See Roberts, *Killing the Black Body*; and Roberts, *Shattered Bonds*.

14. On state violence against Black women, see Haley, *No Mercy Here*; Harris, "'Commonwealth of Virginia vs. Virginia Christian'"; Hartman, *Scenes of Subjection*; Gilmore, *Golden Gulag*; Maynard, *Policing Black Lives*; and Ritchie, *Invisible No More*.

15. Smith, "Counting Frequency," 32.

16. Hartman, *Lose Your Mother*, 170.

17. Gilmore, "In the Shadow of the Shadow State," 229–30.

18. Gilmore, "In the Shadow of the Shadow State," 234.

19. *Lessons from the Damned*, 14.

20. *Lessons from the Damned*, 44.

21. Black Women's Revolutionary Council Sign Up Sheet, 1980; Papers of Pat Parker, 1944–1998, MC 861, folder 13.5, Schlesinger Library, Radcliffe Institute, Harvard University. All quotations in this paragraph are taken from this folder.

22. Gordon, *Hawthorn Archive*, 40.

23. On the expansive uses of the choreopoem and invented languages, see Sullivan, *Poetics of Difference*. On Black feminists' "insurgent grammars," see Edwards, *Other Side of Terror*. On Black feminist musicians and critics as agents of an "intellectual revolution in Black feminist sound," see Brooks, *Liner Notes for the Revolution*, 9.

24. On the Sisterhood as an example of progressive Black feminist literary organizing, see Thorsson, *Sisterhood*.

25. Wall, "Toni's Obligato," 27.

26. Griffin, "That the Mothers May Soar," 485.

27. Quoted in Tate, "Toni Cade Bambara," 60.

28. Edwards, *Other Side of Terror*, 25.

29. Melamed, *Represent and Destroy*, 98.

30. Quoted in Tate, "Toni Cade Bambara," 60.

31. Quoted in Tate, "Toni Cade Bambara," 60.

32. Bambara, "Salvation Is the Issue," 43.

33. Bambara, "Salvation Is the Issue," 43.

34. Holmes, *Joyous Revolt*, 101. Bambara had met Humberto Solás, director of *Lucia* (1968), on a previous trip to Cuba and had featured the essay "Are the Revolutionary Techniques Employed in *The Battler of Algiers* Applicable to Harlem?"

35. Holmes, *Joyous Revolt*, 102.

36. Holmes, *Joyous Revolt*, 127.

37. Bambara, "Why Black Cinema?," 200.

38. Bambara, "Why Black Cinema?," 199–205.

39. Bambara, "Why Black Cinema?," 200.

40. Holmes, *Joyous Revolt*, 206. For more about Bambara's classes at the Scribe Video Center and their influence on other independent Black filmmakers, see Simmons, "Asserting My In(ter)dependence."

41. Holmes, *Joyous Revolt*, 169.

42. Louis Massiah, interview by Randi Gill-Sadler, Zoom, October 14, 2022.

43. Massiah, interview.

44. Massiah, interview.

45. Holmes, *Joyous Revolt*, 170.

46. Field, "Editor's Introduction," 5. See also Field, *Uplift Cinema*.

47. Field, "Editor's Introduction," 7. On Bambara's utopian "reality principle," in which dreams function as a reality to which we hold ourselves accountable, as "a supremely material way of conceiving our relationship to the systems that attempt to control and dehumanize us," see Gordon, *Hawthorn Archive*, 34–49.
48. Stallings, *Afterlives*, 94.
49. Toni Cade Bambara, "Come as You Are," undated typescript, Spelman College Archives. Hereafter cited with parenthetical page numbers in the text.
50. Cervenak, *Wandering*, 23.
51. Harney and Moten, *Undercommons*, 81.
52. Harney and Moten, *Undercommons*, 78.
53. Bambara, "Deep Sightings and Rescue Missions," 174.
54. In the typescript draft, *at every counter* is crossed out and the word *everywhere* is written above it.

References

Bambara, Toni Cade. "Deep Sight and Rescue Missions." In *Deep Sightings and Rescue Missions: Fiction, Essays, and Conversations*, by Toni Cade Bambara and Toni Morrison, 146–78. New York: Pantheon, 1996.

Bambara, Toni Cade. Foreword to *This Bridge Called My Back: Writings by Radical Women of Color*, edited by Gloria Anzaldúa and Cherríe Moraga, xl–xliii. Berkeley, CA: Third Woman, 2002.

Bambara, Toni Cade. "Salvation Is the Issue." In *Black Women Writers (1950–1980): A Critical Evaluation*, edited by Mari Evans, 41–47. New York: Anchor Press/Doubleday, 1984.

Bambara, Toni Cade. "Why Black Cinema?" In *Savoring the Salt: The Legacy of Toni Cade Bambara*, edited by Linda Janet Holmes and Cheryl A. Wall, 199–205. Philadelphia: Temple University Press, 2007.

Bernstein, Elizabeth. "The Sexual Politics of the 'New Abolitionism.'" *differences* 18, no. 3 (2007): 128–51.

Brooks, Daphne A. *Liner Notes for the Revolution: The Intellectual Life of Black Feminist Sound*. Cambridge, MA: Harvard University Press, 2021.

Campt, Tina. "Black Visuality and the Practice of Refusal." *Women and Performance*, February 25, 2019. https://www.womenandperformance.org/ampersand/29-1/campt.

Cervenak, Sarah Jane. *Wandering: Philosophical Performances of Racial and Sexual Freedom*. Durham, NC: Duke University Press, 2014.

Cohen, Cathy J. *The Boundaries of Blackness: AIDS and the Breakdown of Black Politics*. Chicago: University of Chicago Press, 1999.

Covington, Francee. "Are the Revolutionary Techniques Employed in *The Battle of Algiers* Applicable to Harlem?" In *The Black Woman: An Anthology*, edited by Toni Cade Bambara, 313–22. New York: New American Library, 1970.

Crenshaw, Kimberlé. "Mapping the Margins: Intersectionality, Identity Politics, and Violence against Women of Color." *Stanford Law Review* 43, no. 6 (1991): 1241–99.

Edwards, Erica R. *The Other Side of Terror: Black Women and the Culture of US Empire*. New York: New York University Press, 2021.

Field, Allyson Nadia. "Editor's Introduction: Sites of Speculative Encounter." *Feminist Media Histories* 8, no. 2 (2022): 1–13.

Field, Allyson Nadia. *Uplift Cinema: The Emergence of African American Film and the Possibility of Black Modernity*. Durham, NC: Duke University Press, 2015.

Gilmore, Ruth Wilson. *Golden Gulag: Prisons, Surplus, Crisis, and Opposition in Globalizing California.* Berkeley: University of California Press, 2007.

Gilmore, Ruth Wilson. "In the Shadow of the Shadow State." In *Abolition Geography: Essays towards Liberation*, edited by Brenna Bhandar and Alberto Toscano, 224–41. London: Verso, 2022.

Gordon, Avery F. *The Hawthorn Archive: Letters from the Utopian Margins.* New York: Fordham University Press, 2017.

Griffin, Farah Jasmine. "That the Mothers May Soar and the Daughters May Know Their Names: A Retrospective of Black Feminist Literary Criticism." *Signs* 32, no. 2 (2007): 483–507.

Haley, Sarah. *No Mercy Here: Gender, Punishment, and the Making of Jim Crow Modernity.* Chapel Hill: University of North Carolina Press, 2016.

Harney, Stefano, and Fred Moten. *The Undercommons: Fugitive Planning and Black Study.* New York: Minor Compositions, 2013.

Harris, Lashawn. "The '*Commonwealth of Virginia vs. Virginia Christian*': Southern Black Women, Crime, and Punishment in Progressive Era Virginia." *Journal of Social History* 47, no. 4 (2014): 922–42.

Hartman, Saidiya V. *Lose Your Mother: A Journey along the Atlantic Slave Route.* New York: Farrar, Straus and Giroux, 2007.

Hartman, Saidiya V. *Scenes of Subjection: Terror, Slavery, and Self-Making in Nineteenth-Century America.* New York: Oxford University Press, 1997.

Hobart, Hiʻilei Julia Kawehipuaakahaopulani, and Tamara Kneese. "Radical Care: Survival Strategies for Uncertain Times." *Social Text*, no. 142 (2020): 1–16.

Holmes, Linda Janet. *A Joyous Revolt: Toni Cade Bambara, Writer and Activist.* Santa Barbara, CA: Praeger, 2014.

Hong, Grace Kyungwon. *Death beyond Disavowal: The Impossible Politics of Difference.* Minneapolis: University of Minnesota Press, 2015.

Lessons from the Damned: Class Struggle in the Black Community, by the Damned. New York: Times Change Press, 1973.

Maynard, Robyn. *Policing Black Lives: State Violence in Canada from Slavery to the Present.* Winnipeg, MB: Fernwood, 2017.

Melamed, Jodi. *Represent and Destroy: Rationalizing Violence in the New Racial Capitalism.* Minneapolis: University of Minnesota Press, 2011.

Ritchie, Andrea J. *Invisible No More: Police Violence against Black Women and Women of Color.* Boston: Beacon, 2017.

Roberts, Dorothy. *Killing the Black Body: Race, Reproduction, and the Meaning of Liberty.* New York: Knopf Doubleday, 2014.

Roberts, Dorothy. *Shattered Bonds: The Color of Child Welfare.* New York: Civitas Books, 2002.

Sharpe, Christina. *In the Wake: On Blackness and Being.* Durham, NC: Duke University Press, 2016.

Simmons, Aishah Shahidah. "Asserting My In(ter)dependence: The Evolution of NO!" In *Savoring the Salt: The Legacy of Toni Cade Bambara*, edited by Linda Janet Holmes and Cheryl A. Wall, 206–14. Philadelphia: Temple University Press, 2007.

Smith, Christen A. "Counting Frequency: Un/gendering Anti-Black Police Terror." *Social Text*, no. 147 (2021): 25–49.

Stallings, L. H. *The Afterlives of Kathleen Collins: A Black Woman Filmmaker's Search for New Life.* Bloomington: Indiana University Press, 2021.

Sullivan, Mecca Jamilah. *The Poetics of Difference: Queer Feminist Forms in the African Diaspora*. Urbana: University of Illinois Press, 2021.

Tate, Claudia. "Toni Cade Bambara." In *Conversations with Toni Cade Bambara*, edited by Thabiti Lewis, 49–72. Jackson: University Press of Mississippi, 2012.

Thorsson, Courtney. *The Sisterhood: How a Network of Black Women Writers Changed American Culture*. New York: Columbia University Press, forthcoming.

Thuma, Emily L. *All Our Trials: Prisons, Policing, and the Feminist Fight to End Violence*. Urbana: University of Illinois Press, 2019.

Wall, Cheryl A. "Toni's Obligato: Bambara and the African American Literary Tradition." In *Savoring the Salt: The Legacy of Toni Cade Bambara*, edited by Linda Janet Holmes and Cheryl A. Wall, 27–42. Philadelphia: Temple University Press, 2007.

Wynter, Sylvia. "Unsettling the Coloniality of Being/Power/Truth/Freedom: Towards the Human, after Man, Its Overrepresentation—an Argument." *CR: The New Centennial Review* 3, no. 3 (2003): 257–337.

"If You're Going to Be Beautiful, You Better Be Dangerous"

Sex Worker Community Defense

Heather Berg

"We wake up every morning and stretch our bodies," writes the Clandestine Whores Network in a dispatch on "a revolutionary horizon beyond the violent contradictions of a world we wish to leave behind." "There's an understanding of care, everyone knows that the goals to be won are not based on individual but collective skill." Armed cells can be called on for "revenge," and clients who cause harm "are not shown much mercy." The network trains in jujitsu "because learning to defend from the bottom when someone is in your guard is an important way to think about how to defend yourself when you're on your back, on your bed, weighed down being choked." After they train, organizers take time to dance, rest, and strategize. "Tonight," the network writes, "is a great night to refuse our deaths."[1]

The dispatch's language makes it clear that a war is raging. The network is made up of "cadres"; there is a "war room"; it articulates "occupation" as a "generalized . . . tactic."[2] This sense that there is a war on reverberates throughout sex worker radicals' thought. Non–sex workers are dubbed "civilians"; "Stop the war on whores!" reads a popular protest poster each year at International Day to End Violence against Sex Workers marches; sex workers organized in community defense assemble as "armies."

I asked Hookers Army Los Angeles (HALA) founder Vanessa Carlisle about the group's name and whether I was right to read it as a kind of confrontation, a

Radical History Review
Issue 148 (January 2024)   DOI 10.1215/01636545-10846865
© 2024 by MARHO: The Radical Historians' Organization, Inc.

threat. "Yes, yes," they replied, "the threat is the opposite of trying to get protection from the outside through proving ourselves deserving." A lot of policy advocacy seemed to attempt the "humanizing of the sex worker . . . always a woman who deserves to be protected from the harms of out-of-control masculinity." But the appeal never seems to work. Racist and anti-trans exclusions are built in to nominally protective policy, and the state forces being called on for protection are too often the same ones delivering the original harm. HALA refuses that sort of appeal. Instead, it says: "'I don't give a fuck about any of that. If you touch me in a way I don't like, you get hurt." "I really like the idea of us being able to say 'no,' and then backing up our 'nos.' . . . That's foundational for any kind of movement building to me." HALA is inspired here by histories of Black radicalism: "It's why people got so scared of the Panthers, they back up their 'no.'"

HALA is part of a broader movement in sex worker theory and practice. Refusing both sex workers' state-produced vulnerability to violence and the state's monopoly on violence, sex worker radicals articulate self-defense as a practice of community care. They investigate the history and theory of community defense through group study, train in defense tactics, and build networks to keep each other safe. In the process, contemporary sex worker thinkers search for conceptual resources in Black radical and anticolonial traditions of the latter half of the twentieth century—other communities whose members understood that their vulnerability to violence was structurally produced and thought about what it meant to "defend from the bottom." This article explores sex worker community defense with an eye to its relationship to past struggles and contributions to future ones. Chief among those is the contributions of the sex worker Left to the abolitionist struggle for a world beyond prisons and policing.

The essay is based in an archive of interviews with current and former sex workers who responded to my call for thinkers on the (self-defined) sex worker Left. It also draws on writing (e.g., zines, agitprop, and essays) by sex workers on the political Left broadly conceived. Our conversations focused on their thinking around key issues in left politics and on what moving through left spaces as sex-working people has taught them about politics. I approached our transcripts and their writings with an eye to the pressure points that emerge when sex workers read broader left thought against the grain of sex-working life. I also (re)read the texts they identified as formative in their thinking. When interlocutors make direct reference to a text, I cite this as part of the conversation; when their words conjure other thinkers in my own readings, I note these echoes.

Acutely understanding the violence of the carceral state, sex worker radicals come to their abolitionism organically. Sex workers—especially criminalized survivors—are a core abolitionist constituency. Yet sex worker abolitionists point to tenets in popular abolitionist discourse[3] that seem to be "not for us," as Clara, one interviewee in this project's archive, put it. Sex worker abolitionists identify a tension between many abolitionists' preference for a transformative justice that rejects all punitive responses to harm and the sense that transformation may not come without injury to those who profit from the status quo. Seeking historical resources for navigating tactical ambivalence in the present, many wonder if building new worlds will require a transitional program of militant community defense, even retribution. "I'm interested in art, writing and action that calls for autonomy, revenge or extra-legal refusal as opposed to justice, equality or legal recognition," writes Sophia Giovannitti.[4]

Sex workers' visions for what this might look like articulate a revision of "stranger danger" and a set of tactics that treats harm that comes from outside their communities differently than harm that comes from within. Some wonder if the popular abolitionist refrain that individual retribution cannot address structural harms still holds when individual violence does the work of a state that wants sex workers dead. Finally, some thinkers in this archive are frustrated with popular abolitionist discourse's line that punishment from individuals and communities mimics the carceral impulses of the state. They yearn for an abolitionism that views retribution from the people as distinct from violence from the state. If the most publicly visible abolitionist thought tends to treat the utility of violence and the temporality of defense as settled questions, sex worker abolitionists ask us to stay ambivalent.

The abolitionist thinker Dylan Rodríguez responds to a roundtable question on abolitionism's limits with the rejoinder that the better question is "how *multiple abolitionisms* can articulate with each other in a way that poses a legitimate threat to transform the current condition."[5] I am arguing here that sex worker abolitionisms can help do that articulating work. Their interventions can help us think through the politics of justice for sex workers, but also for other targets of harm that comes at the intersection of state and extrastate violence.

Violence as the Work of the State

Sex worker community defense emerges in response to state violence and state neglect, forces that converge to produce vulnerability to harm. The thinkers in this archive hail from criminalized, decriminalized, and legalized regimes and have a range of orientations to leftist politics—from socialist feminist to anarcho-communist. But they overwhelmingly agree that across these contexts and frames, no outside force can be counted on to keep sex workers safe. Yoshi Maximus put it this way: if you're "a sex worker, the police don't care about you. . . . If you're going to be beautiful, you better be dangerous."

Maximus is a sex worker who also moonlights as a bodyguard for other sex workers. Workers in his community have taken to "freestyling" (picking up clients in hotels or bars, rather than through web advertising) more often since the Stop Enabling Sex Traffickers Act (SESTA) undermined their ability to advertise online. But it is harder to screen for safety this way, so friends pay Maximus a small cut to wait outside during sessions, ready to step in if clients become violent. He started this practice because he himself had been "hurt, a lot." People target sex workers for harm, Maximus said, because "we're disposable people." The state manufactures that disposability and, at the same time, criminalizes workers' self-activity geared toward contesting it. Like others in this archive, Maximus has faced pimping charges for his community defense work.

Whether violence comes directly at the hands of state agents, as in the high incidence of police abuse, or from civilians, vulnerability to it is the work of what we might call "the state."[6] Here I am thinking with scholars of settler, anti-Black, and antiqueer and trans violence, who make a case for civilian violence as doing the white supremacist, capitalist state's work for it.[7] This can be true even if we know that the state is not a thing, that its logics are not uniform, and that state agents do not always work in concert.[8] Even in their incoherence, the forces that make up "the state" have a momentum. The state, such as it is, makes sex workers available for death, and then, writes Irene Silt, "our dead bodies serve as justification to fund vice units."[9] Those who cause harm do not work alone. This understanding of civilian violence as doing the work of the state shapes sex workers' critiques of the popular abolitionist line that individualized responses to violence never work; if abusers are not operating as individuals but rather as representatives of a structure, tactics that target the individual might weaken structures too. The *might* here is key because, as we will see, sex worker radicals are ambivalent about this potential.

That violence is state produced is doubly true when nonwhite, trans, poor, and youth workers are made vulnerable to harm. "Racist and sexist state practices" shape "the density and velocity" of the harms sex workers (and other "sexually policed" people) face, writes Anne Gray Fischer.[10] The sex worker theorist and abolitionist Chanelle Gallant told me that reckoning with this reality was politically "catalyzing" for her. Organizing in the wake of the 1980s and 1990s serial murders of forty-nine Vancouver sex workers, mostly Indigenous, she came to understand that "if capitalism and colonialism and patriarchy decide you're not worth anything to them, there's no safety net. You can just be picked off." From this Gallant learned that "sex workers needed to rely on each other to protect ourselves." They know policing offers no protection.

In carrying out the state's violent momentum, citizens take cues about who is available for disposal. "The police hunt down hookers, so the message is that anyone can hunt down hookers," remind the sex worker activists in Fischer's book.[11] The state, meanwhile, maintains its monopoly on violence by punishing sex workers who contest disposability. When carceral systems punish survivors who self-defend, this is to send a message to others who might too. Writing on criminalized self-defense more broadly, Victoria Law cites a 1978 case. The judge sentenced a woman who had shot her abusive husband to twenty years not to rehabilitate her, he said, but to "get the word out to other wives in similar circumstances."[12] This

gets the word out to abusers, too. When this same system metes out harsh punishment to people like Cyntoia Brown, a youth sex trafficking survivor originally sentenced to life for killing her adult assailant in self-defense, this communicates to
other abusers that the state is behind them, and to other survivors that to self-
defend is to risk further violence (this time directly from the state). Feminist antirape activists have long understood self-defense and community vigilantism as direct
challenges to the state's monopoly on violence, one reason the criminalized self-
defenders in Emily L. Thuma's history, sex workers among them, explicitly understood their position as "political prisoners." Thuma figures the Black, Brown, and
Indigenous, the crazy, and the sex working at the forefront of a politics that "analyzed the interrelationship of state abandonment and state violence."[13] Their
everyday acts of community care and self-preservation were the foundation of
the politics that flowed from them.

Though some make a case for "assuming positive intent," as Lady Elizabeth
put it, most of the sex workers in my interview archive had come to believe that the
state has "always wanted us dead."[14] In articulating the experience of living under
state forces that will never serve them, sex worker radicals find affinities with others
(and with overlapping communities) who know that full citizenship is not on the
table. This is the message that "no humans involved"—police code for murdered
sex workers of color—communicates, and many of the sex worker thinkers in this
archive came to radical politics through hearing it.

When the state offers nothing, it also loses some of the power attached to its
performance of protection. This is the risk states take in dealing violence and
neglect—those conditions set the stage for the dreaming up of alternatives. "People
have such a hard time envisioning what community safety looks like without the
state, without police repression," said Lucia Rey. But sex workers already know,
"because the state has failed us consistently." This was in response to my question
about what Rey thought the civilian Left could learn from sex worker organizing.
They added, "I think that leftists have a lot to learn from us, too, about how to organize your own community defense, how to keep your own community safe and do
it in a way that keeps you out of the state's grasp, because we've had to." "At every
turn," Rey said, "the state and all these institutions have failed us, and we have always
found ways to survive and to be resilient. . . . We are keeping each other safe."

On the Politics of Translation

Conceived during the summer of 2020—a moment marked by protests in defense of
Black life, state abandonment surrounding the COVID-19 pandemic, and ever-
increasing assaults on sex workers' livelihoods—Who Revolution ("whore revolution" when spoken) started meeting online to talk theory. The multiracial group's
members represented varied sectors of the sex industry and incomes within it.
Some had already read a great deal of political thought (some self-taught, others

in college courses) and others none at all; all were sex workers invested in anticapitalist struggle. The group's readings were made available for free, and there was a standing offer to reach out to founding members for help thinking them through.

Who Revolution's reading list started with Karl Marx, Vladimir Lenin, and Mao Zedong, then moved to Frantz Fanon, Kwame Nkrumah, and C. L. R. James, parsing the history of racial capitalist state formation and the stakes of revolutionary struggle against it. Next, it moved to Harry Haywood and Milton Howard, Eldridge Cleaver, Huey Newton, and Angela Davis, thinking through the politics of violence and community defense. Sometimes the group talked about how this connected with sex worker politics; at other times they focused on close readings geared toward building a shared theoretical language.

Who Revolution's readings are an exercise in translation at least twice removed—the Panthers salvage what they can from Fanon on self-defense in the Algerian context, and half a century later, a multiracial group of sex workers borrows from the Panthers. As Davis did with Marx, sex worker readers grapple with the politics of borrowing, translation, and citation. This work of extrapolation, scavenging abstract lessons for today's struggles from thinking firmly rooted in the concrete struggles of its own present, is always the task for readers of "militant texts."[15] Who Revolution is just one space where sex workers undertake this project. Other interviewees read alone or with friends in in-person groups loosely formed around those who work at the same strip club, or groups formed around sex worker organizations and mutual aid collectives or sponsored by the sex worker–owned bookstore Bluestockings. Many are studying the same thinkers, and readers here will notice shared affinities in the analyses that follow. This intellectual history is shared, too, with broader abolitionist thought, a framework deeply informed by the Black radical tradition. Part of what is notable in this story is that abolitionist thinkers can engage the same traditions and arrive at sometimes different tactical conclusions.

Sex worker readers approach these texts not in search of a correct line but as tools for grappling with ambivalence. Sex worker abolitionism, like the broader abolitionist project, is not uniform, not finished. Sex worker abolitionists disagree with each other about tactics, and they are open about the ambivalence they feel in their own ideas. SX Noir puts it this way: "I'm giving myself space for conflict within my own thinking. Giving myself the space to say, 'I'm trying to survive under these extreme circumstances. . . . I need space for my ideology to change.'" This embrace of process and contradiction is in the spirit of abolitionist thought more broadly.[16]

Inspired by histories of radical community defense and also cautious of the risk of appropriation, sex worker radicals "acknowledge and honor the hard work, risks, and death endured by many over the past century in order to create a framework for the sex worker specific organizing and political analysis we use today."[17] The Other Weapons collective goes on:

The longevity of our struggle relies on our ability to continue the militant practices of the black radical tradition, to stand in solidarity with those defending their indigenous land from pipeline development and other state-sanctioned genocidal expansions, and to remember that the hope for queer liberation was fought against the police in a riot at Stonewall by black and brown trans women, prostitutes, queens, dykes, and other gender traitors.[18]

Interlocutors echoed these commitments in our conversations. Clara talked about reading Fanon on the utility of violence in her reading group with other Black sex worker radicals, offering the caveat that they were not under the impression that sex workers' struggles in the United States were parallel with anticolonial ones. "I don't want to sound like white women who think [Audre] Lorde's radical self-care was about taking a bath," she joked. Participants in another reading group told me that they take care to "call in" white sex workers who suggest that contemporary sex workers' struggles are akin to struggles for Black civil rights historically, not least because the long civil rights movement is ongoing and not all contemporary sex workers are vulnerable to state violence in the same way. But sex worker radicals echo other thinkers who argue against the tendency to "provincialize" decolonial and Black radical thought, as Eric Stanley puts it, even as they know that this tendency comes in response to real concerns about the risks of bad translation.[19]

From this refusal to provincialize they glean, too, lessons about the risks of what the sex work historian Melinda Chateauvert calls "street justice."[20] These traditions teach what is at stake, and sex worker radicals take up community defense in the shadow of a long history of state repression. In her history of the Black Panthers, Robyn Spencer reminds that "the gun turned out to be a weapon turned on them more than they ever turned it on others"; no serious student of the Panthers reads their history as a romantic story about militancy.[21] So the legacy of Black radical freedom movements informs HALA's practice, but it also highlights the stakes of defense against an abusive state. Still, sex worker thinkers are careful not to confuse the immediate tactical risks of self- and community defense (or even preemptive violence) with ethical arguments against their practice.

Community Defense as Imaginary and Practice

"You're taking a huge risk by defending yourself," Emily said. She talked about "Joey the Player," a serial rapist who targeted sex workers for years. He was all over bad date lists but continued to contact sex workers under new aliases, targeting especially those who were too precarious to do a full screening before meeting. "We couldn't seem to do anything about it," she told me. "My response after the second time this guy contacted me was, 'I'm going to organize a group of women with bats to go meet him.'" But she did not want her friends jailed because of this man, and jailing sex workers for community defense is almost certainly how the state would have responded. "You're fucked no matter what." This was especially so, she said, because a lot of sex workers at the time assumed that Joey the Player was a police officer. He knew too much about how to weaponize the law, and so many of their other abusers had been cops. That did not turn out to be true this time, and unlike most people who harm sex workers, he was prosecuted after years of abuse. Still, the win felt hollow. There would be more people like him, and like most of the thinkers in this project's interview archive, Emily is a prison abolitionist who does not measure success by prosecutions. Community defense is all that is left, but in pursing it "you're taking a huge risk."

Calculating the risk of further criminalization is integral to the theory and practice of sex worker self-defense. The Victorian-era sex worker and madam Josie Washburn described a vision for community defense against rapists but noted that "the unwritten law" of self-defense "benefits the rich only." Washburn anticipated that, were circumstances otherwise, "there would be a sudden increase of male funerals."[22] These are tactical rather than ethical claims. Washburn does not seem vexed by the possibility of this militant backing up of boundaries, just acutely aware that the law is designed to visit yet more violence on survivors who push back. Today the legal stakes figure centrally into sex worker self-defense trainings. This was true for HALA and also for Paris's Sex Worker Antidefense Group (SWAG), where peer trainers teach not just self-defense tactics but also law. SWAG teaches "around" the legal concept of "legitimate self-defense," Charlotte L. told me, even as most of its practitioners do not accept the law's capacity to confer legitimacy. (French law did not affirm sex workers' "legitimacy" as workers until 2016, after all, and continues to undermine it through policy that chips away at their ability to work safely.) SWAG cautions sex workers never to attack abusers from behind because "that could be used against you" in court. The stakes are even higher when the abuser is a cop, Charlotte said. Many of SWAG's trainees are undocumented migrants who work on the street, vulnerable not just to criminalized self-defense but also to deportation. "We definitely make it clear that if you defend yourself against a police officer, you will not be found to be legally legitimate in what you did. . . . We talk about what the law would say, and then people can figure out what they want to do with that information." To warn that some forms of community defense are not safe under current conditions is not to argue against their ethics or political value.

The state is uninterested in protecting sex workers from harm—instead, state agents regularly cause harm—but it also clings tightly to its monopoly on violence. "I think it is truly unjust that the state has the monopoly on legal violence," said Carlisle, "so yeah, I want there to be a sense of self-advocacy around the use of violence in my community." They went on: "We are never allowed to fight back. . . . The fact that you are not allowed to beat the shit out of someone who rapes you is so ridiculous to me. I can barely stand it." If thinkers in this archive calculate that the costs of violent community defense may be too high, it matters that this, not nonviolent ethics in the abstract, is why they retreat. If messaging on transformative justice often condemns vigilante violence on broad ethical grounds, many sex worker thinkers instead caution against vigilantism simply because, under current conditions, vigilante tactics might bring sex worker survivors more harm. The distinction is worth making because it differently hails survivors. It is also something to be strategized around because the balance of risk and urgency might tip. Clara talked about wrestling with exactly this question: "There might come a time," she said, "when the alternative is just to watch your friends die." Clandestine Whores Network's dispatch, and its vision of armed cells prepared to mercilessly "refuse our deaths" is, after all, set in the not-too-distant future of 2026.[23]

For most of the thinkers in this archive, militant community defense is something to dream about that is not safe yet. Maria, who shares self-defense tactics informally in her community of trans sex workers, talked about her vision for justice: "holding people accountable for violence against us." "That doesn't really happen because we're all fucking terrified all the time," she told me, but "at this point, to protect ourselves, we're going to have to commit more crimes." Like many others in this archive, Maria gestured to the story of Aileen Wuornos, the sex worker who killed seven men in self-defense before her 1991 arrest and later state execution. "She fought back and was put to death for it," Maria said. "They were warning the rest of us," she said of Wuornos's execution. Feminist activists at the time of Wuornos's incarceration saw this too, writes Chateauvert, understanding her as a "political prisoner."[24] Wuornos is one of many sex workers who, in the language of the abolitionist project organized to defend criminalized survivors of gendered violence, "survived and [were] punished."[25] Understanding that the cure for sex workers' vulnerability to violence is not intensified contact with the same systems that produce it generates an organic abolitionism among thinkers of the sex worker Left.

Sex Workers on Transformative Justice

"We are keeping each other safe," Rey told us at the start of this story. The tactics they describe—community defense, blacklists, networks of care—answer Ruth Wilson Gilmore's call to think about abolitionism as a project concerned with "presence, not absence," building alternatives rather than simply negating carceral systems as they are.[26] The sex worker radicals in this project's archive disproportionately hail from the Black, Brown, Indigenous, disabled, trans, and poor communities most viciously targeted by the carceral state. Many were politicized through early and violent encounters with policing (or, for those most insulated by relative privilege, navigating its constant threat). Before sex work, and once there, they learn that policing and prisons are more likely to bring harm than remedy. Many of these thinkers were practicing organic abolitionist politics even before they named them, already expert at taking care of each other outside state institutions. Sex workers, writes Gallant, "have a lot to share with the prison abolition movement, because the big boogie man in the prison abolition movement is, 'What about the rapists and murderers?' Well, sex workers know about the rapists and murderers, and have all kinds of strategies to protect themselves."[27] Information sharing, mutual aid, and community defense all do more to keep sex workers safe than the state ever could.

"I'm a mutual aidist. I'm a prison abolitionist," responded Carlisle when I asked how they wanted to be identified politically in writing that came from our interview. Others in this project's interview archive share this sense. In reading groups and in self-study, they read Mariame Kaba, Angela Davis, Andrea Richie, Ruth Wilson Gilmore, adrienne maree brown, and others, and it is here that they find resources for making sense of the criminalization of both sex work as a survival strategy and the community defense that tries to keep people alive once there. Their stories, activist energy, and analysis are at the heart of vibrant abolitionist efforts such as the Survived and Punished project, which Kaba cofounded. They are drawn to abolitionist thought's incisive critiques of the carceral system and its reminder that other ways of being in community with each other are not just possible but already flourishing. While some want sex work decriminalized but the broader carceral apparatus left intact, most join Davis and others in framing decriminalization as part of an expansive abolitionist program; the call is not that "we do not deserve prison" but that "no one does."[28] They also understand deeply the abolitionist refrain that the carceral system extends far beyond the prison's walls. And they know that fellow abolitionists are right when they say that giving people resources reduces harm, not because deprivation creates criminality (as liberals often suggest) but because it makes us more vulnerable to abuse.

These thinkers approach tactical debates as committed abolitionists, not as people skeptical about the possibility of life beyond policing and prisons. It is against that backdrop that I understand the tensions they identify when reading popular abolitionist discourse against the grain of sex worker politics. These tensions are most present when abolitionist alternatives get sutured to a version of transformative justice that is less useful in the wake of the harms sex workers are most likely to experience.[29] If sex worker abolitionists agree with other abolitionists that Joey the Player's incarceration is no win, the vigilante defense (and even retribution) some dream of instead has little place in the nonviolent abolitionist alternatives they see offered up, which are premised on a vision of community that sex workers do not share with perpetrators like him.

This does not account for the diversity of abolitionist thought and the internal debates that flourish in organizing spaces and on the page. There are abolitionisms that do not make the moves that are the subject of interlocutors' comradely critiques.[30] But I was struck by the patterns sex worker radicals identified in our conversations, patterns that dominate the abolitionist appeals that are most visible to them. These appeals frame abolitionist alternatives as principally nonviolent and with the potential to restore community ties between abusers and survivors (or even to destroy the false binary between the two). If there is internal debate about the politics of vigilantism, for example, those conversations are quiet, with a different apparent consensus making its way to the most publicly visible work.

Puzzling out why is not this essay's project, though one answer is in some ways obvious: popular address requires careful calculations about audience, rhetoric, and sometimes even respectability and legality in an increasingly authoritarian moment. At the level of movement strategy, it may not feel safe, or smart, to interrupt the political momentum abolitionist ideas now have by publicly engaging internal debate (not least when that debate includes what might be read as a call for extralegal violence). Not all our tactical debates need to be public facing, but it is not nothing if sex worker abolitionists sometimes feel ignored as a public worthy of address. "I get it," said Clara of appeals to think beyond violence and retribution, "they're writing for civvy liberals—to convince them—not for us."

That is not true of the whole abolitionist project; abolitionism is grounded in the same Black radical tradition that inspires many of the sex worker thinkers in this archive and that informs internal debate on shared questions about the right to violence, the boundaries of community, and so on. Transformative justice emerges not as an appeal to liberal reformists but rather as a tool for intracommunity healing for those who know that state responses will only do more harm. So I read interlocutors' critiques as less about what gets said than about what often does not, less concerned with appeals to think beyond punishment as a response to intracommunity harm (appeals that make a lot of sense in their context) than with the relative absence of a public-facing conversation about those harms (and those perpetrators) that are less amenable to transformative justice responses.

These questions reverberated throughout our conversations: To what tactics should sex worker radicals turn when the rapist and the state agent are the same person? If transformative justice prioritizes a process that understands both victims and perpetrators to be "integral parts of the community who require holding, healing, and support," do perpetrators who do the work of the state merit support too?[31] The chief lesson of transformative justice, said Clara, is that "we need to target structures, not individuals." But, she asked, "what about individual abusers who form a structure?" Can or should they be healed? If transformative justice's invitation is to look toward systems rather than individual acts of harm, what to do with an analysis that sees individual violence as doing the state's work for it?

The theory and practice of transformative justice hinge on a critique of "stranger danger" and a crucial effort to refocus on how to sustainably address intracommunity harm.[32] But sex worker abolitionists remind us that, for some, harm *does* come from strangers who are dangerous. This is, of course, not news to the broader abolitionist movement, with thinkers grounded in the Black radical tradition and its analysis of the white supremacists who (like bad johns) come from outside to do violence that is endorsed by the state. Sex workers' theorizing around the politics of transformation draws on this history together with their particular knowledge about "the rapists and murderers." It does so while avoiding normative renderings of stranger danger, steeped as they are in racist fantasy and a refusal to acknowledge that, for non–sex workers, most harm does come from closer to home. In the history of white-dominated gay and feminist campaigns to "take back the night," writes Christina Hanhardt, community defense figures as a means of defending against outsiders imagined to be men of color.[33] The sex worker community defenders who volunteered for this project take care to avoid this tendency, both because of their political commitments and because it does not serve their needs. For HALA, writes Carlisle, trainings work against the "myth that the most dangerous person is a man (of color, or poor) *out there*."[34] Echoing other abolitionists' critiques of liberal feminist articulations of stranger danger, Carlisle reminds us that most violence comes from "people we know." SWAG likewise found that liberal feminist articulations of self-defense alienated sex workers not just conceptually but also strategically. Those trainings focused on defending against "that guy in the street," Charlotte L. explained, "not on situations when you're already alone with a guy in a room." Still, those people sex workers know—regulars on the vice squad beat, clients known but not really—are usually not members of the communities of which sex workers are a part. Instead, they come from outside to do the violent state's work for it.

Part of transformative justice's force is its invitation to "choose love" in a "monstrous world," as the writer, social worker, and former sex worker Kai Cheng Thom asks us to do in her collection of abolitionist essays and poetry.[35] Most of the thinkers in this interview archive are drawn to the promise of this way of doing politics. When confronting harm within their (overlapping) communities as sex workers, people of color, trans people, anarchists, and so on, many said they work from an abolitionist understanding that revenge does not heal, that transformative justice is possible, and that "no one is disposable."[36] In other moments, though, hopes for justice that transforms at the same time as it leaves all parties intact shatter. When agents of the state perpetrate harm, and when individual abusers self-deputize to do that work for them, some sex worker radicals do want their abusers disposed of. The stakes of prefigurative politics are high; abolitionists—abolitionist sex workers among them—want to respond to harm in ways that prefigure the worlds they hope to build. But prefiguration can start to feel like a trap for sex worker radicals who wonder if transitional programs necessitate different tactics than the ones they hope will animate futures to come. Approaching this possibility through the lens of comradely curiosity, they have more questions than answers: What does a politics informed by desires for revolutionary violence suggest about the abolitionist futures one wants? What futures, conversely, are conjured up in renderings that figure violence and punishment as always belonging to the state? Who is imagined to exist in the future? What happens to sex workers if everyone, including bad johns, gets to stay?

Sex worker abolitionists take up abolitionism's call for a justice that transforms and its insistence that this will not come from the state. But they push back, lovingly, against the core transformative justice principle that violence outside the state replicates the harm we want to render unthinkable.[37] The *army* in Hookers Army gestures to the group's intent to "build a real fighting force in an oppressive system," not one that acts like the state but an "ad hoc guerrilla resistance movement."[38] I am struck by the tensions this brings to light; there is not a lot of space for guerrilla resistance in invitations to refuse abusers' disposal.

adrienne maree brown warns that "judgement and punishment are practices of power over others. . . . The injustice of power is practiced at an individual and collective level." It is from this place that some abolitionists come to the conclusion that to pursue punishment and exile is to take on state-like power. "Instead of prison bars we place each other in an overflowing box of untouchables," writes brown.[39] Sex worker radicals in this project's archive are not so sure that these are the same. Instead, they advocate an analysis of violence that differentiates between its exercise by institutions (or their individual proxies) and by oppressed people. Clara talked about reading Huey Newton in her reading group, and said she had been thinking about what a dictatorship of the lumpenproletariat might look like. It would, to be sure, not look like the carceral systems that uphold the racial capitalist state, but it would require taking real power. Inspired by Newton's critique of liberal pacifism, she pointed to a moment in his "In Defense of Self-Defense" where Newton marks the point of departure between Black radicals and liberal assimilationists: "the principle that the oppressor has no rights that the oppressed is bound to respect." Newton urges readers to "destroy him [the oppressor] utterly," and Clara thought this might be sometimes necessary.[40]

"We're not ready to do anything like this now," Clara said. "The Panthers were crushed." And radicals are surveilled in ways that were unthinkable when Newton wrote in 1967. Contemporary internet surveillance would give a modern COINTELPRO breathtaking new force; sex workers know this because such surveillance is first tested on them. But Clara hoped that organizing might build both capacity and the ability to evade, and her reading group was thinking hard about the ethics and politics of what to do when that time came. They debated "the usual questions," she said: "What harm merits the most extreme response?" "How will we know when we've gone too far?" Earlier in our conversation, Clara had identified as a prison abolitionist. So I asked her how she navigated the tensions between "destroy him utterly" and "no one is disposable." "I'm stuck there," she said. "I have so much love for civilian abolitionists, but every time they say, 'nobody is disposable' I think, 'they haven't met my rapist johns.' I don't know if 'hurt people hurt people' is the best explanation for what they do." Those rapist johns were, "nine times out of ten, white men with money who seek me out because they can." I felt stuck, too. In the spirit of a method that lingers on the encounters that bring us up short, let us spend more time here.

First, a caveat: It reflects the self-selecting nature of this archive that interlocutors focused their analysis (in interviews and in their own writing) on police and white cis men clients (or perpetrators who pose as clients) who do harm—that is, those who are most obviously outsiders and can be most easily understood to be doing the work of a violent state. Broader sex worker discourses are rife with racist ideas that sound a lot like conventional liberal feminists' stranger danger, including the myth that clients of color are more dangerous. I am not arguing that all sex workers avoid this framework, just that the sex worker leftists who volunteered to talk to me did. For white sex workers who felt hailed by my call for participants this might be traced to antiracist practice of the sort Carlisle describes, where part of the work of self-defense training includes teaching against racist ideas of why we need it. It might also be traced to the readings in antiracist thought that multiracial radical reading groups do. Who Revolution, for example, includes readings that help white members unlearn the racist and classist ideas that undergird the "whore-archy." That interlocutors focused on harm that comes from outside also reflects the revolutionary thought they are drawn to, texts whose grounding in anticolonial and antiracist struggle generates a focus on perpetrators not of the community, ones who do the work of a violent state.

Most interlocutors did not turn to what to do about harm in that remaining one time out of ten that Clara identified, when it does come from people who are also targeted by state violence. Those that did advocated different responses depending on the source of the harm. One anonymous interlocutor said she believed deeply in using accountability processes for intracommunity harms in her own community of trans sex workers of color but advocated a "kill your rapist" approach (one that she, like others in this archive, calculated not to be worth the risk right now) outside it. Among the tactical questions left unanswered in these conversations is where exactly to draw the line between inside and out, and what to do when it gets blurry. Abolitionists who condemn punishment as such have resolved those ambivalences in one way, mitigating the risk of retributive harm by turning away from retribution altogether. Some sex worker radicals want to leave these ambivalences open.

Transformative justice practitioners know that politics are about feeling, and much of the work of advocating it operates at the level of affect. How to transform cultures of harm so that not just the state institutions that mete out punishment but our everyday desires for it wither away? How to "kill the cop in your head"? Kaba brings us here in a conversation about the foundations of transformative justice, a practice that could replace the prisons we will tear down. It requires divesting from the carceral state and social services, finding responses to harm that do not create more of it, and prioritizing prevention and structural analysis rather than reactivity and a focus on individuals. Crucially, it "takes as a starting point the idea that what happens in our interpersonal relationships is mirrored and reinforced by the larger systems."[41] We must avoid "mistaking emotional satisfaction for justice," urges Kaba, and, later, "remember again, the systems live within us."[42] These are all good reasons to refuse a distinction between desires for punishment at the hands of the state and outside it. Thinkers in this project's archive suggest, though, that there might elsewhere be good reasons to parse them out.

Transformative justice is also—and this is where sex worker radicals place the greatest distance between their abolitionism and popular frames in transformative justice—"militantly against the dichotomies between victims and perpetrators."[43] Transformative justice emerges directly from communities of color who cannot afford exile when those among them cause harm, who do not want to aid the white supremacist and colonial state by inviting it in, and who know that calling the police will not help anyway. Knowing that "hurt people hurt people," as the maxim goes, and that intracommunity violence is so often a symptom of structural trauma, advocates for transformative justice seek healing over retribution. This hinges on a crucial critique of the myth of stranger danger. If racist fantasies of dangerous outsiders authorize the carceral state, knowing that most harm comes at the hands of people we know (and often love) changes the terms. Most sex worker radicals work from this understanding when confronting violence within their communities. But they also remind us that some perpetrators really are from outside; there is a dichotomy between sex workers and the clients and cops (and client cops) who target them, and another kind of militancy in organizing around the concreteness of that line. Citing Newton citing Fanon, Who Revolution members talked about internal colonialism as a framework for understanding this separateness. There are victims and perpetrators, and only one has the backing of the state. "Our abusers are never part of our community," said Rey. "Clients are clients and sex workers are sex workers."

Rey's abolitionism was hard-earned, first through growing up in an immigrant community where cops brought arrest and deportation, and later as a sex worker who knew that police were more likely to be perpetrators of harm than anyone you would call on for protection. She learned that mutual aid, community defense, blacklists, and outing bad dates are all part of a set of tactics sex workers use to keep each other safe. Some of these tactics sit uneasily alongside abolitionist critiques of violence, banishment, and public shaming as ways to address harm. But Rey reminds us that the core of transformative justice is that it is "tailored to meet the needs of the people who are harmed." They are a reader of Kaba, who takes care to note that accountability processes have their limits. Sex worker radicals have a particular view of those limits: the processes prized in transformative justice responses to harm rely on openings for accountability that do not exist when sex workers confront abusers from outside. Rey puts it this way: "When we fall into the hands of police or clients, neither of which are part of our community, it's difficult to keep them accountable." But, they add, "if accountability doesn't exist, there are still ways to keep our community safe from those people." An abolitionist politics that meets sex workers' needs requires a particular theory of community, one that leaves spaces for an inside and an outside.

This was an ongoing tangle for Gabe, an abolitionist and trafficking survivor who organizes with campaigns for decriminalization that seek to undermine the whole carceral system, not just protect (some) sex workers from some of its violence. "I do want to believe in transformative justice, it's something I've dedicated myself to," he said. But "a lot of our transformative justice in the present moment relies on the social pressure to engage in a process that's only accessible to people who have community supports," and none of Gabe's abusers had been a part of the communities he inhabited. "I definitely used to be more in the 'kill your rapist' camp," he said. "What changed that for me was existing in trans communities for 5–6 years and see-ing mentally ill trans women over and over again get bullied out of their only source of social support after rape accusations—which sometimes were true, sometimes weren't, usually were somewhere in between." He learned that "we can't just aban-don people." Wanting to carry the thread initiated in other interviews, I asked what this meant for abusers who come from the outside. "Yeah, I get stuck on that too. [Transformative justice] is a framework that's built for [perpetrators who are] already marginalized people who are at risk for state violence themselves." This is not the case for clients who do harm with the tacit approval of the state, and it is these perpetrators that are the primary target of interlocutors' concern. This stuck-ness is, then, not a critique of transformative justice so much as it is a reminder of its specificity. Sex worker abolitionism poses a challenge to frames that give all targets of community defense—or revenge, and we will get to whether there is always a clear difference—an equal claim to nondisposal.

Our conversations reverberated with this ambivalence. "I really like transfor-mative justice, at least in theory," said an anonymous thinker in this archive. "In practice, it's messy." It is in confronting client violence, she said, that "I'm more in the anarcha-feminist 'kill your rapist' camp." But, she noted, "there are lots of situ-ations in which that won't work either. I don't really know the answer." Sex worker radicals' embrace of ambivalence (or the stuckness Clara and Gabe marked earlier) highlights what is at stake here: not a contest between abolitionists and carceral lib-erals but a comradely difference among abolitionists who share a commitment to radical world building but have not yet settled on what that looks like. If broader abolitionist movements are to take sex workers seriously in this spirit, these are ten-sions that cannot be explained away with the charge that it is the cops in sex workers' heads doing the talking.

As they wrestle with the politics of community defense and militant texts on its historical practice, sex worker abolitionists suggest that it may be too early to say that violence, even vengeance, has no place in the process of getting from here to there. I wonder if this might meet Kaba's invitation for "a million different little experiments" as we strategize "how we get from where we are to where we want to go."[44] Ambivalence runs through the abolitionist text. In parsing the distinction between "consequences" (an ethical good) and "vengeance" (a political dead end), Kaba writes, "I also don't think that using extreme violence to address extreme violence ever works."[45] But later she wonders whether "we're going to need a war again" to make the next phase of abolitionism possible. Here she's remembering Civil War–era contestations over violence, and Frederick Douglass's insistence that "the war had to come."[46]

Douglass is on Clara's reading group list, too, and she and her comrades charted the shift from his commitment to nonviolence to a belief in violence as one of the tactics enslaved people would need to take up. Like other Black sex workers in this project's archive, and following the through line some abolitionists draw from enslavement to mass incarceration, Clara talked about modern police as "slave catchers." She pointed me to Douglass's words on their predecessors: "The man who rushes out of the orbit of his own rights, to strike down the rights of another, does, by that act, divest himself of the right to live."[47] She was stuck, here again, on how to square this meditation on the ethics of violent community defense with the abolitionist rejoinder that violence will never get us where we want to go. "Even though it feels good to wear the 'kill the rapists' T-shirt," writes the abolitionist organizer Shira Hassan in conversation with Kaba, "that isn't the thing that is actually going to get us the world we want to live in."[48]

It is in abolitionist texts that the sex workers in this archive find the greatest resources for thinking about individual acts of violence as inseparable from their structural contexts. In their foundational document on prison abolition and gender violence, Critical Resistance and INCITE call for antiprison activists to understand the structural roots of individual acts of harm, and this invitation reverberates throughout abolitionist writing.[49] But whereas transformative justice advocates typically frame this reminder as evidence that retribution against individual abusers can never be transformative, some sex worker radicals read it the other way. They overwhelmingly agree with the idea that our tactics should target structures, not individuals. But they push for more clarity on where structures end and individuals who do structural work begin. Thinkers in this article's archive brought me up short at moments when they insist that it is precisely through understanding violence against sex workers as doing the work of an abusive state that the connections among community defense, vigilante punishment, and revolutionary violence become most clear. That is how Cassandra Troyan connects the image of a single sex worker wielding a crowbar to its utopian promise: "You have heard last gurglings of power."[50]

Clara was another student of Malcolm X's thought. She took her understanding of the limits of nonviolent transformative justice from his analysis of the impossibility of moral suasion as a tool against white supremacy. She turned me back to "The Ballot or the Bullet" and its insistence that (she paraphrased) "you can't change a white man's mind." "I'm not sure how to square this with civvy abolitionists' idea that everyone can be healed, brought back in," she said. For Clara, as for Malcolm X, this impossibility applied to individual abusers and to the state as abuser. Again, they are doing the same work. "That whole thing about appealing to the moral conscience of America—America's conscience is bankrupt. She lost all conscience a long time ago," Malcolm X said.[51] "They"—and I think Malcolm X's ambivalence about whether this refers to America or the white man is purposeful here—only eliminate an "evil" "when it threatens their existence." Quoting Kwame Ture—her study group watched *The Black Power Mixtape*, too—another interviewee talked about the tactical problem of nonviolence: "For nonviolence to work, your opponent must have a conscience. The United States has none."[52] "The United States has no consciousness of my humanity," Clara said, and "bad johns don't, either." This is the political landscape that the phrase "no humans involved" conveys. In search of a politics of violence that works on such terrain, sex worker radicals seek out useable pasts from others who theorize self-defense when outside recognition of one's humanity cannot be taken for granted. This is in deep conversation with, rather than antagonistic to, other abolitionist work on self-defense. Black women criminalized for self-defense are understood to have "no selves to defend," as Kaba's zine by that title suggests.[53] Sex worker radicals highlight tactical questions about what routes will best restore those selves.

Against framings of violence as toxic to a politics that is humane and transformative, some are drawn to the idea that violence might be necessary to asserting one's humanness. In this spirit, one anonymous interviewee talked about reading Fanon in the Who Revolution reading group. She was struck by his theory of violence as a "cleansing force" for colonized people.[54] A US-born Latina, she was careful not to claim symmetry between her experience and that of Fanon's colonized subjects. She was not saying that her situation was like that of the people at the heart of Fanon's work, but it resonated when she read that violence can restore the self-confidence of those beaten down by oppression. For Fanon and for her, too, violence has a cleansing force even when it is "symbolic," and at the individual level it pushes against the idea that the problem with violent responses to harm is that they do not get at its root causes. Where transformative justice advocates often warn that violence does not work because it does not reliably function as a deterrent, she wanted to claim the violence as "just for me." "I'm tired of centering johns," she said. Here she echoes another reader of Fanon, Malcolm X, who concluded, "you can't change his mind about us." Of the white man and the white supremacist state, Malcolm X said, "We've got to change our own minds about each other."[55]

Its focus away from trying to change others' minds was part of what drew Charlotte L. to self-defense. In a refreshing departure from sex worker activism that focused on "trying to change someone's mind," self-defense says, "I don't give a fuck what you think, our bodies are worth defending. And we're going to do it."

Where appeals to change civilian minds engendered much division across lines of race, citizenship, and whorearchy, she found that self-defense trainings equalized sex workers: "We're all there for the same thing, we all find ourselves alone in a room or on the street with a man (usually a man). . . . We're all learning from each other's working strategies, without judgement." Whorearchical judgment is a product of tactics that, in seeking to change civilian minds, trade in a politics of respectability.

Healing and community defense might count as transformative ends, whether or not they change abusers' minds (and whether or not those minds are changeable). Thus the historian Catherine Jacquet measures the effects of 1970s feminists' antirape vigilantism by what it did to nurture women's sense of agency.[56] To locate the political value of community defense beyond its deterrent effects is also to make a feminist move against the centering of perpetrators. In this spirit, Hookers Army, said member Lauren Kiley, "doesn't exist for a greater cause, it exists to teach sex workers self-defense, it exists for the people who are in the room that night." "I don't think the point of sharing our stories is limited to the consequences for perpetrators. Otherwise we've already lost," Kiley adds. "We have to shift most of the point to healing and supporting each other. Not because I don't believe in consequences, but because they aren't happening and they wouldn't be enough anyway."[57] If self-defense does healing work, maybe it does not matter if it works to deter.

But if sex worker community defense exists for "the people in the room," it is also true that it has reverberating effects on others, not least those invested in sex workers' undoing. As the history of Black radical thought teaches, people in positions of power rightly understand community defense—in all its manifestations, peaceful and otherwise—as violence because it *does* do violence to dominant systems and those who benefit from them.[58] Troyan echoes this understanding when they name sex worker survival, however won, as "the greatest revenge." Here revenge is the stuff of "joy" and "possibility."[59] Whereas transformative justice theory often strongly disidentifies with revenge, draws a hard line between retribution and self-defense, and insists that revenge only perpetuates harm, many of the sex worker abolitionists in this archive approach the temporality of community defense with some ambivalence. Nods to vengeance emerge too often to ignore this tension.

Other sex worker abolitionists do want to maintain a hard boundary; this is the subject of debate when sex worker radicals gather for group study. For another member of the Who Revolution reading group, a communist and believer in the necessity of violent revolution, such revolution will not be waged through individualized retribution. "Revenge, killing your rapist, isn't revolutionary," she said; we need to focus on "actual healing work." But for others, the blurry line maintains. The armed cells of the Clandestine Whores Network can be called on "when we need revenge, or to show our connective force, maybe just for a ride."[60] "The whore must believe in revenge," Troyan insists.[61] The tension lies in how to square the whore's necessary belief in revenge with the abolitionist rejoinder that, as Thom puts it, "we must not give in to the urge to do harm, even in justice's name."[62] Fiction lets Thom get at exactly this tension; her novel *Fierce Femmes and Notorious Liars*, which follows a vigilante gang of trans sex workers organized in community defense—"creatures out of a suburban businessman's nightmare: Fierce femmes on a mission of vengeance. Trans girls out for blood"—explores the tactical and ethical ambivalences that emerge for them.[63]

The blurry boundary between revenge and self-defense haunts abolitionist feminist history. Thuma's history of anticarceral feminism tells a story grounded in campaigns to defend criminalized survivors—the women and gender-nonconforming people incarcerated for fighting back. Antirape feminists in the 1970s calculated that, faced with a state built to perpetrate and enable abuse, extralegal self-defense was justified. But the line between self-defense and revenge was not solid. Thuma cites a 1974 proposal in the radical feminist publication *Off Our Backs* for "immediate and drastic retaliation against all rapists," for instance, and many of the criminalized survivors whose cases galvanized the movement struggled with the state over exactly the distinction between revenge and self-defense.[64] Contemporary self-defenders, too, confront prosecutors' claims of revenge, not immediate self-defense, a key state strategy for criminalizing survivors for acts of self-preservation judged to be out of time.[65]

If defense of self and community makes the threat "If you touch me in a way I don't like, you get hurt," does it matter whether that hurt comes at the moment of original violence or after? In vigorously defending self-defense at the same time as it condemns vigilantism and revenge, transformative justice theory says yes, that boundary matters a lot. Thinkers in this archive, though, suggest that politicized revenge and defense of self and community are not so easily distinguished on the ground. What becomes of the boundary between revenge and structural transformation when individual violence does the state's work for it? Might individual revenge be better understood as preemptive community defense, given that bad johns so rarely do harm just once? Where one falls determines the shape theories of revolutionary struggle take and the tactics they inform.

"What violence do we need to engage in," asks the sex worker theorist Irene Silt, "to escape the expansive partnership of the making of law and that which conserves it?"[66] This question, and its urgency for a community especially targeted by the deadly partnership of law and those who conserve it, animates sex worker radicals' engagements with the theory and practice of community defense. They ask what it means to "keep each other safe" in the face of a state that marks sex workers as available for harm, and they advance a sex worker theory of transformative justice in the process. To "stop the war on whores" will require stopping the institutions that fuel it and, maybe, the individuals who help.

Heather Berg writes about sex, work, and social struggle. Her first book, *Porn Work* (2021), explores workers' strategies for navigating—and subverting—precarity. Her second project is an intellectual history of the sex worker Left. Her writing appears in *Feminist Studies, Signs*, the *South Atlantic Quarterly*, and other journals. She is an assistant professor of women, gender, and sexuality studies at Washington University in St. Louis.

Notes

Thanks to the sex worker thinkers who shared their time and ideas with me. It is an honor to learn from you. Thanks to Kit Smemo, Rachel Greenwald Smith, Kathi Weeks, and participants at Duke University's Revaluing Care in the Global Economy workshop series for smart comments on an earlier draft, to the anonymous reviewers who gave such comradely reviews, and to Anne Gray Fischer for her keen editorial eye.

1.   Clandestine Whores Network, "Beneath Everything."
2.   Clandestine Whores Network, "Beneath Everything."
3.   I use the term *abolitionist discourse* to describe the abolitionist appeals that have a particularly high profile in popular left publishing, mainstream media, activist sloganeering, and movement spaces and that are most visible to the sex worker thinkers in this archive.
4.   Giovannitti and Hogeveen, "Transactional Dynamics."
5.   Gossett, "Abolitionist Imaginings," 370.
6.   On the ubiquity of police abuse and sexual extortion, see Chateauvert, *Sex Workers Unite*, 173.
7.   See Simpson, "The State Is a Man"; Stanley, *Atmospheres of Violence*; and Gago, *Feminist International*.
8.   See Currah, "State."
9.   Silt, "Tricking Hour," 38.
10. Fischer, *The Streets Belong to Us*, 176.
11. Fischer, *The Streets Belong to Us*, 176.
12. Law, "Sick of the Abuse," 48.
13. Thuma, *All Our Trials*, 3.
14. Silt, "Tricking Hour," 46.
15. Althusser, "From *Capital* to Marx's Philosophy," 33.
16. On contradiction as a resource for abolitionist thought rather than something that should be smoothed over, see Davis et al., *Abolition. Feminism. Now.*, 5. See also Gossett, "Abolitionist Imaginings," 370.
17. Other Weapons Collective, "Sex Workers against Work," 3.
18. Other Weapons Collective, "Sex Workers against Work," 3.
19. Stanley, *Atmospheres of Violence*, 12.
20. Chateauvert, *Sex Workers Unite*, 156.
21. Spencer, *Revolution Has Come*, 2.
22. Washburn, *Underworld Sewer*, 228–29.
23. Clandestine Whores Network, "Beneath Everything."
24. Chateauvert, *Sex Workers Unite*, 166.
25. Survived and Punished, https://survivedandpunished.org (accessed May 15, 2022).
26. Gilmore, "Keynote."
27. In Lam et al., "Roundtable."
28. See Davis, *Are Prisons Obsolete?*, 113.

29. Some sex worker radicals embrace tactics that line up neatly with a nonviolent transformative justice approach. In *Beyond Survival*, a collection of "stories from the transformative justice movement," Gallant interviews activists Elene Lam and Monica Forrester on the tactics sex workers deploy to keep each other safe without police, and they focus on prevention, community healing, and justice defined as political reform ("When Your Money Counts on It").

30. Rafi Reznik, for example, argues that the two alternative approaches to harm most often offered by abolitionists—preventative justice and transformative justice—are inadequate. But retribution, he maintains, is not incommensurate with abolition as such. "Noncarceral punitiveness" is both analytically coherent and defensible ("Retributive Abolitionism," 145, 125).

31. Thom, *I Hope We Choose Love*, 81.

32. Kaba, *We Do This 'til We Free Us*, 154.

33. Hanhardt, *Safe Space*, 87.

34. Carlisle, "How to Build a Hookers Army," 294.

35. Thom, *I Hope We Choose Love*.

36. *No One Is Disposable*.

37. See Mingus, "Transformative Justice."

38. Carlisle, "How to Build a Hookers Army," 302.

39. brown, *We Will Not Cancel Us*, 43, 75.

40. Newton, "In Defense of Self Defense," n.p.

41. Kaba, *We Do This 'til We Free Us*, 149.

42. Kaba, *We Do This 'til We Free Us*, 133, 141.

43. Kaba, *We Do This 'til We Free Us*, 149.

44. Kaba, *We Do This 'til We Free Us*, 166.

45. Kaba, *We Do This 'til We Free Us*, 153.

46. Kaba, *We Do This 'til We Free Us*, 184.

47. Douglass, *Frederick Douglass*, 180.

48. Kaba, *We Do This 'til We Free Us*, 47.

49. Critical Resistance, and Incite!, "Critical Resistance-Incite!," 144.

50. Troyan, *Freedom and Prostitution*, 121.

51. Malcolm X, "The Ballot or the Bullet," 40.

52. In the film Ture is quoted as Stokely Carmichael, the name he used at the time. *The Black Power Mixtape 1967–1975* (dir. Göran Olsson, 2011).

53. Kaba, *No Selves to Defend*.

54. Fanon, *The Wretched of the Earth*, 51.

55. Malcolm X, "The Ballot or the Bullet," 40.

56. Jacquet, "Fighting Back, Claiming Power," 73–74.

57. Kiley, "Red Flags," 138.

58. Sawyer, *Black Minded*, 121.

59. Troyan, *Freedom and Prostitution*, 89, 115.

60. Clandestine Whores Network, "Beneath Everything."

61. Troyan, *Freedom and Prostitution*, 121.

62. Thom, *I Hope We Choose Love*, 89.

63. Thom, *Fierce Femmes and Notorious Liars*, 83.

64. Thuma, *All Our Trials*, 46.

65. Kaba, *No Selves to Defend*.

66. Silt, "Tricking Hour," 18.

References

Althusser, Louis. "From *Capital* to Marx's Philosophy." In *Reading "Capital": The Complete Edition*, translated by Ben Brewster, 9–70. London: Verso, 2015.

brown, adrienne maree. *We Will Not Cancel Us: Breaking the Cycle of Harm*. Chico, CA: AK Press, 2020.

Carlisle, Vanessa. "How to Build a Hookers Army." In *We Too: Essays on Sex Work and Survival*, edited by Natalie West with Tina Horn, 291–302. New York: Feminist Press, 2021.

Chateauvert, Melinda. *Sex Workers Unite: A History of the Movement from Stonewall to Slutwalk*. Boston: Beacon, 2013.

Clandestine Whores Network. "Beneath Everything." *Pinko*, no. 1 (2019). https://pinko.online /pinko-1/clandestine-whores-network.

Critical Resistance, and Incite! "Critical Resistance-Incite! Statement on Gender Violence and the Prison-Industrial Complex." *Social Justice* 30, no. 3 (2003): 141–50.

Currah, Paisley. "The State." *TSQ: Transgender Studies Quarterly* 1, nos. 1–2 (2014): 197–200.

Davis, Angela Y. *Are Prisons Obsolete?* New York: Seven Stories, 2003.

Davis, Angela Y., Gina Dent, Erica R. Meiners, and Beth E. Richie. *Abolition. Feminism. Now.* Oakland, CA: Haymarket Books, 2022.

Douglass, Frederick. *Frederick Douglass: Selected Speeches and Writings*. Edited by Philip Sheldon Foner. Chicago: Lawrence Hill Books, 1999.

Fanon, Frantz. *The Wretched of The Earth*. Translated by Richard Philcox. New York: Grove, 2021.

Fischer, Anne Gray. *The Streets Belong to Us: Sex, Race, and Police Power from Segregation to Gentrification*. Chapel Hill: University of North Carolina Press, 2022.

Gago, Verónica. *Feminist International: How to Change Everything*. Translated by Liz Mason-Deese. London: Verso, 2020.

Gallant, Chanelle. "When Your Money Counts on It: Sex Work and Transformative Justice." In *Beyond Survival: Strategies and Stories from the Transformative Justice Movement*, edited by Ejeris Dixon and Leah Lakshmi Piepzna-Samarasinha, 191–204. Chico, CA: AK Press, 2020.

Gilmore, Ruth Wilson. "Keynote." Presented at "Making and Unmaking Mass Incarceration," University of Mississippi, Oxford, 2019.

Giovannitti, Sophia, and Esmé Hogeveen. "The Transactional Dynamics between Art and Sex in 'Working Girl.'" *Frieze*, June 6, 2023. https://www.frieze.com/article/sophia-giovannitti -interview-2023.

Gossett, Che. "Abolitionist Imaginings: A Conversation with Bo Brown, Reina Gossett, and Dylan Rodríguez." In *Captive Genders: Trans Embodiment and the Prison Industrial Complex*, edited by Eric A. Stanley and Nat Smith, 323–44. Oakland, CA: AK Press, 2015.

Hanhardt, Christina. *Safe Space: Gay Neighborhood History and the Politics of Violence*. Durham, NC: Duke University Press, 2013.

Jacquet, Catherine. "Fighting Back, Claiming Power." *Radical History Review*, no. 126 (2016): 71–83.

Kaba, Mariame, ed. *No Selves to Defend: A Legacy of Criminalizing Women of Color for Self-Defense*. Chicago: Project NIA and the Chicago Alliance to Free Marissa Alexander, 2013.

Kaba, Mariame. *We Do This 'til We Free Us: Abolitionist Organizing and Transforming Justice*. Edited by Tamara Nopper. Chicago: Haymarket Books, 2021.

Kiley, Lauren. "Red Flags." In *We Too: Essays on Sex Work and Survival*, edited by Natalie West with Tina Horn, 131–39. New York: Feminist Press, 2021.

Lam, Elene, Chanelle Gallant, Robyn Maynard, and Monica Forrester. "A Roundtable on Sex Work Politics and Prison Abolition." *Upping the Anti: A Journal of Theory and Action*, no. 18 (2018). https://uppingtheanti.org/journal/article/18-sexworker/.

Law, Victoria. "Sick of the Abuse: Feminist Responses to Sexual Assault, Battering, and Self-Defense." In *The Hidden 1970s: Histories of Radicalism*, edited by Dan Berger, 39–56. New Brunswick, NJ: Rutgers University Press, 2010.

Malcolm X. "The Ballot or the Bullet." In *Malcolm X Speaks: Selected Speeches and Statements*, edited by George Breitman, 23–44. New York: Grove, 1956.

Mingus, Mia. "Transformative Justice: A Brief Description." *Transforming Harm* (blog), January 11, 2019. https://transformharm.org/tj_resource/transformative-justice-a-brief-description/.

Newton, Huey. "In Defense of Self Defense." *Black Panther* 1, no. 4 (1967): n.p. https://www.marxists.org/archive/newton/1967/06/20.htm.

No One Is Disposable: Everyday Practices of Prison Abolition. Barnard Center for Research on Women, 2014. http://www.deanspade.net/2014/02/07/no-one-is-disposable/.

Other Weapons Distro. "Sex Workers against Work." May 26, 2020. https://otherweapons.noblogs.org/post/2020/05/26/sex-workers-against-work/.

Reznik, Rafi. "Retributive Abolitionism." *Berkeley Journal of Criminal Law* 24, no. 2 (2019): 123–94.

Sawyer, Michael. *Black Minded: The Political Philosophy of Malcolm X*. London: Pluto, 2020.

Silt, Irene. "The Tricking Hour." *Tripwire*, no. 7 (2020). https://tripwirejournal.files.wordpress.com/2020/05/tricking-hour-final.pdf.

Simpson, Audra. "The State Is a Man: Theresa Spence, Loretta Saunders, and the Gender of Settler Sovereignty." *Theory and Event* 19, no. 4 (2016). https://www.muse.jhu.edu/article/633280.

Spencer, Robyn. *The Revolution Has Come: Black Power, Gender, and the Black Panther Party in Oakland*. Durham, NC: Duke University Press, 2016.

Stanley, Eric. *Atmospheres of Violence: Structuring Antagonism and the Trans/Queer Ungovernable*. Durham, NC: Duke University Press, 2021.

Survived and Punished. Home page. https://survivedandpunished.org (accessed July 31, 2023).

Thom, Kai Cheng. *Fierce Femmes and Notorious Liars: A Dangerous Trans Girl's Confabulous Memoir*. Montreal: Metonymy, 2016.

Thom, Kai Cheng. *I Hope We Choose Love: A Trans Girl's Notes from the End of the World*. Vancouver: Arsenal Pulp, 2019.

Thuma, Emily L. *All Our Trials: Prisons, Policing, and the Feminist Fight to End Violence*. Urbana: University of Illinois Press, 2019.

Troyan, Cassandra. *Freedom and Prostitution*. Olympia, WA: Elephants, 2020.

Washburn, Josie. *The Underworld Sewer: A Prostitute Reflects on Life in the Trade, 1871–1909*. Lincoln: University of Nebraska Press, 1997.

Organizing for the Decriminalization of Sex Work in South Africa

India Thusi

How have South African sex workers negotiated their relationship with the state? They have organized and demanded the decriminalization of sex work, even as some feminists have questioned this demand. Sex worker advocacy groups have focused primarily on advocating for decriminalization as the agenda for sex work reform.[1] The Sex Workers Education and Advocacy Taskforce (SWEAT) and Sisonke, the leading sex work activist organizations in South Africa, have demanded the decriminalization of sex work, arguing that sex workers have agency and autonomy and should be allowed to choose their occupation without the state criminalizing this choice.[2] A report by SWEAT and Human Rights Watch argues that "the criminalisation of sex work undermines the health and dignity of sex workers and exposes them to violence and abuse. The South African government should act urgently to end criminalisation of sex work and work with sex workers to protect their rights."[3]

Decriminalization would eliminate the criminal sanctions that people who sell services experience for being sex workers, including arrests and constant police surveillance. It is a demand for state recognition of sex workers' autonomy to make choices regarding how they employ their bodies. Advocacy groups argue that the continued criminalization of sex work endangers sex workers by exposing them to law enforcement officials who selectively enforce prostitution laws and target sex workers by arresting them, soliciting bribes, and/or sexually exploiting them. Moreover, advocates argue that criminalization stigmatizes sex workers by labeling their

Radical History Review
Issue 148 (January 2024)   DOI 10.1215/01636545-10846879
© 2024 by MARHO: The Radical Historians' Organization, Inc.

conduct as unlawful, pushing them further to the margins of society, and making it difficult for sex workers to access state resources. Advocates argue that removing the threat of imminent arrest and/or criminalization would bring sex workers a little closer to a better material reality and would make them less fearful of interacting with the state. However, decriminalization would not solve all the problems that sex workers encounter; it would merely eliminate some of the most harmful aspects of criminalization, which include confinement, arrest, and caging. Thus decriminalization would only be a first step in addressing the needs of sex workers. Sex worker advocates have favored decriminalization as a form of harm reduction for sex work while also highlighting the individual autonomy of sex workers, embracing an approach that has garnered widespread support across the women's rights sector in South Africa.[4]

In 2013 the Commission for Gender Equality released a report embracing decriminalization of sex work and outlining the various ways that criminalization violated the human rights of sex workers.[5] This report details how criminalization violates sex workers' individual rights and argues that sex workers should have autonomy to select their occupation.[6] The emphasis on criminalization in this area is less about using criminal law to protect sex workers and more about freeing sex workers from the violence of criminal law by decriminalizing their activities. The Women's League, the women's wing of the African National Congress, also adopted a rights-based approach in discussing sex work. In 2012 the Women's League stated its support of decriminalization of sex work: "Whatever the ideal approach would be going forward, it is imperative and critical that it embraces the dignity of women, increases job opportunities and decent work for all women; and affords sex workers their human rights, human dignity and access to health care and social justice."[7] The treasurer for the organization, Hlengiwe Mkhize, confirmed that this statement was a show of support for decriminalization. The support for decriminalization provides recognition of the violence created by policing and punishment. For example, in noncriminal labor environments, workers can more easily report employers who sexually harass them because they need not fear that they would in turn be arrested because their labor involved criminal conduct. If sex work were decriminalized, sex workers might be better able to seek assistance from social workers without fearing that they might lose their children because their labor made them "criminals." Sex workers might less frequently be the targets of patrolling police officers who are directed to enforce the prostitution laws. Marginalized people, especially marginalized women who experience subordination on multiple axes, are often profiled and subjected to discriminatory outcomes within the criminal legal system. While poor women engaged in lawful labor face many challenges, they generally do not need to hide in the bushes to avoid police while they are working, nor do they need to lie about their employment because it is criminal. They are generally not the objects of lawful arrests based on their labor. Sex worker–led groups fear that more criminalization facilitates more punishment, more arrests, and more harm.

By contrast, the South African nonprofit organizations Embrace Dignity and the New Life Centre for Girls have opposed the decriminalization of sex work. "Embrace Dignity recognizes prostitution as a form of violence against women. In conditions of gender inequality and deep poverty, it is false to assume that people involved in prostitution are exercising free choice and agency."[8] This organization is committed to the abolition of sex work in South Africa and does not support an individual sex worker's choice to engage in sex work. Similarly, the New Life Centre for Girls "rehabilitates children and women who are commercially sexually exploited and trafficked in South Africa. It was established in April 2005 as a response to the high influx of children and women who are involved or at risk of being involved in prostitution due to child sexual abuse, trafficking, poverty, unemployment, lack of family structure and Orphans."[9] These organizations focus on the moral regulation of sex work and treat sex work as inherently undignified. The South African Christian Lawyers' Association, a socially conservative organization, has also argued that reform efforts should focus on ensuring that sex work never occurs.[10]

The problem with this approach to sex work, which opposes decriminalization, is that it fails to contend with the state violence that marginalized sex workers experience when sex work is criminalized. A report by SWEAT and Human Rights Watch found that "the criminalisation of sex work contributes to and reinforces stigma and discrimination against sex workers. Many [sex workers] interviewed for this report described multiple experiences of stigma and discrimination, ranging from being denied access to housing to verbal abuse by members of the public."[11] The continued criminalization of sex work tends to be most harmful to sex workers, who deal with intersectional subordination and are already marginalized just for existing. For sex workers who are women, Black, queer, migrants, or any intersection of those identities, any form of criminalization brings a host of consequences that harm the populations that criminalization aims to protect. These women are marginalized not just as women but also as Black women, women with disabilities, or women who are poor.

For two years I conducted ethnographic fieldwork with sex workers in Johannesburg, South Africa, and Amanda was one of my key informants. Amanda's story highlights some of the complexities of relying on criminal law to address the harms of sex work. When she first arrived in South Africa from Zimbabwe, Amanda had to "squat" with her aunt for some time because she didn't have a place to stay. She eventually began working as a domestic worker and was paid very little, no more than R1,500 each month (about US$100 a month at the time). As a domestic worker, she was working for a married man and his wife, and the wife was justifiably suspicious of her husband. The husband told Amanda that she was a "pretty girl" and promised to take care of her. While Amanda could have reported her employer or sought state protection to address her situation, she instead left this employment.

One day Amanda saw a group of male friends with some "beautiful ladies who worked at Royal Park." The ladies bought drinks for all the men and told Amanda,

"You can use your body to do that yourself." Amanda asked the guys she was with where to go, and she soon started working at the Hillbrow Inn. Amanda described the money she was earning as "too much." Amanda bought a fridge for R4,000 (about US$400 at the time), which she earned in one week. She went to restaurants, like Ocean Basket (a South African restaurant similar to the American restaurant Red Lobster) in Eastgate and enjoyed life in ways she did not before she became a sex worker. Amanda has two brothers, a mother, and two kids. She became the breadwinner for her family and stated that she "sacrificed for the family."

As Amanda frequently told me, "It's not about men or sex, just money. . . . It wasn't easy [to do this]. This work can sometimes be humiliating." One client failed to pay her for services, which really upset her because she went to his place for the transaction. When she confronted him, she said: "I need my money, and you wasted my time. I can't waste time." She had been with this client for two days. His wife learned of his infidelity and returned home early from a family trip to her mother's house. When the wife arrived, Amanda informed the wife that she was just a friend and did not want her husband. Amanda, who is in her early thirties, said that she was just passing through and that both the wife and the husband were younger than her. "Why would your husband want me? I'm old." However, the husband had not yet paid her for the services she had rendered, and Amanda waited there from 10:00 a.m. to 4:00 p.m. as the husband and wife argued. She finally left, but not before she had an opportunity to take the husband's identification and cellular phone as insurance of future payment. Once the husband realized that he was missing his personal items, Amanda was compensated. Amanda had found a strategy for adapting to the uncertainty of future payment for services that had already been rendered.

Amanda eventually quit working at Hillbrow Inn after a couple of years and became a domestic worker earning R4,000 per month. However, when I met with her, she was reconsidering her decision to leave the sex industry, because she earned significantly less money as a domestic worker than as a sex worker. She also told me that she missed the companionship, albeit performative, that came during sex work encounters. She had grown accustomed to constant physical contact and numerous dates with new people. Amanda's story was echoed by the dozens of sex workers I interviewed during my ethnography. Most of the sex workers did not actively desire to do sex work, but they enjoyed the financial freedom it afforded them. Sex work allowed them to provide for their families but also exposed them to various occupational hazards. Yet such hazards were negotiated through a system of coping mechanisms that allowed sex workers to minimize the risks. Sex workers often recounted working several sex work hot spots before settling on a location where they felt comfortable. They often worked with friends and could check out potential clients before entering their cars. Several sex workers had police clients whom they would call if they were having issues with other clients. They found ways to manage the risks of their occupation.

Amanda was not merely a victim; she made choices but nonetheless had to manage real risks and dangers associated with her job. Treating sex workers as victims is an understandably attractive option. After all, victims fit into neat narratives that portray women as needing protection. However, we must question whether some feminists, when they denounce sex work and relegate sex workers to victimhood, reinforce male sexual hegemony and paternalism predicated on the assumption that women are helpless and require protection because they cannot remain emotionally detached during sex. Men are not perceived as victims in sex work transactions because they are presumed to be emotionally detached from the sex, viewing it merely as physical release. The feminist narrative that opposes sex work discounts the possibility that men can be sex workers or that men might be the less powerful actors in a sex work transaction. It does not consider whether women can be similarly detached from sex and can view sex as a mere physical act for obtaining money. Some of this narrative's premises strengthen arguments that underlie patriarchy and systems that deny women's open expressions of sexuality and ability to exploit their sexuality.

Several domestic workers in South Africa have told me that they felt degraded by their work or would choose other work under more favorable circumstances. Should their form of labor also be criminalized to protect their dignity? Should all forms of "undignified" labor expose its participants to the violence of criminalization and policing? Should sex work be unique in this respect? While the noncriminalized nature of domestic labor has not eliminated all the vulnerabilities that people engaged in domestic labor experience, domestic workers are free from the discriminatory policing that sex workers regularly encounter; they can report their earning and obtain pension benefits when they retire; they can provide an employment letter to landlords when they seek housing because their labor is lawful; and they can freely go to the local labor board to report unsafe working conditions without fearing that police officers would be waiting outside the labor board to arrest them after they make their complaint. The civil remedies available to noncriminalized laborers do not eliminate all the unsafe conditions laborers encounter, but they do provide an avenue for workers to seek state assistance without fearing that they will lose their liberty for doing so.

Whether dignified or not, sex work can change lives and create greater freedom from patriarchal structures in its ability to change the economic reality of sex workers. The history of sex work in South Africa reveals that women have used sex work for economic gain since the 1650s. There are reports of female slaves purchasing their freedom with the proceeds of their work as sex workers.[12] While these women were undoubtedly in a position of diminished power, such a power imbalance does not erase the fact that sex work was a tool of empowerment for them. This raises the question of whether feminist debates around sex work need to consider more thoroughly the pragmatic considerations and consequences of the varying stances on it.

Remarkably, I found some convergence of interests between sex workers and police officers during my ethnography. All but one police officer whom I interviewed favored the decriminalization of sex work, and police officers often described its criminalization as a distraction from addressing more serious conduct. Members of the police indicated that there should be a policy to protect sex workers and address their concerns:

INDIA: What are your thoughts on prostitution?

APRIL (POLICE OFFICER):   I think there must be a system or a department that deals with it because they are humans and they need to be helped, so that they can deal with the challenges that they are facing. If need be, they can be put in a very secure place so that they can trade.

Sex workers frequently displayed autonomy and agency in their relationships with police, evincing dispersed power relations and showing that even those who have been labeled as "vulnerable" or marginalized retain the power to resist and act on others.[13] Engagement with the state is complex, and power can be harnessed by various actors, even the seemingly vulnerable.

In many instances during my study, police officers abused their authority and failed to protect sex workers. However, the relationship between police and sex workers was complicated. Sex workers often recounted times when they called on the police for assistance and indicated that their relationship with police "just depends." Police officers generally expressed a willingness to improve their relationship with sex workers and indicated that their current relationship was quite poor.

CARY (CENTRAL JOHANNESBURG SEX WORKER):   We meet some bad guys on the streets. . . . Guys were trying to rob us, and they [South African Police Service] helped so many times. . . . Metro [Metropolitan Police Service] is full of shit. They chase us away, if you don't run it's a problem.

INDIA: Do prostitutes call police for assistance?

CHRIS (HILLBROW POLICE OFFICER):   Yes, they do. When they need help, they do.

INDIA: Have you responded to prostitutes' calls for assistance?

CHRIS: Yes, once. He [the client] slept with someone else so the guy didn't pay the lady. So they came to the police station. She [the sex worker] wanted to open a case, but it was an argument between two parties. I talked to the guy to give the lady the money that she deserves.

Some sex workers indicated that the criminalization of sex work prevented them from seeking police assistance:

ANNIE (CENTRAL JOHANNESBURG SEX WORKER):   Clients are beating us sometimes, taking our money.

INDIA: Do you feel comfortable going to the police?

ANNIE: No, [they're] going to say [I'm] selling my body, they [police] took something [my money]. . . . [I would] feel embarrassed.

Both the police officers and sex workers I encountered understood decriminalization as the removal of the state's ability to arrest and use violence to prevent people from selling sexual services.

However, the state would also have obligations to protect sex workers and validate their human rights under the South African Constitution beyond preventing the violence that stems from criminalization. This aspect of decriminalization is much less developed. What comes after criminal sanctions are removed? The state would need to invest resources to address income inequality and provide the social benefits that all workers need, including mechanisms for ensuring that they work in safe environments and are paid fairly. The state would need to ensure that the criminalization of sex work was not replaced by a civil system of fines and tickets that similarly punished sex workers for their work. There would need to be a commitment to destigmatize sex work, so that sex workers are less vulnerable to exclusion and exploitation. The continued criminalization of sex workers makes it difficult for them to seek assistance for their client disputes.

Advocates frequently argue that sex workers need to have access to the police for criminal remedies, but when they experience violence by clients, little attention is paid to the civil remedies that would be available to them if sex work were decriminalized. Formal decriminalization might improve access to justice by encouraging sex workers to enforce contracts that they have with others in the sex industry and to be forthcoming about the nature of their disputes when seeking police assistance. They might be able to bring civil lawsuits or seek administrative remedies that address their working conditions.

But South Africa is a nation that struggles with income inequality, and many people live in poverty. There is xenophobia. There is social inequality. There is sexism. Decriminalization of sex work would not eliminate these systemic problems. Sex workers would likely to continue to experience the harms of social inequality even if sex work were decriminalized. Nevertheless, decriminalization would eliminate the threat of being arrested and the stigma of being a criminal. Decriminalization might allow sex workers to imagine the material reality that they would want the state to provide for them in a post-decriminalization world. In fact, decriminalization might be the necessary first step for sex workers to live in a material world where they feel safer and in better control of their lives.

India Thusi is a professor of law and Charles L. Whistler Faculty Fellow at Indiana University Bloomington's Maurer School of Law as well as a senior scientist at the Kinsey Institute. Her research adopts an anthropological methodology and examines racial and sexual hierarchies as they relate to policing and criminalization. Her articles have appeared in the *Harvard Law Review*, the *Northwestern Law Review*, the *NYU Law Review*, and other journals. Her book *Policing Bodies* (2021) examines the policing of sex workers in South Africa.

Notes

1. See Richter et al., "Sex Work and the 2010 FIFA World Cup," arguing for decriminalization.
2. Fick, *Coping with Stigma*; Manoek, *"Stop Harassing Us!"*
3. Human Rights Watch, *Why Sex Work Should Be Decriminalised in South Africa*.
4. See, e.g., Boudin and Richter, "Adult, Consensual Sex Work in South Africa," discussing the practical realities of sex workers and the need for sex worker autonomy in choosing to engage in body work.
5. Commission for Gender Equality, *Decriminalising Sex Work in South Africa*, 6: "The current legal regime harms the interests of sex workers by denying them their human and constitutional rights to protection as well as preventing access to legal assistance and enjoyment of their labour rights. However the current legal context has led to harassment and abuse of sex workers at the hands of the police."
6. The Commission for Gender Equality position brief further explains the rationale for its advocacy for sex work decriminalization and, like other sources, in part relies on the narrative that decriminalization will protect the sex worker against police harassment. See Commission for Gender Equality, "Position Paper on Sex Work," 9: "The criminalization of sex work harms sex workers and denies them access to the rights contained in our constitution. Sex workers are subjected to numerous human rights violations, predominately harassment and abuse at the hands of police officers, and are not able to access and exercise legal or labour rights, or social protections."
7. African National Conference, discussion paper.
8. Embrace Dignity, https://www.facebook.com/EmbraceDignity/ (accessed August 15, 2023).
9. New Life Centre for Girls, https://www.facebook.com/p/New-Life-Centre-For-Girls -Midrand-100079518696201/ (accessed August 15, 2023).
10. Davis, "ANC Women's League."
11. Human Rights Watch, *Why Sex Work Should Be Decriminalised in South Africa*.
12. Trotter, "Dockside Prostitution in South African Ports," 677.
13. Foucault, *History of Sexuality*.

References

African National Conference. Discussion Paper on Gender Based Violence, 14. 2012.

Boudin, Chesa, and Marlise Richter. "Adult, Consensual Sex Work in South Africa: The Cautionary Message of Criminal Law and Sexual Morality." *South African Journal on Human Rights* 25, no. 2 (2009): 179–97.

Commission for Gender Equality. *Decriminalising Sex Work in South Africa: Official Position of the Commission for Gender Equality*. 2013. https://cge.org.za.

Commission for Gender Equality. "Position Paper on Sex Work." January 16, 2013.

Davis, Rebecca. "The ANC Women's League and the World's Oldest Profession." *Daily Maverick*, March 27, 2012. https://www.dailymaverick.co.za/article/2012-03-27-the-anc-womens-league-and-the-worlds-oldest-profession/.

Fick, Nicolé. *Coping with Stigma, Discrimination, and Violence: Sex Workers Talk about Their Experiences*. Cape Town: SWEAT, 2005.

Foucault, Michel. *The History of Sexuality*. Translated by Robert Hurley. Vol. 1. New York: Pantheon, 1978.

Human Rights Watch. *Why Sex Work Should Be Decriminalised in South Africa*. 2019. http://www.sweat.org.za/wp-content/uploads/2020/01/Why-Sex-Work-Should-be-Decriminalsed.pdf.

Manoek, Stacey-Leigh. *"Stop Harassing Us! Tackle Real Crime!" A Report on Human Rights Violations by Police against Sex Workers in South Africa*. Women's Legal Centre, August 2012. http://wlce.co.za.

Richter, Marlise L., Matthew F. Chersich, Fiona Scorgie, Stanley Luchters, Marleen Temmerman, and Richard Steen. "Sex Work and the 2010 FIFA World Cup: Time for Public Health Imperatives to Prevail." *Globalization and Health* 6 (2010). https://globalizationandhealth.biomedcentral.com/articles/10.1186/1744-8603-6-1.

Trotter, Henry. "Dockside Prostitution in South African Ports." *History Compass* 6, no. 3 (2008): 673–90.

Embodying Revolution

Situating Iran within Transnational Feminist Solidarities

Manijeh Moradian

The revolution that began in Iran in the fall of 2022 under the slogan "Women, Life, Freedom" has placed gender equality and sexual and bodily freedoms at the pulsing heart of a broad, multiethnic movement to transform the Iranian government from a theocratic dictatorship to a secular democracy. It has also engendered modes of solidarity characteristic of transnational feminist organizing. Ignited that September by the death in police custody of a twenty-two-year-old Kurdish woman, Jina (Mahsa) Amini, who was arrested and beaten for allegedly wearing "improper hijab," the protests began in Amini's hometown of Saqqez, in Iranian Kurdistan, where her family had the prescience to engrave the following message on her tombstone: "Dear Jina, you won't die. Your name will become a symbol." That is, she would be not a "martyr," a word deeply embedded in the official lexicon of the Islamic Republic of Iran (IRI), but a symbol—of everything that is unjust and cruel and of everything that is worth fighting for. The slogan "Women, Life, Freedom" (*Jin, Jiyan, Azadi* in Kurdish) comes to Iranian Kurds and to all of Iran from the ideological orientation known as Jineology, which was adopted by Kurdish organizations in Turkey and Syria.[1] The Partiya Karkerên Kurdistan (PKK) deliberately eschewed patriarchal nationalism in favor of "democratic confederalism" and developed a socialist politics rooted in the self-emancipation of women.[2] The slogan "Women, Life, Freedom" thus indexes regional affiliations and solidarities and

Radical History Review

Issue 148 (January 2024)   DOI 10.1215/01636545-10846893

© 2024 by MARHO: The Radical Historians' Organization, Inc.

also operates as an intersectional demand to recognize that "Iranian women" face different experiences of marginalization and repression because of ethnic, linguistic, religious, and class hierarchies.

From Kurdistan, the uprising spread with a breadth and speed that defied prediction. Young women and girls were at the forefront, and they were quickly joined by young men. Together this generation, drawn from the working and middle classes, has crossed all of the "red lines" of the IRI. Women have removed and burned their state-mandated headscarves. Women and men have violated gender segregation in public spaces and bans against socializing with unrelated members of the opposite sex. Girls as young as elementary- and middle-school age have shouted down government officials, disrespected the supreme leader, and insisted on their right to decide for themselves what to wear and what to believe. Images of revolt went viral, galvanizing all of Iran and the Iranian diaspora: young, uncovered women and men dancing together in the streets around bonfires, defending the streets with hastily assembled barricades, fighting off security forces, trying to save each other from arrest, taking over their campuses and schoolyards, singing, marching, chanting. This collective defiance suddenly made it possible to reimagine and reorient a society, a culture, a consciousness, a body, or rather the relations between and among many bodies shaking off the accumulated weight of fear, shame, alienation, and despair.

These actions expressed the resolute conviction that no other woman should die or go to prison or be tortured or "reeducated" over the issue of hijab. This militant stance quickly catalyzed an outpouring of all other social, political, and economic grievances, drawing in wide sections of the population that would likely hesitate to call themselves feminists. Rather than diluting the cause, however, in the initial weeks and months of the uprising, the right to freedom from patriarchal state violence gained widespread legitimacy within Iran as a baseline measure of the future that protesters, including striking students and workers, were trying to create. This was a stark reversal of the dynamics of the 1979 revolution, when thousands of Iranian women poured into the streets of Tehran on International Women's Day to protest the first gestures toward mandatory hijab by the provisional government, rightly understanding this attack on women's bodily autonomy as a harbinger of a broader authoritarian turn.[3] While the issue of women's equality was sidelined in the name of national unity forty-four years ago, this new uprising generated such a widespread understanding of gender and sexual oppression as central to the operations and structures of authoritarian power as a whole that a nationwide uprising ensued.

Less than two weeks into the uprising, news came from the impoverished southeastern province of Sistan and Baluchestan that a fifteen-year-old girl had been raped by a local police chief in the city of Chabahar. The "Chabahari girl" became a symbol for Baloch women activists such as the group Voice of Baloch Women, which issued a statement connecting the patriarchal violence of the state, the clergy, and the clan with the systemic impoverishment and marginalization of Baloch people.[4] The use of sexual violence by the state against jailed protesters— women and men—is a long-standing tactic of the IRI, and the particularly brutal targeting of ethnic minorities, including the "Bloody Friday" massacre in the Baloch city of Zahedan, made headlines as the government attempted to suppress the uprising.[5] Coming just a couple of years after Iran's #MeToo movement shook up the country by breaking social taboos against talking about sexual assault and by naming names of perpetrators in positions of power, this new uprising takes aim at gender and sexual violence within the public as well as the private sphere.[6]

The revolution has gone beyond merely asking that women be equal to men. On February 15, 2023, a coalition of twenty labor, student, and civil society organizations based in Iran issued a charter that including the following among its demands:

> The immediate announcement of complete equal rights between men and
> women in all political, economic, social, cultural, and familial fields. All forms
> of discrimination and discriminatory laws against any gender, sexuality, or
> sexual orientation must be abolished. We demand the official recognition of the
> LGBTQIA+ community and the decriminalization of any gender or sexual
> orientation. The unconditional commitment to grant women total rights over
> their bodies and choices, and the prohibition of the enforcement of patriarchal
> control.[7]

Such a capacious call for equal rights for all genders and sexual orientations is part of what makes this uprising different than previous opposition movements. Furthermore, these and other demands must be understood as the culmination of many decades of organizing, when women's groups, unions, and student organizations tried valiantly to work within the system for change, including through the electoral process and through legal and judicial channels.[8] This new uprising is a response to the IRI's violent resistance to reform and has quickly generated a profoundly feminist understanding of the goals of revolution and of the meaning of freedom unprecedented in the history of Iran.

Rather than view the movement in Iran in isolation, as commentators and supporters in the West—both Iranian and non-Iranian—generally do, a transnational feminist approach that takes into account the national and historical specificity of the uprising and also situates it as one leading edge in a global fight against patriarchy and authoritarianism would be far more productive. What would it mean to analyze Iran in relation to other regional movements that pinpoint the intersections between state repression and gender and sexual oppression and seek revolutionary self-determination in response, for example in Afghanistan, Iraq, or Palestine? What if we look beyond the region to Latin America, the scene of mass feminist mobilizations and strikes? How might this perspective allow for a cross-pollination among movements, an exchange of ideas and strategies, the learning of lessons that might be transposed from one context to another, and the strengthening of grassroots South-South solidarities? Can we imagine the feminist uprising in Iran as part of the "feminist international" that, as Verónica Gago explains, "is made up of alliances that defy the limits of nation-state geometry" and that contest "abstract notions of class (in which shared 'interests' are assumed a priori) or the people (in which an amalgam of homogenous national affection is taking as a given)"?[9]

Addressing these questions will involve reexamining some of the frameworks and practices developed under the sign of transnational feminism. Feminists residing in countries that have waged the "war on terror" and systematically targeted Muslim populations domestically will have to find ways of condemning Islamophobic racism and Islamic fundamentalism at the same time. A starting point must be a principled stance in solidarity with the efforts of women and LGBTQ people, from all national, ethnic, religious, and class backgrounds, to assert full equality and bodily freedom from state repression everywhere. On the hypervisible, hyperstigmatized issue of hijab, this principle requires a defense of the right of women not to wear hijab when it is imposed on them under threat of violence, as well as a defense of the right of women to wear hijab free from legal and extralegal discrimination and violence. The notion of voluntary, rather than mandatory, hijab should be fully compatible with opposition to the modes of US imperialism that rely on gendered anti-Muslim logics. It is the project of feminists everywhere to challenge and change the repressive aspects of the dominant cultures of their societies. This work need not undermine national sovereignty but instead can deepen and strengthen the work of demilitarization, decolonization, and democratization from below.

The militant stance of Iranian women and men against patriarchal state violence in Iran has already resonated with other feminist movements and created new forms of transnational and diasporic activism. A global perspective is already in operation for some Iranian women eager to break Iran's relative isolation and to be connected to feminist practices that have emerged in other contexts. For example, Feminists for Jina, a network of Iranian feminists living outside Iran that formed in September 2022 in solidarity with the "Jina Revolution" in Iran, drew inspiration from women's resistance to gendered violence and dictatorship in many locations, including in the Caribbean and Latin America. Distinct from the established Iranian diasporic population that fled the 1979 revolution, Feminists for Jina is composed predominantly of Iranian women who grew up in the Islamic Republic, left as adults, and remain deeply connected to contemporary Iranian society.

In an effort to emphasize and support the feminist elements of the uprising, the network prepared to lead protest rallies in multiple cities in Europe and North America on November 25, the International Day for the Elimination of Violence against Women. On this day in 1960, the Mirabal sisters were assassinated for their resistance to the Trujillo dictatorship in the Dominican Republic, and the ritual of marking their deaths was taken up by feminist groups before eventually gaining recognition from the United Nations.[10] In the days before the November 25 actions, Feminists for Jina activists and their supporters organized, documented, and posted on social media Persian-language performances of the Chilean song "A Rapist in Your Path." Somewhere between a song and a chant, with coordinated choreography, this piece was initially created by the Chilean feminist group Las Tesis and performed on November 25, 2019, the result of careful research and strategizing about how to enable feminist theory to circulate widely and inform larger social movements against neoliberal austerity.[11] As Verónica Dávila and Marisol LeBrón have argued, "The song speaks to the particularities of gendered violence" and has also "struck a chord around the globe."[12] Since 2019 thousands of women across Latin America and the Caribbean have performed the piece, as well as women in India, Turkey, and Iran on International Women's Day 2021, a phenomenon Ana López Ricoy calls "South-South symbolic transnationalism."[13]

Feminists for Jina performances of "A Rapist in Your Path" in Berlin, London, New York, and elsewhere built on the 2021 Iranian iteration but further adapted the Persian translation of the words to amplify the revolutionary activity of Iranian women since September 2022.[14] As Paula Serafina has argued, "Participants in the performance are speaking truth to power in a collective act of denunciation that marks a point of no return: We are no longer silenced, and you are no longer shielded."[15] The uprising in Iran shifted where this point of no return is located politically. Whereas the Persian lyrics from 2021 reflected the Iranian context by naming hijab, forced marriage, and acid attacks against women as part of the overarching system of patriarchal state oppression in Iran that the song exposed, the November 2022 diasporic version named the security forces (Sepah) and the supreme leader (*rahbar*), the top authority in the IRI, thereby injecting an explicit call for revolution into the piece.

Transnational performances of "A Rapist in Your Path" expressed what I have elsewhere called "revolutionary affects," those embodied intensities that remain after encounters with repression and resistance and that can later be tapped as sources of energy fueling new attachments to revolutionary struggle.[16] Following the young women in Iran whose revolutionary affects set the collective mood for street protests when they took off their hijabs and fought back against security forces, Iranian women in diaspora wanted to throw their own bodies into this fight.[17] More than ordinary rallies and chants, the performances of what has come to be called "The Rapist Is You" provided this opportunity. As López Ricoy notes, "The performance meant reinforcing a collective identity by sparking a sense of embodied catharsis. It was not only a moment of collective unity but also of embodying a shared grievance."[18] The Feminists for Jina performances expressed solidarity with women in Iran, Latin America, and elsewhere. But they were also a vital chance for participants to express their own accumulated experiences of patriarchy and gender and sexual violence. The videos of these November 2022 performances were posted and shared widely on social media, making it possible to incorporate the new Iranian uprising into transnational feminist circuits of affect, solidarity, and militancy.

As I write, the task of sustaining the movement in Iran against brutal state repression, foreign machinations, and diasporic efforts at co-optation remains daunting, especially in the absence of established opposition parties or ideologies within Iran. It is precisely in this context that the efforts of networks like Feminists for Jina to build solidarity from below matter most, and the question of whether or not Iran becomes a legible site of solidarity for other revolutionary feminist movements takes on great urgency. The body is both a powerful tool of resistance and an archive of revolutionary affects that remain, even during periods of backlash. As Débora de Fina Gonzalez argues, "Performance-based protests reflect embodied dimensions of social struggle. What they generate, despite their ephemeral nature, goes beyond protest events."[19] Even while the IRI remains in power, it is at the level of the body that a historical impasse has been broken.

Manijeh Moradian is an assistant professor of women's, gender, and sexuality studies at Barnard College, Columbia University. She is the author of *This Flame Within: Iranian Revolutionaries in the United States* (2022).

Notes

1. Askew, "Words Have Power"; Tasdemir, "Feminization of Pro-Kurdish Party Politics in Turkey."
2. Düzgün, "Jineology."
3. Moradian, *This Flame Within*, 215–46.
4. Slingers Collective, "Why Is Chabahari Girl Our Code Name?"
5. Ghadarkhan, "Activist Reports Mass Sexual Abuse in Iran's Detention Centers." On the "Bloody Friday" massacre, see Human Rights Watch, "Iran."
6. Yaghoobi, *The #MeToo Movement in Iran*.
7. Zamaneh Media, "Twenty Independent Trade Unions and Civil Organisations."
8. Hedayat, "'Revolution Is Inevitable.'"
9. Gago, *Feminist International*, 182.
10. United Nations, "International Day."
11. Serafini, "'A Rapist in Your Path,'" 292. See also de Fina Gonzalez, "'A Rapist in Your Path,'" 595.
12. Dávila and LeBrón, "'Un Violador en tu Camino.'"
13. López Ricoy, "South-South Symbolic Transnationalism."
14. For the 2019 performance in Iran, see Fem Rebel, "متجاوز تویی—The Rapist Is You (Farsi)."
15. Serafini, "'A Rapist in Your Path,'" 294.
16. Moradian, *This Flame Within*, 7–9.
17. For a participant's account of revolutionary activity as embodied and transformative in the new Iranian feminist revolution, see "L," "Figuring a Woman's Revolution."
18. López Ricoy, "South-South Symbolic Transnationalism," 501.
19. de Fina Gonzalez, "'A Rapist in Your Path,'" 597.

References

Askew, Joshua. "Words Have Power: What Are the Origins of Iran's Protest Chant 'Woman, Life, Freedom'?" *Euro News*, January 2, 2023. https://www.euronews.com/2023/01/11/words-have-power-what-are-the-origins-of-woman-life-freedom-iran-protest-chants.

Dávila, Verónica, and Marisol LeBrón. "'Un Violador en tu Camino' and the Virality of Feminist Protest." *NACLA*, December 27, 2019. https://nacla.org/news/2019/12/27/un-violador-en-tu-camino-virality-feminist-protest.

de Fina Gonzalez, Débora. "'A Rapist in Your Path': Feminist Artivism in the Chilean Social Revolt." *Feminist Studies* 47, no. 3 (2021): 594–98.

Düzgün, Meral. "Jineology: The Kurdish Women's Movement." *Journal of Middle East Women's Studies* 12, no. 2 (2016): 284–87.

Fem Rebel. "تجاوز تویی—The Rapist Is You (Farsi)." YouTube video, posted March 8, 2021. https://www.youtube.com/watch?v=zFupilELupo.

Gago, Verónica. *Feminist International: How to Change Everything*. Translated by Liz Mason-Deese. New York: Verso, 2020.

Ghadarkhan, Samaneh. "Activist Reports Mass Sexual Abuse in Iran's Detention Centers." *Iranwire*, November 30, 2022. https://iranwire.com/en/prisoners/110654-activist-reports-mass-sexual-abuse-in-irans-detention-centers/.

Hedayat, Bahareh. "'Revolution Is Inevitable': Bahareh Hedayat's Letter from Evin Prison in Tehran, Iran." *Jadaliyya*, January 4, 2023. https://www.jadaliyya.com/Details/44720/Revolution-is-Inevitable-Bahareh-Hedayat%E2%80%99s-letter-from-Evin-Prison-in-Tehran,-Iran-December-2022.

Human Rights Watch. "Iran: 'Bloody Friday' Crackdown This Year's Deadliest." December 22, 2022. https://www.hrw.org/news/2022/12/22/iran-bloody-friday-crackdown-years-deadliest.

"L." "Figuring a Woman's Revolution: Bodies Interacting with Their Images." Translated by Alireza Doostdar. *Jadaliyya*, October 5, 2022. https://www.jadaliyya.com/Details/44479/Figuring-a-Women%E2%80%99s-Revolution-Bodies-Interacting-with-their-Images.

López Ricoy, Ana. "South-South Symbolic Transnationalism: Echoing the Performance 'A Rapist in Your Path' in Latin America." *Gender and Development* 29, nos. 2–3 (2021): 493–511.

Moradian, Manijeh. *This Flame Within: Iranian Revolutionaries in the United States*. Durham, NC: Duke University Press, 2022.

Serafini, Paula. "'A Rapist in Your Path': Transnational Feminist Protest and Why (and How) Performance Matters." *European Journal of Cultural Studies* 23, no. 2 (2020): 290–95.

Slingers Collective. "Why Is Chabahari Girl Our Code Name?" November 1, 2022. https://slingerscollective.net/why-is-chabahari-girl-our-code-name/.

Tasdemir, Salima. "The Feminization of Pro-Kurdish Party Politics in Turkey: The Role of Women Activists." PhD diss., University of Exeter, 2013.

United Nations. "International Day for the Elimination of Violence against Women: 25 November." https://www.un.org/en/observances/ending-violence-against-women-day/background.

Yaghoobi, Claudia, ed. *The #MeToo Movement in Iran: Reporting Sexual Violence and Harassment*. New York: Bloomsbury, 2023.

Zamaneh Media. "Twenty Independent Trade Unions and Civil Organisations Issued a Joint Charter of Basic Demands." February 15, 2023. https://en.radiozamaneh.com/33695/.

Feminist Intifada

Palestinian Women through a Century of Organizing

Jennifer Mogannam

In examining various stages of one hundred years of Palestinian women's and feminist organizing, it becomes apparent that Palestinian feminism is not a new phenomenon. Though the most recognized formations that have adopted feminist language in collective mobilizing have emerged in the twenty-first century, a Palestinian anticolonial feminist politics has been brewing since modern, Western forms of colonialism were imposed on the lands and peoples of Palestine. While the development of such a feminism has changed shape and been undermined by shifting colonial and imperialist policies meant to repress the Palestinian liberation struggle, Palestinian feminist political praxis has been mobilized throughout. Each phase of mobilizing has shaped a practice of feminism grounded in how women have inserted themselves into the anticolonial struggle against both British and Zionist colonial forces, and through this practice a feminist politics of liberation and care has emerged. While the term *feminism* remains contentious in Palestinian spaces, Palestinian feminist praxis has been built through every moment of intifada in the Palestinian liberation struggle. *Intifada* is an Arabic term that translates to "uprising" and is largely specific to moments of Palestinian insurgency. As I think through different historical moments of Palestinian intifada, I note the various roles women have played and how those mobilizations create a nonlinear yet necessary trajectory of Palestinian anticolonial feminism. I argue that this trajectory, while not widely accepted due to multidirectional challenges to the concept and language of

Radical History Review
Issue 148 (January 2024)   DOI 10.1215/01636545-10846907
© 2024 by MARHO: The Radical Historians' Organization, Inc.

feminism, is in fact compatible with, and even necessary for, the struggle to actualize Palestinian liberation and freedom.

Palestinian Feminist Formations

On September 26, 2019, *tal'at* emerged across Palestine, through calls for mobilization in response to the intercommunal, gendered murder of the Palestinian woman Israa Gharib.[1] Palestinian feminists situate this murder within a global rise in femicide that results from patriarchal hierarchies that deem women's bodies property and connect family honor to control over women's bodies.[2] The Zionist state further perpetuates the familial anxieties around honor and poses a threat to women's physical safety through infiltration practices for the purposes of blackmail.[3] As my comrade and colleague Shadia[4] narrated to me, the idea of *tal'at* began to form earlier in 2019 and, following some smaller, localized protests, *tal'at* ("We're going out," in the feminine)[5] was used as a slogan to call for nationwide protest in response to growing cases of gendered violence in Palestine. The original intent of this mobilization was a singular day of aligned protest; however, through the immense force, power, and energy of this moment, organizers realized the necessity of continuing to organize this feminist front in a fascinating display of the power of both spontaneity and organization.[6] *Tal'at* mobilized not just women but Palestinians of all genders,[7] and the profound impact rippled across Palestine, the region, and the Palestinian *shatat* (translated most often as "diaspora" but more literally meaning "dispersal" to connote the transnational community of Palestinians outside their homelands). It also evoked a power that women came to assume in organizing spaces that are typically overpowered by male leadership.

The emergence of *tal'at* challenged the social and political culture that perpetuates gender-based violence in Palestinian infrastructures while also calling into question the lack of effective prevention, intervention, and accountability processes for engaging such gendered questions. In turn, this moment reflects a twofold challenge to the patriarchal order. First, it contests Zionist colonial, ideological underpinnings of violence based on gender that have insurmountable effects on Palestinians and serves as a tool for emasculating Palestinian men. There are many instances in which Zionist colonialism genders its colonized subjects. Some examples include the use of sexual violence as a torture practice on Palestinian political prisoners and unequal access to health care that has resulted in mothers birthing their babies at checkpoints because they are not allowed to pass—often resulting in birth complications, including death of the mother, the baby, or both. Second, this moment challenges Palestinian society and political culture to take seriously the egregious consequences of gender inequity and particularly femicide as structurally enabled through Palestinian governing bodies and social status quos. Within Palestinian social and legal structures, there are no clearly defined repercussions for instances of femicide or other forms of gender-based violence, yet solicitations like catcalling in the streets have been monitored by morality police, thus furthering the cultural view that protecting women is an issue of honor and violence against them is a family matter. These pressures are further exacerbated by the technologies of Zionism that prohibit a life of dignity for Palestinians, often prohibiting Palestinian men from their aim of providing economic stability to their families, threatening their sense of masculinity and thus producing an expression of masculinity in the family through regulations of honor, gender, and violence.

This moment of uprising in 2019 left many Palestinians across the *shatat* wondering why there had been such a void in contemporary Palestinian feminist mobilizing. As *tal'at*'s efforts continued to resonate, some organizers in the United States, including me, remained in contact with the organizers in Palestine whom we had encountered in other Palestinian organizing spaces. This relationship was crucial for thinking through the shared need for an explicitly feminist platform in the diaspora. After almost a year of foundational work and process, the Palestinian Feminist Collective (PFC) publicly launched on March 15, 2021, pledging that "Palestine is a feminist issue."[8]

This pledge immediately gained public traction; signatories stepped forward in the hundreds to thousands and are still trickling in nearly three years later. As Palestinian and Arab women and feminists committed to liberation in its multilayered forms, we came together around an idea and a void that we felt. The pledge came out just before the emergence of the unity intifada in 2021, which signified a renewed resurgence of Palestinian resistance to defend land and lives across Palestine's entire geography, from Jerusalem to Gaza and from Nablus to Haifa, as well as retaliatory escalations of violence by the Zionist regime. In this moment the PFC decided to write "A Love Letter to Our People in Palestine."[9] This public letter was in part a response to a letter we learned of from *tal'at* to the women of Jerusalem defending their homes from demolition and lands from confiscation. These initiatives and this moment of heightened resistance led to the mobilization of a letter from gender studies departments in support of the PFC.[10] This unexpected and welcome initiative was released alongside an influx of university departments issuing public statements in support of Palestine. At this moment it became clear, at least in my view, just how critical the need was for a Palestinian feminist formation, both for the Palestinian community and for US-based radical feminist allies, and how deeply felt the PFC message was as it aimed to fill that void.

Historicizing Palestinian Feminism

In tracing historical iterations of Palestinian feminism, we must examine women's organizing spaces, which housed this work almost exclusively until the early 2000s. The queer organizing spaces that emerged in Palestine articulated their organizational trajectories as overtly feminist. Palestinian women's organizing dates back over a century and therefore is far from a new phenomenon. To take the question of Palestinian feminism seriously, we must honor this continuity and the different formations that house this trajectory. Highlighted in the PFC's Feminist Futures 2023 calendar project is this century-long legacy Palestinian women and feminists have created. The work of this project is featured in the physical calendar, in corresponding social media posts, and through programmatic events accompanying the physical calendar.[11] The first iterations of Palestinian and Arab feminisms predated the British Mandate, as we see with women's resistance against the construction of a settlement in Afula as early as 1893 and through to the establishment of women's societies including, most notably, the Arab Women's Association in Jerusalem and localized Arab and Palestinian women's unions across Palestine in the early 1920s.[12] In the early years of resistance under both British and Zionist rule, to the foundations of the Palestinian student movements and emergence of the parties, to the establishment of the Palestine Liberation Organization (PLO) and the anticolonial national liberation movement, women have persisted in their organizing; they have inserted themselves in spaces not relegated to them and paved the way for the participation of more women, signifying an anticolonial, feminist practice of visibilizing and strengthening demands and participation from a broader social base. During the British Mandate, Palestinian women were committed to Palestine as an autonomous and contiguous land-based formation and were unequivocally consistent in their criticisms of colonial migration, militarism, and rule, both British and Zionist, as a foundational part of their principles in organizing.[13] This legacy of Palestinian and Arab women's organizing persisted in multiple forms across the past century.

During the peak of the liberation movement, known as the *thawra*, or revolution, from the 1960s to the 1980s, Palestinian women largely mobilized through the General Union of Palestinian Women (GUPW) as well as the various political parties and PLO unions. At this time, the Palestinian liberation movement was consolidated under the PLO, one united infrastructure that housed political parties, popular resistance unions, guerrilla organizations, and executive infrastructures that moved forward a united project and strategy of liberation. In this period, in particular, the aims of women's movements were in line with those of the national liberation struggle, and women inserted themselves within male-dominated spaces to pave the way for more broad-based women's participation in revolutionary activities. These activities centered the creation of a Palestinian national infrastructure in exile to contest the Zionist state's violence and its colonial existence altogether through political party organizing, popular refugee mobilization, and cross-border armed resistance. The national movement at the time, including many revolutionary women active in the movement's organizations, subscribed to the framework that Palestine must be liberated before women can be liberated. While you can read this work through a feminist lens both as a sort of feminist nationalism and as shortsighted in feminist imagination for its relegation of women's issues to a postliberation chronology, the language of feminism was not used as such in either regard. However, women were central to conceiving of a feminist cultural practice from within the movement, putting forth a politics of care and sustaining the revolutionary current through their gendered labor.

Women were central to the organized resistance against colonial, military, and state rule inside Palestine as far back as the 1936 Great Revolt (and preceding it), which lasted three years. In all waves of Palestinian resistance, especially in what has been communally labeled the first intifada in the late 1980s, coordinated popular resistance from within Palestine strongly contested Zionist state violence and militarism. Both the 1936–39 Great Revolt and the first intifada are important moments, in a century of ongoing anticolonial intifadas, for the organized formations that emerged in these two moments as grassroots defenders of Palestinian life, land, and dignity. During the late 1980s Palestinian Islamic movements emerged and women found their way into organizing in these spaces as well, resisting in direct confrontation with Zionist state militarism. Following the early 1990s peace processes, which ultimately resulted in the Oslo Accords[14] and the formation of the Palestinian Authority (PA), a process of both political collapse and an influx of money from foreign nongovernmental organizations (NGOs), particularly from the West, shifted the landscape of women's organizing. This occurred not only in Palestine under the PA but also across the region where Palestinians were displaced, especially in the refugee camps.

This transition reflects the move from a radical nationalist women's organizing modality, whereby women's labor fueled revolution and intergenerational survivance, to a more politically restrictive phase, whereby the collapse in the organizing institutions, coupled with liberal funding with strings attached, created a "women's empowerment" boom across the newly established NGO sector.[15] Many women who were leading the GUPW and the women's movements found themselves moving into NGO positions with narrowly defined women's empowerment foci.[16] As Islah Jad explains, NGOization enables a new, growing form of dependency on the West and is a tool to expand Western hegemony. She argues that a process of decentralizing and fragmenting sociopolitical issues from one another ensues and mobilizes state-building frameworks, localizing women's struggles and decoupling them from the broader liberation struggle.[17] The frameworks brought forth by the funding networks of United Nations and international development organizations revert women's empowerment "back [to] the old dichotomies of West versus East" and inscribe the Westernized notion of women as the model of empowerment to follow.[18] This NGOization move, in combination with the conditions set through the Oslo Accords for Palestinian political elites and wealthy exilees to return to the PA territories, produced a new elite class in Palestine that ushered in a new wave of economic instability through the facade of growing capitalism under occupation. The influx of NGO and PA funding forged a deeper wealth gap as well as reliance on these types of employment opportunities, creating a dependence on colonial and imperialist funding circuits and governing structures to ensure economic stability and survival. Following the counterrevolutionary engagement of the peace process, in which we see the national bourgeoisie become figureheads for a governing body that maintains the colonial regime instead of offering an alternative, and the fracturing of a unified liberation project, a void was deeply felt in terms of Palestinian mobilizing, which, I argue, is still felt today. Of course, this dissolution of organized liberation struggles impacted women as it impacted all of Palestinian society. It created a vacuum of revolutionary infrastructure, leadership, and vision, all of which have continued to devolve incrementally into further fragmentation from the 1990s to today.

Palestinian Feminism Today

While women have continuously been part of Palestinian political life, whether in the PLO, the PA, the secular parties that make up the PLO, or the Islamic parties that emerged in the 1980s, the first Palestinian queer organizations—Aswat and Al-Qaws—emerged in the 2000s, at a time when women's organizing through NGOs was in full force.[19] However, these organizations did not immediately become public, and their work was met with heavy social and political backlash that continues today. While queer organizing situates its work within the conditions of settler colonialism and through feminist visions, it, like feminism, is still not fully integrated into the larger social and political landscape in Palestine or the shatat.

Tal'at and the PFC also face backlash in Palestinian community spaces. Feminism is a challenging concept for Palestinian communities, because the most common iteration of feminism is Western, imperialist feminism. Therefore, using the language of feminism connotes for some an alignment with imperialist aims. This association is as much linked to the anti-imperialist politics of the Palestinian *thawra* as it is to the current phase of NGOization and strings-attached funding streams for women's (and other) organizing. As has been reflected in countless comments on the social media platforms of the PFC as well as *tal'at* and other formations, there are multidirectional challenges to the concept of feminism as a vehicle for anticolonial resistance.

However, the Palestinian feminism that both *tal'at* and the PFC offer stands in stark contrast to imperialist and white feminisms, though in our communities the concept of feminism is often seen as imperialist and Western. In fact, if one engaged in the concepts and politics the PFC is putting forth, one would find that the commitment to Palestinian resistance in all forms, to anticolonial struggle, and to decolonization is central to its feminism. In turn, PFC's feminism is compatible with, and arguably offers necessary frameworks for, the struggle for Palestinian liberation and freedom. What *tal'at* and the PFC offer organizationally, as far as liberation is concerned, is to conjoin political and social struggles and aims as inextricably tied and coconstitutive in the fight for liberation. This is exemplified through *tal'at*'s popularized slogan "no free homeland without free women."[20] These two collectives account for very real material conditions being felt by women and queer Palestinians as multiply and intersectionally oppressed through the duality of being a subject of both colonialism and patriarchy and the entanglement of the two. The feminism put forth by the PFC and *tal'at* are not new among intergenerational Palestinian conversations. However, they articulate a Palestinian feminism of twenty-first-century relevance, building on over a century of Palestinian women's mobilizations and accounting for the material conditions and social struggles central to the Palestinian gendered experience as we mobilize toward actualizing decolonized liberation through sustained Palestinian feminist intifada.

Jennifer Mogannam is an assistant professor of critical race and ethnic studies at the University of California, Santa Cruz. She is a former UC President's Postdoctoral Fellow and a founding member of the Palestinian Feminist Collective.

Notes

1. Rosa Luxemburg Stiftung—Palestine, "Discussion about the New Palestinian Feminist Initiative"; Hawari, "Israa Gharib's Murder Has Nothing to Do with Honour"; Marshood and Alsanah, "Tal'at."
2. Abueish, "Israa Ghareeb."
3. Ben David and Ben David, "'I'd Rather Die in the West Bank'"; Mahmoud, "Film about Israel Collaborators"; O'Connor, "Gay Palestinians Are Being Blackmailed"; Council on American-Islamic Relations, "Israeli Guards Rape Palestinian Women"; Rapoport, "The Disturbing Story from Within"; Mohsen, "Decolonization of Palestine."
4. *Shadia* is used as a pseudonym for someone still actively engaged in the community that *tal'at* created and is part of the leadership community of *tal'at*.
5. Since Arabic is a gendered language, the gendering of the term is an important part of its significance.
6. Fanon, *The Wretched of the Earth*.
7. Giovannetti, "Palestinians Demand Legal Protection."
8. Palestinian Feminist Collective, "Pledge That Palestine Is a Feminist Issue."
9. Palestinian Feminist Collective, "Love Letter."
10. Gender Studies Departments in Solidarity with Palestinian Feminist Collective, "Gender Studies Departments in Solidarity."
11. Palestinian Feminist Collective, "Calendar."
12. Palestinian Feminist Collective, "Calendar."
13. Mogannam, *Arab Woman and the Palestine Problem*.
14. The Oslo Accords were a Western-facilitated attempt at diplomatic resolution between Palestinians and the Zionist state. However, the agreements disregard the refugee question and the question of Jerusalem and have upheld colonial military rule through elaborate mobility-control infrastructures like checkpoints, sniper towers, and the annexation wall and through the rapid expansion of settlements, which continue to confiscate lands and bantustanize West Bank Palestinian territories. See Palestine Remix, "The Price of Oslo."

15. Jad, "The 'NGOization' of the Arab Women's Movements." The concept of intergenerational survivance has been elaborated by Indigenous feminists on whom I draw strongly, including Linda Tuhiwai Smith. See Vizenor, *Survivance*.

16. Hindi, "Narratives of National Struggle."

17. Jad, "'NGOization' of the Arab Women's Movements."

18. Jad, "'NGOization' of the Arab Women's Movements," 46.

19. ASWAT, "Palestinian Feminist Center for Gender and Sexual Freedoms"; Al Qaws, "AlQaws for Sexual and Gender Diversity in Palestinian Society."

20. Rosa Luxemburg Stiftung—Palestine, "Discussion about the New Palestinian Feminist Initiative."

References

Abueish, Tamara. "Israa Ghareeb: A Palestinian Woman Who Lost Her Life in the Name of 'Honor.'" *Al Arabiya English*, September 4, 2019. https://english.alarabiya.net/features/2019/09/04/-We-are-all-Israa-Ghareeb-Death-of-Palestinian-woman-sparks-public-outrage-.

AlQaws. "AlQaws for Sexual and Gender Diversity in Palestinian Society." http://alqaws.org/siteEn/index (accessed March 15, 2023).

ASWAT. "Palestinian Feminist Center for Gender and Sexual Freedoms." https://www.aswatgroup.org/home (accessed March 15, 2023).

Ben David, Tamar, and Lilach Ben David. "'I'd Rather Die in the West Bank': LGBTQ Palestinians Find No Safety in Israel." *+972 Magazine*, September 17, 2021. https://www.972mag.com/lgbtq-palestinians-israel-asylum/.

Council on American-Islamic Relations. "Israeli Guards Rape Palestinian Women." May 20, 2004. https://www.cair.com/cair_in_the_news/israeli-guards-rape-palestinian-women/.

Fanon, Frantz. *The Wretched of the Earth*. Translated by Richard Philcox. New York: Grove, 2004.

Gender Studies Departments in Solidarity with Palestinian Feminist Collective. "Gender Studies Departments in Solidarity with Palestinian Feminist Collective." http://genderstudiespalestinesolidarity.weebly.com/ (accessed March 15, 2023).

Giovannetti, Megan. "Palestinians Demand Legal Protection after 'Honour' Killing of Israa Ghrayeb." *Middle East Monitor*, September 1, 2019. https://www.middleeastmonitor.com/20190901-palestinians-protest-for-legal-protection-of-women-after-killing-of-israa-gharib/.

Hawari, Yara. "Israa Gharib's Murder Has Nothing to Do with Honour." *Al Jazeera*, September 4, 2019. https://www.aljazeera.com/opinions/2019/9/4/israa-gharibs-murder-has-nothing-to-do-with-honour.

Hindi, Zaynah Patricia Munther. "Narratives of National Struggle: Exploring Gender, Empowerment, and the Palestinian National Movement through the Life Stories of Four Palestinian Women." MA thesis, American University of Beirut, 2012.

Jad, Islah. "The 'NGOization' of the Arab Women's Movements." *Al-Raida Journal* 2 (2004): 38–47.

Mahmoud, Amany. "Film about Israel Collaborators Sparks Outcry in Palestine." *Al-Monitor*, April 2, 2022. https://www.al-monitor.com/originals/2022/03/film-about-israel-collaborators-sparks-outcry-palestine.

Marshood, Hala, and Riya Alsanah. "Tal'at: A Feminist Movement That Is Redefining Liberation and Reimagining Palestine." *Mondoweiss*, February 25, 2020. https://mondoweiss.net/2020/02/talat-a-feminist-movement-that-is-redefining-liberation-and-reimagining-palestine/.

Mogannam, Matiel E. T. *The Arab Woman and the Palestine Problem*. London: Joseph, 1937.

Mohsen, Tamam. "The Decolonization of Palestine Demands Dismantling Patriarchal Prejudice." *Mondoweiss*, April 1, 2022. https://mondoweiss.net/2022/04/the-decolonization -of-palestine-demands-dismantling-patriarchal-prejudice/.

O'Connor, Nigel. "Gay Palestinians Are Being Blackmailed into Working as Informants." *Vice*, February 19, 2013. https://www.vice.com/en/article/av8b5j/gay-palestinians-are-being -blackmailed-into-working-as-informants.

Palestine Remix. "The Price of Oslo." https://remix.aljazeera.com/aje/PalestineRemix/mobile /films/the-price-of-oslo/ (accessed August 18, 2023).

Palestinian Feminist Collective. "Calendar—Palestinian Feminist Collective." https://palestinian feministcollective.org/calendar/ (accessed March 15, 2023).

Palestinian Feminist Collective. "A Love Letter to Our People in Palestine." *Jadaliyya*—جدلية, May 14, 2021. https://www.jadaliyya.com/Details/42739.

Palestinian Feminist Collective. "Pledge That Palestine Is a Feminist Issue." https:// actionnetwork.org/petitions/pledge-declaring-palestine-is-a-feminist-issue (accessed March 15, 2023).

Rapoport, Meron. "The Disturbing Story from Within." *Middle East Eye* (French ed.), February 12, 2015. http://www.middleeasteye.net/opinion/disturbing-story-within.

Rosa Luxemburg Stiftung—Palestine. "A Discussion about the New Palestinian Feminist Initiative, Tal'at—Part of the Revolutionary Feminist Tradition." March 24, 2020. https://www.rosalux.ps/2992-2992/.

Vizenor, Gerald. *Survivance: Narratives of Native Presence*. Lincoln: University of Nebraska Press, 2008.

"We Came Together and We Fought"

Kipp Dawson and Resistance to State Violence
in US Social Movements since the 1950s

Jessie B. Ramey and Catherine A. Evans

For over sixty years Kipp Dawson has built coalitions on the front lines of major social movements confronting state-sponsored violence. Dawson's collaborative leadership in the Vietnam antiwar campaign and movements for civil rights, women's rights, gay liberation, labor, and education justice challenged forms of active harm and death (fig. 1). Operating alongside others, she resisted powerful systems of discrimination, staggering divestment, and purposeful neglect. Her astonishing career—and marginalized identities as a lesbian, Jewish, working-class woman from a multiracial family—demonstrates the radical power of ordinary people engaged in collective, transformative action.

In this visual essay, we share material from two new archival collections our team helped curate: the Kipp Dawson Papers, housed at the University of Pittsburgh, and over thirty interviews with Dawson, now part of the Women Miners Oral History Project at West Virginia University. These materials span the remarkable breadth and depth of Dawson's intersectional feminist activism and suggest rethinking leadership as a concept to fully appreciate the scope, interconnectedness, and efficacy of resistance to state violence. Rather than view her work through a traditional, patriarchal leadership lens—locating a solo leader at the top of a power hierarchy—we approach Dawson's lifetime of work through a framework of "radical collaboration." Women have often performed the invisible labor of this intentional,

Radical History Review
Issue 148 (January 2024)   DOI 10.1215/01636545-10846922

Figure 1.   Dawson's collection of buttons from movement organizing. Courtesy of Kipp Dawson.

transformational, and diffuse form of leadership. Radical collaboration prioritizes relationship building, fosters networks of community care, and redefines movement goals. In the following chronological sections, we present excerpts from interviews with Dawson along with historical context and archival items to demonstrate the role of women's radical collaboration in organizing both resistance to state violence and alternative visions for the nation.

Civil Rights Movement

In 1960, at the age of fifteen, Dawson cofounded the first civil rights club at Berkeley High School with Brenda Malveaux (now Freeman) and Tracy Sims (now Tamam Tracy Moncur). The three young women started their group, Students for Equality, in solidarity with the southern sit-in movement and the newly forming Student Nonviolent Coordinating Committee (SNCC). After being outed for having a romantic relationship with another woman, Dawson graduated from high school at sixteen and enrolled in San Francisco State College. Convinced that socialism provided the necessary space for collective action and an alternative vision for the future, she joined the Young Socialist Alliance and the Socialist Workers Party (SWP), affiliations she maintained until the late 1980s. By 1963–64 Tracy Sims was leading the Ad Hoc Committee to End Discrimination in Hiring, and Dawson helped co-organize large-scale sit-ins, including those at Mel's Diner, the Sheraton-Palace Hotel, and Auto-Row, challenging racist hiring practices in San Francisco (fig. 2).[1]

Figure 2. Dawson and Tracy Sims circa 1964 at their arraignment following an arrest for a sit-in demonstration. The small black button on Dawson's sleeve says, "Ad-Hoc's COMIN'!" Unless otherwise indicated, the photographs in this essay are found in Kipp Dawson Papers, 1951–2021, AIS.2022.10, Archives and Special Collections, University of Pittsburgh Library System.

Arrested six times, Dawson served twenty-nine days in the San Francisco County Jail. During one arrest, the guards threw Dawson and two others into solitary confinement for singing in the holding cell. The remaining women protested together by rhythmically banging their mattresses on the floor, demonstrating what Dawson emphasizes as the power of solidarity to confront state violence:

> They won and none of them thought that she had done anything really unusual
> because, really, she hadn't. Each of them recognized that their strength was
> *collective* rather than individual and that when they put their strength together
> they could do things that they might not have ever thought or imagined that
> they would ever be called on to do. And they freed us.[2]

The Bay Area civil rights protests activated students, leading directly to the launch of the Free Speech Movement at the University of California Berkeley, and then, under Dawson, at San Francisco State College.[3] With thousands of students participating in acts of mass disobedience, the effort won the lifting of university bans on political activity and created free speech zones, further supporting movement organizing. Dawson credits the success of these reform efforts to women's collaborative leadership, especially the legacy of Black women's solidarity networks (fig. 3):

> Behind the scenes, doing the grunt work—the work, really—and organizing
> the communication, organizing the backup, and then putting bodies on the
> line, too . . . it was women who stood out. . . . [Black women] established the
> networks of communication and solidarity that have made such huge transitions
> possible. . . . And just like all those women . . . who got me out of the hole in
> the jail . . . those women didn't stop with that event: they got energized by
> that, and they went on to organize other things.[4]

Figure 3. On her 1975 album Bernice
Johnson Reagon, a founding member of the
SNCC Freedom Singers, featured a photo of
Dawson among a crowd taken days after the
Selma march. Courtesy of Kipp Dawson.

Despite the promise and possibilities opened by organizing, resistance created perils, too. Dawson was deeply influenced by the generations of women in her family who fought state violence, including her grandmother, whose husband had been murdered in a wave of Ku Klux Klan violence empowered by the US government's Palmer Raids. Because her mother was a Communist Party member and a labor organizer and her stepsister was a founder of the Black Panther Party, government agents regularly harassed Dawson's family. The FBI accumulated an enormous file on Dawson, and a journalist, testifying before the US House Un-American Activities Committee (HUAC), named her a subversive and "red diaper baby."[5] Yet Dawson kept her own prolific files, documenting radical collaboration and offering a counternarrative in the face of shifting state violence.

Vietnam Antiwar Movement

In 1965, Dawson began to focus on the Vietnam antiwar movement. She helped to found the Vietnam Day Committee in Berkeley with Jerry Rubin and Abbie Hoffman and co-organized the first International Days of Protest against American military intervention, leading to the formation of the National Coordinating Committee to End the War in Vietnam. By the following spring, she had dropped out of college to work full-time in the movement, becoming executive director of the West Coast Spring Mobilization Committee to End the War in Vietnam (SMC). Dawson also served on the SMC staff in New York City, co-organizing the 1967 National March on the Pentagon and the 1968 International Student Strike against the War. In 1972, she worked with the National Peace Action Coalition, raising money and support for the large April action in New York City against the war. These efforts drew hundreds of thousands of people to teach-ins and marches across the United States and internationally and, crucially, sustained that level of engagement for several years.

Dawson explained the kind of radically collaborative efforts necessary to build a significant antiwar movement:

> The reason that it was such a successful movement in the United States is that people came together with all different kinds of ways of looking at society . . . and put those aside in order to build common actions. . . . The National Coordinating Committee convention . . . happened in 1966 in Washington, D.C. . . . There were people there from the Communist Party, the Socialist Party, the Socialist Workers Party, the Socialist Labor Party, the Unitarian Church, the American Friends Service Committee, the Student Peace Union. People from the traditional pacifist organizations all came together . . . [who] had a history of calling each other opponent organizations. To get back to work took a lot of thought, and a lot of quiet discussions off the main floor meetings, and a lot of patience, but also a vision that it was possible to build something that we would all work in together. And I believe that the Socialist Workers Party's vision of that happening was one of the things that made me most excited about being involved with the SWP.[6]

Creating unity was especially difficult because the federal government sowed divisions among organizations through misinformation campaigns and outright violence. The FBI covertly released flyers accusing the SWP of harming the antiwar movement and targeted Dawson by saying she was not trustworthy because she "smiled too much."[7] The government campaigns were effective, and, in a particularly painful division, the SMC distanced itself from socialism, ejecting Dawson. Yet she persisted, motivated by a "deep belief in the power of people to resist, together, and sometimes even to win against repressive governmental forces."[8] She later raised money, as a staff member for the Political Rights Defense Fund, to support the SWP lawsuit against the FBI, the CIA, and other federal agencies that exposed COINTELPRO operations. The lawsuit was successful and—officially, if not in practice—ended government infiltration of organizations.[9]

Women's Movement and Gay Liberation Movement

Struggling with her sexual identity, Dawson tried to "live a straight life" and, in 1966, married Leslie Evans, a fellow activist.[10] She became pregnant and obtained an underground abortion, as the state deemed this health care illegal. Collaborating with a network of women across the United States, Dawson and countless others took their own reproductive health into their collective hands. After moving to New York City in 1967 to work in the antiwar movement, Dawson was increasingly involved in the fledgling women's movement, connecting her own identities and movement work. She participated in the first and second Congresses to Unite

Figure 4. Dawson and her mother at the July 9, 1978, Equal Rights Amendment march in Washington, DC.

Women in 1969 and 1970. And as a representative of the SWP, she helped coordinate the 1970 Women's Strike for Equality, meeting in Betty Friedan's living room with Ivy Bottini, Ruthann Miller (now O'Donnell), Bella Abzug, Kate Millett, Flo Kennedy, Gloria Steinem, and others. That same year she ran for the US Senate on the SWP ticket and organized local and national marches for abortion rights, serving on the staff for the Women's National Abortion Action Coalition during the two years leading up to *Roe v. Wade* (figs. 4 and 5).

As antifeminists lesbian-baited the women's movement and Friedan famously told the media she opposed "the lavender menace," Dawson joined protesters in the streets donning armbands declaring, "We are all the lavender menace." Now fully out as a lesbian, separated from her husband, and serving as a representative of the SWP, she joined the steering committee for the 1971 Christopher Street Liberation Day in commemoration of the second anniversary of the Stonewall Riots, which became the annual pride parade. Some in the nascent gay rights movement rejected involvement by the SWP, which was known for its homophobia.[11] However, Dawson openly criticized the socialist leaders and women's movement leaders who attacked Kate Millett and her sexual identity following her violent outing by mainstream media (fig. 6).[12]

Figure 5. Dawson and fellow United Mine Workers of America (UMWA) women marching for abortion rights at the 1989 March for Women's Lives in Washington, DC.

Figure 6. The SWP's Pathfinder Press published Dawson in 1971 and 1975.

Figure 7. Dawson
participated in UMWA
strikes against Massey
and Pittston and
supported numerous
other labor events,
including the air traffic
controllers (PATCO) in
1981.

While much of Dawson's movement leadership was public, her work with the growing LGBTQ+ movement shifted to the personal level. For instance, Dawson and her partner fought for recognition as a family unit in a groundbreaking legal case; the precedent-setting victory allowed her to adopt her own child and legalized gay families in Pennsylvania.[13]

Labor Movement and Education Justice Movement

Still active with the SWP, Dawson moved to Pittsburgh and, in 1979, started working as a coal miner. During her thirteen years in an underground mine, she organized with other women leaders through the United Mine Workers of America (UMWA) and the Coal Employment Project (see figs. 7 and 8). Dawson's efforts also extended internationally: she traveled to El Salvador and to South Wales and England to support Women against Pit Closures (see fig. 9).

After Dawson's final layoff from the mines, she returned to college, finished her degree in history, and taught in public schools for twenty-two years. Becoming

Figure 8. The women of UMWA Local 1197 consistently used radical collaboration to support striking workers, their families, and each other.

active in the education justice movement, she advocated against massive state divestments in public education and served on the executive board of the Pittsburgh Federation of Teachers (fig. 10). Dawson also cultivated coalitions to fight the devastating impact of such government policies as high-stakes testing mandates, overpolicing of students, and the school-to-prison pipeline, all of which disproportionately harm BIPOC children. While she considers electoral politics "too swampy," she consistently emphasizes the importance of elections and voting and more recently has worked to build movements by energizing people within campaigns, ranging from local school board races to congress. Advocating door knocking and phone banking to cultivate solidarity among people, Dawson believes that it is not the individual elected official who will make the change but "an aroused and mobilized populace and movement of people who are trying to get things to happen."[14]

Dawson continues her activism today, rooted in the same motivation she has had since the 1950s: "When people can experience and feel the beauty of struggling together for one another and leave behind the 'me-myself-and-I' paradigm at the heart of exploitation and isolated misery, all good things are possible." Though she parted ways with the SWP, she maintains that her work in every movement "deepened [her] belief that the future of life on the planet, and of human

Figure 9. In 1985, Dawson (*center left*) was among a delegation of US unionists whose presence ensured Salvadoran unionists' safety in an above-ground conference where Febe Elizabeth Velásquez (*center*) was elected president. Four years later, Velásquez was killed in a bombing of the FENASTRAS union headquarters.

Figure 10. Dawson (*center*) with fellow teachers at a 2013 rally in Harrisburg, Pennsylvania. Courtesy of Kipp Dawson.

society, demands replacing capitalism with a society based on human and planet need, as opposed to privatized property and personal wealth."[15] Dawson consistently references the love, hope, and joy that powered and continues to nurture her collective work. Reflecting on the central role of radical collaboration, even when wins were elusive, Dawson notes, "The biggest victory is that we did fight . . . that we came together and we fought. And that we have that history to build on."[16]

As the documents and interviews in the new archival collections represented here demonstrate, women like Dawson have radically collaborated to lead coalitional movements against state violence since the 1950s. Her lifetime of labor illustrates a long tradition of intersectional organizing, persistence in the face of intramovement bigotry, and optimism for the future despite devastating setbacks. Her movement work is also a call to action for today's activists, inspiring a new generation to understand the stakes and to refuse to cede power to systems of harm. As Dawson reminds us: "Our history is not one straight line . . . not a direct line from bad times to good ones. . . . It's a spiral, and sometimes as we're going up the spiral, we're going what looks [like] backwards. But we are still moving forward." Dawson insists that we do not know when the spiral ends, "but we know what the goal is: a world where everyone and the planet itself are shared with love and dignity."[17]

Jessie B. Ramey is the founding director of the Women's Institute and associate professor of women's and gender studies at Chatham University. She is the author of *Childcare in Black and White: Working Families and the History of Orphanages* (2012).

Catherine A. Evans is a PhD candidate in literary and cultural studies at Carnegie Mellon University. She served as the archival intern for the Kipp Dawson Papers.

Notes

We would like to thank Kipp Dawson, a teacher and librarian by training and historian at heart, for preserving an extraordinary archive of social movement work and for her continued leadership, mentorship, and inspiration.

1. Alqatari, "Ad Hoc Beatniks."
2. Dawson, interview, October 10, 2021. All interviews cited in this essay are found in Kipp Dawson, Interviews (2021–2023), Women Miners Oral History Project, West Virginia and Regional History Center, West Virginia University.
3. Freeman, "From Freedom Now! To Free Speech."
4. Dawson, interview, October 10, 2021.
5. HUAC, *Subversive Influences*.
6. Dawson, interview, March 9, 2022.
7. Dawson, interview, March 9, 2022.
8. Dawson, email to Jessie B. Ramey, January 31, 2023.
9. Blackstock, *COINTELPRO*.
10. Dawson, interview, March 30, 2022; Evans, *Outsider's Reverie*.
11. Dawson, interview, March 20, 2022.

12. Dawson, *Kate Millett's Sexual Politics*.
13. Dawson, interview, April 6, 2022.
14. Dawson, interview, March 15, 2023.
15. Dawson, email, January 31, 2023.
16. Dawson, interview, April 13, 2022.
17. Dawson, interview, April 6, 2022.

References

Alqatari, Ammar. "Ad Hoc Beatniks." FoundSF: Shaping San Francisco's Digital Archive, 2019. https://www.foundsf.org/index.php?title=Ad_Hoc_Beatniks.

Blackstock, Nelson. *COINTELPRO: The FBI's Secret War on Political Freedom*. 3rd ed. New York: Pathfinder, 1988.

Dawson, Kipp. *Kate Millett's Sexual Politics: A Marxist Appreciation*. New York: Pathfinder, 1971.

Evans, Leslie. *Outsider's Reverie: A Memoir*. 2nd ed. Los Angeles: Self-published, 2019.

Freeman, Jo. "From Freedom Now! To Free Speech: How the 1963–64 Bay Area Civil Rights Demonstrations Paved the Way to Campus Protest." Paper presented at the annual meeting of the Organization of American Historians, San Francisco, CA, April 19, 1997. https://www.jofreeman.com/sixtiesprotest/baycivil.htm (accessed July 22, 2022).

HUAC (House Un-American Activities Committee). *Subversive Influences in Riots, Looting, and Burning. Part 6, San Francisco–Berkeley: Hearings before the United States House Committee on Un-American Activities*. 90th Cong., 2nd sess., June 27–28, 1968.

Keep up to date on new scholarship

Issue alerts are a great way to stay current on all the cutting-edge scholarship from your favorite Duke University Press journals. This free service delivers tables of contents directly to your inbox, informing you of the latest groundbreaking work as soon as it is published.

To sign up for issue alerts:

1. Visit **dukeu.press/register** and register for an account. You do not need to provide a customer number.

2. After registering, visit **dukeu.press/alerts**.

3. Go to "Latest Issue Alerts" and click on "Add Alerts."

4. Select as many publications as you would like from the pop-up window and click "Add Alerts."

read.dukeupress.edu/journals

Printed and bound by CPI Group (UK) Ltd, Croydon, CR0 4YY

13/04/2025

14656480-0004